OUR SUFFICIENCY IS OF GOD

MERCER
UNIVERSITY PRESS

Endowed by
TOM WATSON BROWN
and
THE WATSON-BROWN FOUNDATION, INC.

OUR SUFFICIENCY IS OF GOD

ESSAYS ON PREACHING IN

HONOR OF

GARDNER C. TAYLOR

Edited by

Timothy George, James Earl Massey, and Robert Smith, Jr.

Mercer University Press
Macon, Georgia

MUP/H806

© 2010 Mercer University Press
1400 Coleman Avenue
Macon, Georgia 31207
All rights reserved
First Edition.

Books published by Mercer University Press are printed on acid free paper that
meets the requirements of American National Standard for Information Sciences—
Permanence of Paper for Printed Library Materials.

Dust jacket photograph of Gardner Taylor courtesy of
Richard C. Choe©

Mercer University Press is a member of Green Press initiative
(greenpressinitiative.org), a nonprofit organization working to help publishers and
printers increase their use of recycled paper and decrease their use of fiber derived
from endangered forests. This book is printed on recycled paper.
ISBN: 978-0-88146-206-7
Library of Congress Cataloging-in-Publication Data

To the four congregations served by Dr. Gardner C. Taylor

Bethany Baptist Church, Elyria, Ohio (1938–1941)

Beulah Baptist Church, New Orleans, Louisiana (1941–1943)

Mount Zion Baptist Church, Baton Rouge, Louisiana (1943–1947)

Concord Baptist Church of Christ, Brooklyn, New York (1948–1990)

And I will give you pastors according to mine heart, which shall feed you with knowledge and understanding.
—Jeremiah 3:15

CONTENTS

INTRODUCTION

HONOR TO WHOM HONOR IS DUE

Timothy George

Over the past century, Gardner Calvin Taylor has cut a swath unmatched by any other Protestant minister across the landscape of American Christianity. In 1990, he retired as pastor of the 14,000-member Concord Baptist Church of Christ in Brooklyn after forty-two years of service. Though Taylor is now in his tenth decade, his active ministry continues through preaching, writing, and enduring influence in the guild of homiletics and beyond. That influence is rooted in the many and various roles Taylor has played throughout his long career, which began in the Great Depression and perdures through the economic crisis of recent times. Gardner Taylor has been a pastor, a church administrator, a ministry entrepreneur, an educator, writer, lecturer, social critic, civil rights activist, political leader, denominational statesman, and citizen of the world. But first and foremost, he has been a preacher of the gospel of Jesus Christ. Among the many roles he has been asked to play, he has found his basic calling in "the sweet torture of Sunday morning," as he once referred to his pulpit work.[1] The essays in this volume focus on the preaching ministry of Gardner Taylor. They are offered with affection and esteem, by colleagues, students, and friends—fellow preachers all—whose own attempts to speak the unsearchable riches of Christ owe so much to the life and labors of Gardner C. Taylor. This

---

[1] Terry Muck and Paul Robbins, "The Sweet Torture of Sunday Morning: An Interview with Gardner C. Taylor," *Christianity Today Leadership* 2/3 (1 July 1981): 16–29.

introductory chapter consists of two parts: a brief biographical overview and a short review of the essays contained in this volume.

Gardner Calvin Taylor was born on 18 June 1918 in Baton Rouge, Louisiana,[2] the only child of Reverend Washington Monroe Taylor, a Baptist preacher, and his wife, Selina Gesell Taylor. Young Taylor grew up as the adored son of strong, loving parents. Three streams of influence merged in the formation of young Gardner. His father, "Wash," was born only five years after the end of slavery in 1865. He frequently reminded his son of what it was like to grow up in those times when, as Taylor often reported, "you could almost still hear the echo of hounds baying on the trail of runaway slaves." As a young man, Gardner Taylor knew personally many of those who had survived the dark night of slavery. Their stories of heartbreak and hope, of struggling but not losing, inspired and informed Taylor's view of the world and gave him a social conscience that would shape his life's work.

The crucible of this formation was the black church. Wash Taylor was a distinguished preacher and pastor of the Mt. Zion Baptist Church in Baton Rouge, one of the largest congregations in the state. He was said to preach in "the old style, much emotion and power, but with eloquent language."[3] Like his son in later life, Wash Taylor's ministry extended far beyond the bounds of his local church.

----

[2] A full-length biography of Gardner Taylor has yet to be written. I am indebted to the research of Gerald Lamont Thomas, *African American Preaching: The Contribution of Dr. Gardner C. Taylor* (New York: Peter Lang Publishing, 2004), esp. 82–106. Numerous autobiographical allusions can be gleaned from Taylor's sermons and lectures. See the six-volume collection compiled by Edward L. Taylor, *The Words of Gardner Taylor*, 6 vols. (Valley Forge: Judson Press, 1999–2002).

[3] Gerald Thomas's interview with C. D. Simmons, who heard Wash Taylor preach in Washatau Parrish, Louisiana, in 1924. See Thomas, *African American Preaching*, 83.

He offered a prayer at the inauguration of the governor of Louisiana and was later elected as president of the Louisiana Baptist State Convention and a vice president at-large in the National Baptist Convention, USA, Inc.

When Wash Taylor died in 1931, Gardner was only thirteen years old. His mother went to work to support her son and to help him complete his studies. She was assisted in this endeavor by her aunt, Gert, a disciplinarian of "flinty tenderness" who put "steel in a little boy's spine," as Taylor later recalled. Selina was a teacher, very bright and well read, and she conveyed her love for the English language to her precocious son. From both of his parents, but especially from his mother, Taylor learned what might be called the sacramental power of language. Though not highly educated by later standards, his parents, Taylor recalled, "had a natural feel for the essential music of the English language wedded to an intimate and emotional affection for the great transactions of the Scriptures."[4] This is reflected not only in the fact that Taylor's sermons are among the most literate in the history of preaching, but also in his attention to the performative nature of language. Words not only convey meaning; they also embody reality. Through the power of the Spirit, the preacher's words make present in time things that are separated in space, the realities of judgment and mercy, origins and end, paradise and perdition. For this reason, Taylor says, "words must make definite suggestions, not only in their definition but in their sound. There are words that caress, words that lash and cut, words that lift, and words that have a glow in them."[5] In his poem *East Coker*, near

---

[4] Gardner C. Taylor, *How Shall They Preach: The Lyman Beecher Lectures and Five Lenten Sermons* (Elgin IL: Progressive Baptist Publishing House, 1977) 13.

[5] Michael Duduit, "Preaching and the Power of Words: An Interview with Gardner C. Taylor," *Preaching* 9/4 (January–February 1994): 2, 4-8. Also, "The Sweet Torture of Sunday Morning: An Interview with Gardner C. Taylor in *Leadership* 2/3 (Summer 1981): 27. For more on this, see also, Gardner C. Taylor,

the end, T. S. Eliot describes the art of learning to use words as "a raid on the inarticulate," and Taylor applies this definition to the craft of preaching as well.

Richard John Neuhaus, who served for many years as a pastoral colleague of Taylor in Brooklyn, described how the great preacher's love of language contributed to the depth and richness of his sermons:

> Gardner Taylor begins by picking up the word, such as *reconciliation,* or *communion,* or *sisterhood.* First he just says it, but then you can see him warming up to it. Clearly he *loves* that word and he is going to do wonderful things for it and to it. He tries just rolling it out of his mouth; then, staccato-like, he bounces it around a bit; then he starts to take it apart, piece by piece, and then put it together in different ways. And pretty soon you have a lot of people engaged in wondering and puzzling with Dr. Taylor, trying to figure out what this word and idea of *reconciliation* is all about. They walk around the word, looking at it from different angles. Taylor gets on top of it, and looks down, then he lifts up a corner and peeks underneath; you can see this is going to be a difficult word to get to know. He whispers it and then he shouts it; he pats, pinches, and probes it; and then he pronounces himself unsatisfied, and all the people agree. "It's time to look at what the great apostle Paul has to say about this here word *reconciliation.*" And all the people agree.[6]

Although he was brought up in the church as the son of a well-known pastor, it was not Gardner Taylor's intention to follow in his

---

"Preaching and the Power of Words," in *Communicate with Power: Insights from America's Top Communicators,* Michael Duduit, ed. (Grand Rapids: Baker Books, 1996) 206-15.

[6] Richard John Neuhaus, *Freedom for Ministry* (Grand Rapids: Eerdmans, 1979) 177.

father's footsteps. As a young man, his ambition was to become a criminal lawyer, even though no African American had ever been admitted to the Louisiana State Bar at that time. One of his friends asked where he thought he was going to practice law, in the middle of the Mississippi River? Nonetheless, he was accepted at the University of Michigan law school.

John Calvin, who was also attracted to the study of law, once described his acceptance of the evangelical gospel as a "sudden conversion," though it was no doubt prepared for by years of reflection and inward struggle. The same may be said of Taylor's call to the ministry, which was not only sudden but also dramatic and unexpected. While Taylor was a student at Leland College, a historic black school not far from Baton Rouge, he served as a chauffeur for Dr. James A. Bacoats, who had succeeded his father as pastor of Mt. Zion Baptist Church. Taylor later described the incident that would change his life forever:

> Late on a Spring afternoon of my senior year at Leland, I was rushing back to campus along Highway 61 in Dr. Bacoats' car when Death brushed ever so close. Two white men in an old Ford suddenly veered across the highway. I slammed the brakes and steered the car toward the ditch. Too late! One man was dead or dying, blood gushed out of his nostrils and mouth and ears. The other was lying groaning on the side of the road. The only witnesses were a poor farmer plowing in his field by the road and a local Baptist preacher named Jesse Sharkey who was on his way from work at the Standard Oil Company. Remember, this was rural Louisiana and the year was 1937. Lynching was then more than a dark memory in the national reflection. However, a strange calm came over me that April afternoon and a Strong Figure whom my father and mother had first mentioned to me came back to stand at my side. God was real again, very real. The next morning at the inquest, both of these poor white men testified that I was in no way responsible for the fatal accident. My quick brush with death that afternoon, either from the accident

or at the hands of a mob, turned me imperiously toward consideration of the meaning of my life and the ultimate purpose of human existence. Consequently, upon the recommendation of Dr. Bacoats, I went on to the Oberlin Graduate School of Theology, sure that the "Old Blessed Figure," God, about whom I had first heard about from my parents, willed it so.[7]

Since its founding in 1833, Oberlin College had a policy of admitting students regardless of their race, creed, or color. Under the presidency of the revival preacher Charles Grandison Finney, the school became a center of the antislavery movement. Still, Gardner Taylor was only the eighth person of African-American descent to graduate from Oberlin School of Theology. In addition to receiving a thorough grounding in the classical theological disciplines, Taylor had opportunities to preach in nearby churches. In his second year, he was called as the pastor of Bethany Baptist Church in Oberlin. While a student at Oberlin, Taylor fell in love with and married Laura Bell Scott, who was also a graduate of Oberlin and, like his mother, a very gifted teacher. Until her untimely and tragic death in 1995, Laura Scott Taylor shared with her husband a life of service to Jesus Christ and his church. In 1996, Gardner Taylor married Ms. Phyllis Strong, who, like his first wife, had a distinguished career as an educator. Forty years before their marriage in 1996, Phyllis Strong had been baptized by Gardner Taylor at his church in New York.

Following two pastoral charges in Louisiana, Taylor was called in 1948 to be the pastor of Concord Baptist Church of Christ in the Bedford-Stuyvesant section of Brooklyn. At the age of thirty, Taylor stepped into one of the most prestigious pulpits in the country. Although the church had an active membership of 5,000 when he

---

[7] Gardner C. Taylor, "Why I Believe There Is a God," in *Why I Believe There Is a God: Sixteen Essays by Negro Clergymen*, ed. Howard Thurman (Chicago: Johnson Publishing Company, 1965) 86.

arrived, it would grow to almost three times that size under his leadership. In the dead of winter 1952, due to faulty electrical wiring, the entire church structure burned to the ground. Taylor led the congregation to rebuild, and the new church edifice was dedicated on 1 April 1956. Concerned about educational opportunities for the rising generation, Taylor also led his church to establish the Concord Elementary Day School, which, under the principalship of his wife Laura, became fully accredited. The church also sponsored a federal credit union, a clothing exchange, a 121-bed nursing home, and a retirement center. Taylor put down deep roots in Brooklyn and New York and was elected to serve on the city of New York's board of education and the Citywide Committee for Integrated Schools.

Never one to shy away from political involvement, Taylor nonetheless knew the difference between prophetic preaching and political moralizing. "Prophetic preaching arises out of the Scriptures," he said. "Moralizing is self-generated and arises from social mores or personal predilections."[8] When Taylor became too involved in politics, his wife Laura told him that his preaching was getting very thin. On one occasion, he was encouraged to run for Congress but backed away after due consideration, believing that he could make a greater difference in the lives of his people through his ministry of influence as their pastor. Taylor never understood his mission as bringing the kingdom of God on earth, the utopian goal of nineteenth-century liberalism, but rather the prophetic task of "making straight in the desert a highway for our God." From this perspective, Taylor addressed the great personal and social issues of the day, calling into question secular solutions to serious problems. His declarations often had a disquieting effect on entrenched partisans of varied perspectives. For example, on the controversial issue of abortion, he said, "All of life is sacred. It is no more

---

[8] Gardner C. Taylor, *Lectures, Essays, and Interviews*, vol. 5 of *The Words of Gardner Taylor*, comp. Edward L. Taylor (Valley Forge: Judson Press, 2001) 79.

permissible to destroy life six months before birth than five years after birth. Many people claim that they are interested in human life and fight for the child's right to be born. But the same people are often nowhere to be found when the child's body is stunted by poor nutrition and its mind is affected by poor education."[9]

As a son of the South, educated in the North and tested in the crucible of a large urban ministry, Gardner Taylor was uniquely suited to address the crisis of civil rights in the burdensome decades of the fifties and sixties. A longstanding friend of the King family, he invited young Martin Luther King, Jr., to preach at Concord in 1952 when he was en route to graduate studies at Boston University. Later, Taylor raised funds for King's efforts in the South and was arrested with him during demonstrations in the 1960s.

Taylor's support for the cause of civil rights led to a major confrontation with Joseph H. Jackson, the longstanding president of the National Baptist Convention, USA, Inc. Jackson was well acquainted with Taylor and had earlier recommended him as a pastoral candidate at Concord, but as a social conservative, Jackson opposed King's use of marches and demonstrations in the crusade for civil rights. The issue came to a head in 1961 when Taylor was nominated to oppose Jackson for the presidency of the denomination. In a court-supervised election, Jackson prevailed. However, this episode led to a rupture among African-American Baptists and the emergence of the Progressive National Baptist Convention. Taylor later served as both vice president and president of this new denomination, though he has maintained close ties of friendship and is held in highest esteem across this religious divide.

Martin Luther King, Jr., greatly admired Gardner Taylor and learned much both from his courageous example and his fusion of eloquence and passion in the art of preaching. Richard Lischer has

---

[9] Ibid., 85–86.

described Taylor's influence this way: "What King and many young preachers besides would have learned from Taylor was the genius for channeling evangelical doctrine and the great stories of the Bible into socially progressive and prophetic utterance."[10] In March 1992, Taylor delivered a sermon at Howard University, "Another Look at the Crucifixion," which demonstrates his ability to speak with power and poignancy to the quest of African Americans for justice and human rights in the light of Jesus Christ and His gospel:

> I am among the last of the living links with the great aspirations of the fathers. I shared a public platform with Mordecai Johnson and Benjamin Mays and Charles Wesley, to name but three. I knew some blacks who had fought in the Union Army. My grandfather fought in the Civil War, but I did not know him directly. And I remember on what we call Declaration Day—really Memorial Day—how they would gather at the National Cemetery at Port Hudson and put on those old blue uniforms with GAR on it—Grand Army of the Republic—and even though bent of limb and slow of step, how proudly they would look back upon their aspirations, upon the fact that they had fought for their liberty.
>
> I knew people, as I said, who came out of that tragic time with the almost rancid odor of slavery in their spirits. But, my God, they were not defeated nor beaten down. I can see them now across the chasm of the years in their little churches on the plantations and the cane breaks and the cotton fields. Gnarled hands, wrinkled brows, bent shoulders, with all of the disallowances and the intimidations, Nathan Bedford Forrest's Ku Klux Klan in its first wave of terrorism—all of that. You know what they were singing? I wish you could have heard them—"We Are Climbing Jacob's Ladder." Hardly with ground to stand upon, disallowed in the society, called "Nigger"

---

[10] Richard Lischer, "Gardner C. Taylor," in *Concise Encyclopedia of Preaching,* ed. William H. Willimon and Richard Lischer (Louisville: Westminster John Knox Press, 1995) 466.

on every hand—we are climbing Jacob's ladder. With no number to speak of, "every round going higher and higher." Looking at the long road ahead of them they raised the question, "Do you think I'll make a soldier?" "Do you think"—they'd sing it three times—"I'll make a soldier, soldier of the Cross?" And they were not talking about any indifference, any capitulation, any laziness. They went on, "Rise! Shine! Give God the glory, Soldier of the Cross." Then they'd sing that last line—"Do you want your freedom, soldier of the Cross?" They did not use the sickle and hammer, it was not the stars and bars, it was not the stars and stripes, it was Soldier of the Cross. And with that they marched, opened their little schools, started their little grocery stores and their insurance companies, built their churches. Soldier of the Cross! It was their confidence that in Jesus Christ there is power.

He is light for darkness.

Strength for weakness.

Peace for confusion.

Hope for despair.

Bread for the hungry.

Water for the thirsty.

And at last the way to a taller town than Rome and an older place than Eden.[11]

Gardner Taylor has brought to his pulpit work an intimate knowledge of the history of preaching in both its classical and contemporary expressions. In the 1940s, he and the famous Southern Baptist orator Robert G. Lee shared the same platform. When Taylor came to New York in 1948, he joined a cadre of extraordinary preachers, all of whom became his close friends and colleagues— Sandy Ray, Paul Scherer, George Buttrick, Adam Clayton Powell, Jr., Robert McCracken, Ralph Sockman, and Samuel DeWitt Proctor

---

[11] Ibid., 467.

(with whom he wrote the book *We Have This Ministry*). Taylor learned much from these ministry peers. His sermons are also sprinkled with quotations and references to many of the pulpit greats of previous eras whose work he knew so well one might have thought he was their contemporary—Charles Haddon Spurgeon, R. W. Dale, Harry Emerson Fosdick, P. T. Forsyth, Frederick W. Robertson, Alexander MacLaren, John Jasper, William Holmes Borders, John H. Jowett, and others. In 1976, Taylor was invited to present the 100th Lyman Beecher Lectures on Preaching at Yale Divinity School, which were published in his book *How Shall They Preach*. In preparation for this assignment, Taylor spent hours in the library of Union Theological Seminary reading *seriatim* through the ninety-nine previous lectures presented in this distinguished series.

With his deep biblical knowledge, seasoned pastoral wisdom, and poetic genius for the English language, Taylor breathed the same air as the grand masters of preaching in former days. But his feet always remained firmly planted on the ground, in touch with the flesh-and-blood realities of everyday life. And his heart remained ever attuned to the distinctive emphasis and pathos of the African-American preaching tradition, "a kind of accent which black people have given to the faith."[12] In a series of lectures at Duke University on "The Preaching of the Black Patriarchs," Taylor spoke about the great biblical themes of redemption and deliverance refracted through long years of the heartbreak of slavery and the joy-sorrow of a faith made strong on the anvil of anguish. Taylor concluded these lectures by quoting the words of the prophet Isaiah, rehearsed by St. Paul in his Epistle to the Romans concerning the "beautiful feet" of those entrusted to bring good tidings (Isaiah 52:7; Romans 10:14–15):

> Now that reference is not to the shapeliness of the feet of the courier. It has nothing to do with that. It has nothing to do with

---

[12] Taylor, vol. 5 of *The Words of Gardner Taylor*, 199.

bunions and calluses or corns or deformity, something else all together. It is the figure of someone long imprisoned in a damp, dark dungeon out of which there is but one narrow slit which looks out upon the mountain highway. And that prisoner knows that a great and crucial battle is being fought. Upon that battle turns the fate of the prisoner, and then on a certain day he looks out and sees on the ledge of the mountain road a courier whose uniform tells him he is the courier of his own government, of his own sovereign. The pace, the urgency, the movement of the courier tells him that he brings quickly a good word. And so the word "how beautiful upon the mountain are the feet of them that bring good tidings." You will then face your future with confidence, knowing that you bear to troubled prisoners the tidings of their liberation—by God's grace come to earth in the Lord Christ.[13]

I first met Gardner Taylor in the mid-1970s when I was a student at Harvard Divinity School and he was a visiting professor of homiletics. In those days, preaching was not a regular part of the curriculum at Harvard. As the pastor of a multiracial, inner-city congregation, I was eager to learn all I could about the craft of preaching. A number of us engaged in ministry looked forward each week to Dr. Taylor's lectures on "the purpose of preaching in the plan of God." He shared with us vivid recollections of his own involvement in the history and craft of preaching across the years, from his preaching in rural churches on the bayous of Louisiana to his pastoral work, then at its prime, in New York City. He also guided the class into the process of sermon formation, how to prepare, deliver, and listen to sermons. Dr. Frank Reid, pastor of the Bethel African Methodist Episcopal Church in Baltimore, who also studied with Taylor at Harvard, recalled how Taylor would listen to the students' sermons in the class: "Once a student had gone through

---

[13] Ibid., 218.

all the preliminaries and taken their text, he would close his eyes, lift up his head to the heavens, and put his right hand on his chin and with the index finger of his right hand, he would either rub his chin or sometimes go to his brow, but invariably his eyes would be closed for the entire message. It was one of the most spiritual experiences I ever had, just watching him listen to a sermon."[14]

Taylor taught similar preaching courses at Colgate Rochester Divinity School (1969–1972) and Union Theological Seminary (1973–1974). Several years after Beeson Divinity School was established in 1988, Taylor presented the inaugural William E. Conger, Jr., Lectures on Biblical Preaching. We have included with this volume an audio CD of two of the Conger Lectures presented on this occasion. Taylor's Conger Lectures at Beeson are one of many such lectureships he has devoted to the signature work of his ministry. In 1997, a Baylor University survey in *Newsweek* magazine named Taylor one of the twelve greatest preachers in the English-speaking world. His name had appeared on earlier listings of this sort in *Time* magazine (1979) and *Ebony* magazine (1984). In 2007, the Gardner C. Taylor Archive and Preaching Laboratory opened at the Interdenominational Theological Center in Atlanta.

We open this volume with the moving "Tribute to a Titan," by James Earl Massey, a younger contemporary and fellow Oberlinian with Taylor. Like Taylor, Massey is a master of the preaching tradition and shares with him a high view of the preacher's calling and stewardship.[15] Taylor, ever the student, has been a close reader of Massey's many books on preaching and commends his *Designing the Sermon* for young preachers. Massey suggested to Robert Smith and me the concept for this festschrift and also furnished the title, *Our*

---

[14] Gerald Thomas's interview with Frank Reid, 23 November 1991. See Thomas, *African American Preaching*, 106.

[15] Among James Earl Massey's many books, see especially his *Stewards of the Story: The Task of Preaching* (Louisville: Westminster John Knox Press, 2006).

Sufficiency Is of God, a response to St. Paul's piercing question, "And who is sufficient for these things?" (2 Corinthians 2:16). Taylor has often spoken of the foolishness and presumptuousness of preaching, a fact every herald of the gospel must confront before daring to speak in the name of God. Each of the essays in this volume reflects Taylor's lifelong struggle and the answer he found in the response the great apostle gave to his own question: "This is a terrific responsibility. Is anyone confident to take it on? No—but at least we don't take God's Word, water it down, and then take it to the streets to sell it cheap. We stand in Christ's presence when we speak; God looks us in the face. We get what we say straight from God and say it as honestly as we can" (2 Corinthians 2:16–17, *The Message*).

We have also included a tribute to Gardner Taylor by Neville Callam, general secretary of the Baptist World Alliance. Shortly before Taylor received his pastoral call to New York, he traveled to Copenhagen, Denmark, to attend the Baptist World Alliance. On the Sunday morning of that meeting, he preached at the Second Baptist Church of Copenhagen, a remarkable honor for a twenty-nine-year-old. In subsequent years, Taylor would speak at four consecutive meetings of the Baptist World Alliance, in Cleveland, London, Miami Beach, and Tokyo. His work on behalf of Christian unity and human rights found an eager response within the world community of Baptists. Along with his near-contemporary Billy Graham, he has represented the cause of Christ across many countries, cultures, and confessions.

The effect of a sermon depends on what is said, on how it is said, and on who says it. The essays in this volume are divided into three parts, each reflecting one of these priorities: Crafting the Sermon, Honoring the Scriptures, and Voicing Truth with Grace. A superb musician as well as a great preacher, James Earl Massey appeals to the musicality inherent in the task of "Composing Sermons That Sing!" Drawing on his own experience, as well as the pulpit work of George

W. Truett, Peter J. Gomes, and Taylor himself, Massey discusses
three essential requirements for sermonic composition: a talent to
create, a controlling sense of order, and an honest concern for people.
Massey's lyrical essay quotes and comments on the admonition of
Thomas Carlyle: "See deep enough and you see musically."[16]

In his essay "Measuring a Preacher's Creativity with a Borrowed
Ruler," Joel C. Gregory applies to the field of preaching certain
psychological research measurements. In doing so, he points out that
creativity is not without boundaries, such as the canon of scripture,
ecclesial traditions, and the limits of the preacher's own personality.
Still, Gregory analyzes the creative nature of preaching by examining
divergent thinking, anamorphic perspectives, and the larger *gestalt* of
the preacher's own life storyline. Gregory also points to the
significance of the creative community as the shaping context for
sermons with depth and power. Taylor's preaching exemplifies each
of these traits while avoiding the effects of rhetoric in the vulgar sense
of that term—artificial eloquence and showiness: "Although a
rhetorical giant, Taylor displays an attitude toward preaching that is
more like one of an ambulance attendance trying to get humanity
some urgent help than someone who enjoys polishing the ambulance
and blowing the siren."

Our next two essays examine the intersection of preaching, the
arts, and storytelling. Picking up on the theme of musicality
introduced by James Earl Massey in his lead essay, Donald E.
Demarray looks at various ways the preaching imagination is enriched
through music, the visual arts, and the metaphoric use of language
that suffuses pulpit utterances of great masters such as Gardner
Taylor. He draws on the work of Lewis Carroll, C. S. Lewis, and
Eugene Peterson to show how "great preaching brings together
knowledge and beauty of expression." Michael Duduit, the

---

[16] Thomas Carlyle, *On Heroes, Hero-Worship and the Heroic in History*, ed.,
Archibald MacMecham (Boston: Ginn and Co., 1901) 90.

distinguished editor of *Preaching* magazine, offers practical wisdom about the use of story in the work of preaching. In his "Doctrine That Flies: Using Story to Communicate Truths," he reminds us that stories are more than good illustrations. They have an integrity of their own and convey the truth of the text in a way that "makes ideas stick." Well told and properly used, stories also have power to convey doctrinal content, especially in a culture wary of didactic, linear communication.

In his brilliant essay "Preaching Doctrine, Sermon Genre: Gardner Taylor's Sense of Providence," Thomas G. Long places Taylor's preaching against the background of the Puritan model of doctrine-reason-use, a multivalent concept of the sermon that has ceased to cohere in contemporary culture. Long shows how the shifting of genres has led to the neglect of doctrine. He calls for a reinvigorated role of the preacher as teacher, but one that does not bypass the lure of skepticism in a world of evil, suffering, and finitude. Using Taylor's sermon "Providence: The Control and Care of God," first preached in the 1960s, Long shows how George Lindbeck's cultural-linguistic understanding of doctrine can provide a framework for making the sermon "less a recitation of theology and more an improvised performance of theology." For example, Gardner Taylor's sermon on providence is not an explanation or an argument, but a performance, not in the sense of entertainment, but rather an accomplishment, something performed. This approach allows Taylor to take seriously the listening situation of his hearers, but also to affirm what the Christian church has taught, believed, and confessed about the providence of God:

> There is a hand which guides our footsteps if we will but trust God, no matter what anybody may say or do. The world may try to hurt us, but God keeps our souls. Evil influences may try to block our way, but God tears down obstacles or makes us leap over them. The

enemy may wound us, but God will heal our wounds. Strong winds may blow, but they speed us to port.[17]

In his 1976 Lyman Beecher Lectures at Yale, Gardner Taylor responded to the question "How many points should there be in a sermon?" with a provocative if humorous answer: "At least one!" In the opening essay of Part Two of this volume, Marvin McMickle extends Taylor's answer to say that "a sermon should have only *one* central point." Drawing on the homiletical studies of Tom Long, Fred Craddock, and Haddon Robinson, McMickle provides his own definition of preaching: "Every sermon needs to make one clear, compelling, biblically centered and contextually relevant claim that sets some aspect of God's will and God's Word before some specific segment of God's people. This is done with a hope that those people will be challenged, informed, corrected, or encouraged as a result of the words set before them that day."[18] A sermon may have several component parts, but each will serve one central truth or teaching, the "sermonic claim." McMickle contends that time is too precious to be wasted on pointless preaching, and he calls on preachers to begin their sermon preparation with a careful consideration of the biblical text: "The sermon should be based upon the truths that are being taught and the lessons that can be learned from the biblical text that has been chosen or assigned." Such preaching, if it is faithful to its mission, will engage the culture in which it goes forth without becoming captivated to it. To those fearful of proclaiming the truths of an ancient text to a postmodern generation with little respect for absolute verities of any kind, McMickle reminds the preacher that

---

[17] Gardner C. Taylor, "Providence: The Control and Care of God," *The Scarlet Thread: Nineteen Sermons* (Elgin IL: Progressive Baptist Publishing House, 1981) 34.

[18] Marvin A. McMickle, *Shaping the Claim* (Minneapolis: Fortress Press, 2008) 6.

such resistance has been encountered before in earlier epochs of the church's history. He admonishes preachers to set forth a central claim of the scriptures in a clear, unintimidated manner. "Our task," he writes, "is to be an instrument through which a word of ultimate significance claims our congregations in a transformative manner."

William E. Pannell explores Gardner Taylor's *oeuvre* in terms of what it means for a preacher's work to be determined by "a sense of the Scriptures." While this phrase includes the conviction that the Bible is God's inspired word and the only rule for faith and practice, it means much more than this. It incorporates the preacher's special calling to the ministry and his or her felt need for the Spirit's presence and power. Pannell's essay points to the linkage between preaching and spiritual formation in the task of theological education. He recalls Taylor's admonition to young preachers not to neglect their own spiritual lives. When this happens, the preacher is left with "nothing but a second-hand story, an arm's length dealing with truths." The preacher who finds spiritual sustenance for a lifetime of ministry will be able to share out of such abundance with others, to live a grace-filled life of gratitude to God, and to bequeath to the rising generation a legacy of faithful service to be carried forward into the future.

Until her death in 2008, Ella Pearson Mitchell and her husband, Henry H. Mitchell, were a dynamic ministry team who shared together their lifelong work of preaching, teaching, and writing. In his essay "Preaching as Experience of the Gospel," Henry Mitchell describes his personal friendship with Gardner Taylor and the impact this relationship has had on his own understanding of the preaching task. The essay includes a reference to a memorable sermon by Gardner Taylor presented at the annual convention of the American Baptist Churches in 1954. In that tortured time in American race relations, the year of *Brown vs. Board of Education*, Taylor spoke on the topic of justice and race to the 10,000 delegates of the convention. Taylor concluded his sermon with the spiritual "Let Us Break Bread Together." At the end of the sermon, Taylor was embraced by his friend C. Oscar Johnson, a white minister from St. Louis, and the two of them led the assembly in the celebration of the Lord's Supper.

Robert Smith, Jr., in "Preaching as a Contemplative Theological Task," probes beyond Taylor's eloquence, passion, and exegetical mastery to discover a deeper impulse in his pulpit work. Smith defines contemplation as "being available to God, brooding over God, and hovering over God and God's Word; delighting in God." Contemplation in this sense encompasses the components of adoration, consideration, illumination, aurality (in the sense of depth hearing), and singing. Contemplation leading to doxology marks the preaching work of Gardner Taylor and helps to describe the genius he has brought to this art. If Taylor's preaching is contemplative, it is also incarnational, and Wallace Charles Smith explores this aspect of Taylor's work. Drawing on Phillips Brooks' famous definition of preaching as "divine truth communicated through a personality," Wallace Charles Smith calls for the preacher to develop a homiletic lifestyle that allows God's story, revealed in the Bible and Jesus Christ, to intersect with the preacher's own story. This calls for a meditative study of the scriptures as well as a life of prayer, journaling, and self-examination.

In his essay "Pulpits without Purpose," Cleophus J. LaRue reflects on the difficulty of preaching in a time of rapid change within the church as well as the culture. In a post-traditional age, mainline churches stand alongside seeker churches, cell churches, mall churches, seven-day-a-week churches, next churches, and para-churches of various sorts. The challenges for preaching are unmistakable, yet churches and their ministers have always had to find their bearings in the tension that lies between the poles of identity and adaptability. LaRue finds guidance in the work of the missiologist Andrew Walls, who commends three guidelines for purposeful preaching in a time of flux: the church test, the kingdom test, and the gospel test. He concludes with this admonition: "In our everchanging world if we forget to preach Jesus and him crucified, we run the risk of preaching from pulpits without purpose even though our churches may be on the cutting edge of change and bubbling over with worldly success. To preach Jesus in this post-Christian world is our most compelling challenge and charge for there is still power in the heart of that old story."

In his essay on "Gardner Taylor as Interpreter of Scripture: Hermeneutics for Homiletics," William H. Willimon explores the ways scripture functions in Taylor's preaching and finds therein a guide to others who seek to do faithful biblical exposition. He notes that Taylor, in all of his preaching, manages to be "ever so much more interested in the Word than in himself or even his listeners." This leads him to practice an "eyewitness hermeneutics," *stepping into* the text rather than *back from* it. This process requires preachers to un-learn the methods of reductionistic historical criticism they have been taught. As a case study of this approach, Willimon analyzes in depth Taylor's sermon "In His Own Clothes," based on Mark 15:20. He finds the practice of Taylor a corrective to much contemporary preaching that panders to the less-than-ultimate needs of mostly well-off listeners and, in the process, misses the prophetic edge of the Bible and pares down the gospel.

Part Three of this volume, "Voicing Truth with Grace," opens with David Buttrick's "When Preachers Preach, Does God Speak?" This essay is about the authorization of preaching: To what extent can the frail words of human messengers present the authentic voice of God? Buttrick plumbs the Reformation traditions to find there precisely this claim. As the Second Helvetic Confession (1563) put it, "The preaching of the Word of God is the Word of God." Drawing on the contemporary work of Nicholas Wolterstorff and Fred Craddock, Buttrick concludes that while preachers have no personal authority, they are nonetheless under authorization, not only from ecclesiastical judicatories but from God. Buttrick finds this sense of the preacher's vocation more resonant in the African-American church tradition, exemplified by Gardner Taylor, than among Anglo churches of mainline constituents in North America today.

Like Gardner Taylor, Duke professor Richard A. Lischer has presented the Lyman Beecher Lectures on Preaching at Yale. He is also the author of a landmark study of Martin Luther King, Jr.: *The Preacher King: Martin Luther King, Jr., and the Word That Moved America* (1995). In his essay for this volume, "Anointed with Fire: The Structure of Prophecy in the Sermons of Martin Luther King, Jr.," Lischer analyzes the anatomy of a prophetic sermon as well as the characteristics of a prophetic preacher. He also points out the biographical and homiletical parallels between King and Taylor, along with some of the differences that marked their mutually sympathetic but divergent ministries: King's prophetic witness burned brightly like a meteor against the night while Taylor's more theological and exegetical approach was shaped by a ministry of preaching and pastoral care sustained over many decades.

O. C. Edwards, Jr., begins his essay, "A Good Man Speaking Well: The Holy Rhetoric of Gardner C. Taylor," by quoting Quintilian's classic definition of the perfect orator and proceeds to analyze Taylor's preaching in light of this standard. Having read all of Taylor's sermons in the set of six volumes compiled by Edward L. Taylor, Edwards subjects to close scrutiny "Three Days That Changed the World," a sermon based on 1 Corinthians 15:3–4. Edwards identifies eight "move statements" in this sermon. He also shows how Taylor adeptly incorporates the rhetorical devices of adynaton, paralipsis, and ecphrasis, all in a natural, unself-conscious way. Teresa L. Fry Brown gives us a portrait of Taylor's personal forcefulness and his ability to convince others in her essay "Poetic Persuasion: A Master Class on Speaking Truth to Power."

For Taylor, the preacher stands in the Quaker tradition of

"speaking truth to power." The "truth" in this case is not the preacher's own, but that derived from the biblical text. Such "revelant" (as Taylor elsewhere calls it) preaching becomes "relevant" preaching as the sermon is addressed to the lived experiences of those who listen. The poetry in this process comes through in what Brown calls Taylor's *metamorphic boldness,* an approach that destabilizes (in the sense of challenging the status quo) a hearer without dehumanizing him or her. In this way, preaching becomes a holistic communicative act that leads to transformation.

Martha Simmons is the publisher of *The African American Pulpit,* a leading journal in the field of homiletics, and Brad R. Braxton was the senior minister of Riverside Church in New York City. Both bring a distinguished career of publishing and teaching to their collaboration on their essay in this volume, "What Happened to Sacred Eloquence?" More than any other quality, they declare, Gardner Taylor's preaching was marked by sacred eloquence. They expound on this theme through a review of the formative influences on his preaching career, including that of his father. Eloquent preaching, as Taylor practices it, is marked by three traits, each of which is essential to the kind of eloquent pulpit work that is persuasive: (1) a speaker who is filled with and guided by the Holy Spirit; (2) a speaker who is authentic and original; and (3) a speaker who is a persuasive and highly skilled wordsmith. In a culture where words are inflated and language dumbed down, Simmons and Braxton recognize that eloquent preaching is a rare commodity in the post-Taylor age. Still, they believe its recovery is worth working for, and they offer practical suggestions for theological educators engaged in this task of ministry formation.

Cheryl J. Sanders is an ordained minister in the Church of God (Anderson) and professor of Christian ethics at Howard University School of Divinity. In her essay "The Measure of Prophetic Ministry: Trajectories in Contemporary African-American Preaching and the

Legacy of Gardner C. Taylor," she places Taylor in the lineage of the African-American prophetic preaching tradition. This tradition goes back to the age of slavery and includes such celebrated proclaimers as David Walker, Sojourner Truth, Frederick Douglass, and Maria Steward. She analyzes a series of sermons published in *The African American Pulpit* by several outstanding contemporary preachers. Also, drawing on her earlier scholarly work on sermons preached by African-American women, she argues for mutual appreciation and shared learning between men and women of the pulpit. Gardner Taylor admits that he himself was slow to accept the rightful place of women as proclaimers of the Word. However, Sanders quotes from Taylor's sermon "Three Women and God" (1991) to show how his prophetic orientation has been enlarged to include the support of the preaching ministry of women. Taylor was fond of quoting words of Thomas Graham, his theology dean at Oberlin, who said, "Faith is reason gone courageous." Sanders' essay is a reminder that prophetic ministry always requires such courageous, reason-informed faith. Gardner Calvin Taylor remains a model of such ministry across lines of race, class, gender, nation, and denomination.

Gardner Taylor concluded his sermon "Three Women and God," originally preached to the students and faculty of Princeton Theological Seminary, with an overview of his own life, the many miles he has traveled, and the work he has done—*pro Christo et ecclesia*—across nearly a century of life on this planet. Each of the contributors to this volume has been greatly blessed to know Dr. Taylor and to travel a few steps with him on that mighty long journey toward that city with foundations. We all take heart from these words of our beloved friend:

> I want to say to you something that I do not often say. I have come now to the evening of my life. It has been a wonderful day. I never dreamed, having been born when I was and where I was, ninety miles from where land runs out in the deepest South, that

such wide opportunities should have opened to me. However, let me say this to you from my heart, my young friends. The faith that I now have, I have not won in any bucolic cloistered surrounding. I have won my faith in the toughest arena in the world, in the thrust and counter-thrust of public life in the city of New York. I've known people of great wealth, but I'd rather have Jesus than silver or gold; I'd rather have Jesus than riches untold. I have heard great auditoriums echo with acclaim from one end of the earth to the other. You name it—New York, Cleveland, Chicago, London, Tokyo, Miami—but I'd rather have Jesus than people's applause.

I have known great people—Malcolm and Martin. Once, preaching in Old First Church here in Princeton about twenty-five years ago, I spent a morning with Albert Einstein. But I'd rather hear the gospel of Jesus Christ than all of the wisdom of scientific genius. No matter how famous or obscure the preacher, no matter whether highly educated or prayerfully self-taught, no matter whether male or female, I'd rather hear from him or her the riches of the pure and simple gospel than all of the astonishing insights of science. I'd rather have Jesus; I'd rather have Jesus than anything this world affords. I'd rather have Jesus.[19]

---

[19] Gardner C. Taylor, "Three Women and God," in *Quintessential Classics, 1980–Present*, vol. 3 of *The Words of Gardner Taylor*, comp. Edward L. Taylor (Valley Forge: Judson Press, 2000) 201.

TRIBUTE TO A TITAN

James Earl Massey

Dr. Taylor, when I graduated from Oberlin Graduate School of Theology, a large measure of the pride I felt was associated with my knowledge that, twenty-four years earlier, you had graduated from there. You and I did not know each other then, but your graduation had a lot to do with mine.

I vividly recall a visit you made to Oberlin Seminary during my student days there. I was looking out of a first-floor classroom window, pondering a statement the professor had just made, when I noticed Dr. Walter Marshall Horton standing on the walkway beside one of the colonnades leading to the Bosworth Quadrangle. He was talking to someone I recognized—you. The two of you stopped briefly at several capitals along the colonnade, and Dr. Horton was talking as he successively pointed upward to the limestone facial likenesses of graduate school faculty peering down above the two of you; the newest likeness there was that of Leonard Stidley, one of your teachers.[1] I watched it all as you listened attentively and looked up appreciatively and admiringly. You might or might not recall that visit and that happening, but I clearly do. Watching it all gave me a sense of the regard your remaining teachers held for you, and I took note of your respect for them. That watching also allowed me a brief reprieve from wrestling with the intricacies of some difficult coursework and from thinking about the burden I then carried as the founding pastor of a steadily growing church. Seeing you there at that time, Dr. Taylor, and aware of your already legendary ministry, I

---

[1] For a story about the stone likenesses adorning the Boswell Quadrangle colonnades, see John Kearney, "Carved in Stone," *Oberlin Alumni Magazine* 92/2 (Spring 1996): 14–17, with cover illustrations.

remembered that you once "sat" where I was then sitting. Your visit was for me a providential happening. It quickened my faith, encouraged my hope, and strengthened my diligence. I thanked God and took courage.

So, Dr. Taylor, as a figure of encouragement for me at that difficult time in my life, your prior graduation from Oberlin Seminary in 1940 had a lot to do, twenty-four years later, with mine.

Interestingly, it was during an Oberlin alumni gathering that we later met formally, and that fact of tie has been one of the many factors that has blessed the bond between us across more than thirty years.

You have led and nurtured numerous congregations through your ministry, and you have inspired generations of preachers both by what you *say* as well as what you *represent* every time you step into a pulpit. I have always admired your avid preparation to preach and how you have balanced a focused word with a sense of space for the hearer. Unlike some, indeed unlike many, you never drown hearers in a roiling sea of words; through apt imagery, you rather supply rafts of meaning to keep people afloat during the storms in their life. Your mastery of descriptive language continues to tutor multitudes of ministers about how to speak meaningfully to common experience. You have used strict forms in your sermonizing, and yet your preaching has remained dynamically flexible and accomodating as to timing, approach, voice levels, and styles of utterance. The evolution of your craftsmanship has been duly studied and rightly honored in academic treatments, especially in the more recent treatments by Gerald Lamont Thomas and L. Susan Bond.[2]

You have shown a gift for prioritizing what matters most in treating a text: respect, trust, centeredness, conciseness, clarity,

---

[2] See Gerald Lamont Thomas, *African American Preaching: The Contribution of Dr. Gardner C. Taylor* (New York: Peter Lang Publishing, 2004), esp. 2–5, 81–144; L. Susan Bond, *Contemporary African American Preaching: Diversity in Theory and Style* (St. Louis: Chalice Press, 2003) 49–63.

conviction, and readiness to climax the message with a Christ-honoring call to faith and hope. Your sermons have never seemed to be self-regarding; when you preach, nothing ever seems to say, "Well, here I am!" Avoiding selfish ambition and calculated maneuvers, you have remained faithful in the service of the gospel. While the individual quality of your gifts has been nurtured with care, you have had the wisdom to look beyond those gifts for God's enabling. Yours has been a voice dedicated to spreading the gospel, helping people know the nurturing challenge and assuring benediction of God's grace.

Dr. Taylor, my final years as dean at Anderson School of Theology coincided with your final years as senior pastor of Concord Baptist Church of Christ in Brooklyn, and there were occasions when some of our students followed my urging and traveled to Concord Church to see and hear you before you retired. You received them all with characteristic openness. They all returned confessing their joy in having experienced the claiming ambiance of that worship setting, the integrity of your preaching, the nobility of your craftsmanship, and the graciousness of your hospitality. I wanted those seminarians to experience through you what I have long known and admired about you, namely the radiance and contagion that attends "a worker who has no need to be ashamed, rightly explaining the word of truth" (2 Timothy 2:15).

Dr. Taylor, we the editors and contributors to this volume thank God for you, an exemplary preacher, kind mentor, and dear friend! You are truly a *Titan*, standing tall and strong after great struggles and exemplary service across many years.

TRIBUTE TO THE REVEREND DR. GARDNER C. TAYLOR

Neville Callam

Dear Dr. Taylor,

> "It was he [Christ] who gave some to
> be…pastors and teachers."
> (Ephesians 4:11 RSV)

The worldwide family of Baptists greatly appreciates the opportunity to greet you, Dr. Taylor, on the occasion of the presentation of this festschrift in your honor.

As a beloved Baptist pastor, preacher, and teacher, you have encouraged us over the years through your strong and steady support of the Baptist World Alliance, your unwavering example as a pastor, and your faithful stewardship as a preacher of the gospel.

We celebrate the fact that you were cradled in a church graced with gifted preaching by your own father, and we thank God that, if even against your earlier inclination, you answered the call and have become the quintessential preacher of your generation. You have achieved greatness because of the way in which you cultivated the gift God gave you, and you have proclaimed the good news without ever seeking to achieve fame through doing so.

How well do I recall the memorable sermon you delivered on 7 November 1983, when the Baptists of Jamaica gathered at the historic Sabina Park in Kingston for the closing service in the celebration of the bicentenary of Baptist work in their country! That was the first time I heard you preach.

We recall that you were born to parents who came from homes that knew the injustice of chattel slavery, and we are grateful that your concern for faithfulness to the Christian ministerial vocation was not confined to the pulpit. Your prophetic consciousness yielded not only critical, theologically based social commentary, but also a life of service aimed at arresting the vicious tide of injustice and manifesting redemptive engagement in the name, and for the sake, of Christ Jesus.

We rejoice that God has sustained you over these years during which you have served, faithfully and well, both the Lord who called you into this ministry and the people to whom God has sent you.

The Baptist World Alliance celebrates the gift not only to Baptists, but also to the wider Christian family, that our Lord has provided in you, Dr. Taylor. As you celebrate the blessing of advancing years, may the God who determines the span of our years grant you grace to experience the boundless love and the ceaseless faithfulness of the one we proudly claim as our Lord.

Sincerely in Christ,
Neville Callam
Baptist World Alliance General Secretary

CURRICULUM VITAE OF GARDNER CALVIN TAYLOR

Robert Smith, Jr.

1918	Born: June 18, in Baton Rouge LA Son of the Reverend Washington Taylor and Selina Taylor
1934	Graduated: McKinley High School, Baton Rouge LA
1937	Graduated: Leland College, Baker LA
1940	Graduated: Oberlin Graduate School of Theology, Oberlin OH [B.D.]
1941	Married: Laura Bell Scott of Oberlin OH
1938–1941	Student Pastorate: Bethany Baptist Church, Elyria OH
1941–1943	Pastor: Beulah Baptist Church, New Orleans LA
1943–1947	Pastor: Mt. Zion Baptist Church, Baton Rouge LA
1947	Preached at Baptist World Alliance, Copenhagen, Denmark, at age twenty-nine (he was honored by invitations to appear five times before the Baptist World Alliance)
1948–1990	Pastor: Concord Baptist Church of Christ, Brooklyn NY
1950	Preached at Baptist World Alliance, Cleveland OH
1954	Preached at American Baptist Convention on "Christ and Civil Rights"
1955	Preached at Golden Jubilee of the Baptist World Alliance, London, England
1958	Preached throughout Australia

1959–1970	Preached on National Radio Broadcast (NBC)— (twice he served as National Radio preacher on NBC programs)
1961	Exchange preacher in England and Scotland
1961	Founding member Progressive National Baptist Convention
1963	Arrested for demonstrating against job discrimination in the building industries in Brooklyn NY
1967	Delivered the president's message to the Progressive National Baptist Convention, Cincinnati OH
1969–1972	Adjunct professor of preaching at Colgate Rochester Divinity School, Rochester NY
1973–1974	Adjunct professor of preaching at Union Theological Seminary, New York
1975–1976	Adjunct professor of preaching at Harvard Divinity School, Cambridge MA
1976	Delivered the 100th Lyman Beecher Lectureship on Preaching at Yale Divinity School, New Haven CT
1979	Delivered E. Y. Mullins Lectures on Preaching at Southern Baptist Theological Seminary, Louisville, Kentucky
1979	Named by *Time* magazine as one of the seven greatest Protestant preachers in America
1980	Named by *Time* magazine "The Dean of the Nation's Black Preachers"
1983	Preached for the closing service in the celebration of the bicentenary of Baptists' work in Jamaica
1984	Named by *Ebony* magazine as one of America's fifteen greatest black preachers
1988	Recipient of honorary D.D., Oberlin College [commencement speaker]
1990	Retired from the pastorate of Concord Baptist Church of Christ in Brooklyn

1990	Recipient of honorary degree, Dillard University
1993	Preached at Inaugural Prayer Service for President William Jefferson Clinton
1993	Inaugurated the William E. Conger, Jr., Lectures on Biblical Preaching at Beeson Divinity School
1994	Dubbed "The Poet Laureate of American Protestantism"
1995	His wife of fifty-five years, Laura Scott Taylor, killed in a traffic accident (he has since remarried [Phyllis Strong] and moved to Raleigh NC)
1997	Recipient of honorary degree, Hum.D., Tuskegee University
1997	A Baylor University survey in *Newsweek* Magazine named him one of the twelve greatest preachers in the English-speaking world (Great Preachers Series in Gateway Films/Vision Video)
1997	Offered the benediction at President William Jefferson Clinton's second inauguration
1999	Recipient of honorary degree, D.H.L., Medgar Evers College of City University of New York (CUNY)
2000	President William Jefferson Clinton bestowed upon him the nation's highest honor, "The Presidential Medal of Freedom"
2007	The Gardner C. Taylor Archive and Preaching Laboratory opened at the Interdenominational Theological Center, Atlanta GA

PART ONE:

CRAFTING THE SERMON

COMPOSING SERMONS THAT SING!

James Earl Massey

In common parlance, "composing" is something we associate with poets and musicians, but that action, albeit in other forms, is something all humans regularly do. To "compose" is to create by mental or artistic labor; it is to form something by putting elements or parts together.

Some years ago, Mary Catherine Bateson, a professor of anthropology and English at George Mason University in Fairfax, Virginia, published a book in which she explained how "composing" is germane to daily human experience. Based on the stories of several well-known women who, gifted in their own right, had successfully managed to improvise their own careers so as to relate meaningfully with the life and work of their spouse, the book was titled *Composing a Life*. Although written for women, the insights Bateson shared in that book were important as well for men in comparable situations, and the main insight shared is that improvisation must play a major role in the conscious shaping of a life. "Improvisation can be either a last resort," Bateson stated, "or an established way of evoking creativity."[1]

Our concern here is with composing the sermon and how creativity is evoked to do so. As a composition, the sermon is something consciously created, and purposefully and personally composed, so it is essential for preaching that the means for evoking creativity for sermon making be clearly understood and utilized.

What, then, is required on our part for such creativity, such composing, to occur? I suggest three essentials.

---

[1] Mary Catherine Bateson, *Composing a Life* (New York: Penguin Books, 1990)
4.

1. The first essential requirement in composing a sermon is *a talent to create*. There is a direct relationship between a person's talent and that person's creative act. A talent is an innate ability or aptitude, a capacity for acting, an endowment, a dispositional trait. When that talent is operative by responding to some stimulus, whatever it shapes as a response usually gives the creative person what Bateson refers to as "a joyous self-recognition."[2]

It takes talent to create a sermon, a talent whose capacities are stimulated by an encounter with some truth, experience, some aspect of life, but usually an encounter with a biblical text. Engaged attentiveness to a text is essential to creating a sermon because empowerment to preach is linked with engagement with the truth spoken within the text.

Peter J. Gomes, longtime minister in the Memorial Church at Harvard, has spoken often, and has written lately, about preaching as an activity that depends upon trust: trust in oneself (as someone God has called to preach), trust in the text, trust in people, and trust in God. With respect to trusting a text, Gomes commented,

> Many young preachers ask themselves when confronted with textual preaching, "What can I do to make this interesting? How can I make this text talk?" Or, in other words, "How can I make this text say what I want to say?" These, I suggest, are the wrong questions, as any good exegesis and interpretation course will demonstrate. The question really is, first, "What is this text saying?" then, "What does it give me permission to say? How have others dealt with this? What did they know that I do not? What do I know that they did not?"... Trust that the text not only spake, but speaks.[3]

The texts of scripture do speak, and they speak openly, clearly, and loudly to those whose interest is to hear, those who trust the text

---

[2] Ibid., 225.

[3] Peter J. Gomes, "Preaching as a Matter of Trust: Recovering the Nerve of the Pulpit," in *Theology in the Service of the Church: Essays in Honor of Thomas W. Gillespie*, ed. Wallace M. Alston, Jr. (Grand Rapids: Eerdmans, 2000) 105.

enough to touch and taste its message. As for "touching" the text, I am reminded of a statement Joseph A. Fitzmyer quoted from Jerome, when he, that learned ancient, said that in scripture "the Spirit has been joined to the letter; and whatever at first sight seems to be cold, if you touch it, grows hot."[4]

The more intense the encounter with the text through "touching" it, the greater the impact of the text on the preacher's consciousness and talent to shape its message within a sermon.

A truly close touching of the text goes beyond the face of the text to encounter the substance, the soul, of the text. Sermons that sing are sermons shaped from such an encounter. Thomas Carlyle, in his classic study *Heroes, Hero-Worship, and the Heroic in History*, has lauded the effectiveness of those whose words have an attractive musicality in them, when the words used reflect the depths that are in the thing spoken about, and when what is spoken (or written) is soulfully done and highlights its "essential point." In connection with that concern for effectiveness, Carlyle emphasized the need for a "great heart, [and] the clear deep-seeing eye."[5] Here, also, is another pertinent thought of his on the matter: "The gifted man is he who *sees* the essential point, and leaves all the rest aside as surplusage."[6]

The sermon that sings is one that has been shaped and floated on the tide of meaning contained in a text. When the essential point of the text has been *seen, heard,* and *felt,* then the preacher can word it musically so that it sings. A sermon should be more than a shared thought; it must be a shared feeling as well, so that the preacher's encounter with the text allows a hearer's encounter with its essential point. And basic to it all is a talent to respond creatively to what is touched in a text. The psychoanalyst Rollo May once noted about

---

[4] See Joseph A. Fitzmyer, *The Gospel According to Luke X–XXIV*, Introduction, Translation, and Notes (Garden City NY: Doubleday, 1985) xi.

[5] Thomas Carlyle, *On Heroes, Hero-Worship, and the Heroic in History*, ed. Archibald MacMecham (Boston: Ginn and Co., 1901) 90.

[6] Ibid., 107.

poet W. H. Auden: "The poet marries the language, and out of this marriage the poem is born."[7] In the same way, the preacher marries the text, and from that union the sermon is born.

2. A second essential requirement for composing a sermon is to have *a controlling sense of order.* "Order" has to do with how the sermon elements—the stages, "points," or "moves"—are arranged, fitted together, sequenced, and timed. In *Designing the Sermon: Order and Movement in Preaching,* which was published almost thirty years ago and has remained both in print and in use, I treated the classic forms traditionally utilized in the preparation of sermons.[8] That book was part of the Abingdon Preacher's Library, a set of volumes published in the 1980s to serve those whose background in homiletics might be spotty or who needed help in some specific area of their preaching task. I was assigned the topic of sermon design.

A sermon's "design" is the plan devised, mapped out, to order its elements to serve its intended purpose, and there are traditional forms that are valuable as guides as the preacher composes. Basically, sermon design has to do with relating form to function. There is a dialectical relationship between form and content in any creation, and the sermon as a creation is no exception.

This is not the time to treat the tradition of sermon forms in any extended discussion, but it must be said that composing a sermon does require, at some point, that some form must be adopted for it, even if that form is arbitrarily or necessarily *adapted.* I want to illustrate what I mean, and to do so I must refer to the subject of *form* as it *affects* two other creative fields, *music* and *writing.*

---

[7] Rollo May, *The Courage to Create* (New York: W. W. Norton & Co., 1975) 85.

[8] See James Earl Massey, *Designing the Sermon: Order and Movement in Preaching* (Nashville: Abingdon Press, 1980); see also James Earl Massey, *The Sermon in Perspective: A Study of Communication and Charisma* (Grand Rapids: Baker Books, 1976), esp. ch. 4, "The Sermon as Creation," 71–99.

The unique compositions of Ludwig van Beethoven (1770–1827) have received repeated treatment across the centuries. That he was a musical genius was evident from an early period in his life. Beethoven's musical output is all the more remarkable as one recognizes his achievement despite the limitations of the traditional forms for the music of his time. Beethoven adopted those traditional forms and composed within them. In time, however, he creatively adapted some of those forms. Guided in his later years by a sense of some larger significance, Beethoven began writing music in expanded patterns that redefined his legacy as a composer. Basic sonata form had been adequate earlier in writing for the piano, for instance, but his "late" style expanded that form to express his greater vision. Instead of sonatas in the traditional three-movement form, he composed one with four movements, the "Hammerklavier," that pianistically demanding sonata in B-flat, Op. 106, and later, in his last sonata, in C-minor, Op. 111, he used only two movements. He had composed two-movement sonatas before (the two of Op. 49, and the Op. 54 in F and the Op. 90 in E), but these were not on the exalted plain of the sonata in C-minor, Op. 111. Pianist pedagogue Robert Taub has commented, "Opus 111 is the apotheosis; with its conclusion Beethoven has done everything that could be done with the sonata as a genre."[9] Beethoven's creativity had overflowed the banks of traditional sonata form, and his content demanded an altered form. Form serves function, and Beethoven wanted a form that would quicken sensibilities to the substance he was sharing in his music.

Maynard Solomon, a noted Beethoven scholar, has explained that in his later years Beethoven was always seeking "to find a final or good enough form for his creative idea."[10] There were instances when

[9] Robert Taub, *Playing the Beethoven Piano Sonatas* (Portland: Amadeus Press, 2002) 240.

[10] Maynard Solomon, *Late Beethoven: Music, Thought, Imagination* (Berkeley: University of California Press, 2003) 214.

he deconstructed what he had completed in order to recast portions of it in another form. That was the case when he separated a movement from his piano sonata in C, Op. 53, which exists now as that independent portion familiar to us as the "Andante favori, WoO 57." He did so for reasons of form.[11] Beethoven's revising and restructuring the form of what he had composed was necessary to prepare and share what he understood as the "essential point" of a composition. The right form must be found to serve one's function.

Writers and novelists also know this, and when that right form eludes a writer's grasp, anxiety abounds until that needed form is found or shaped. In this regard I am thinking about novelist Ralph Ellison (1913–1994), whose *Invisible Man* so skillfully treated the effects of race distinctions in American culture that he achieved both national and international fame. Informed by surrealism, symbolism, and real life, Ellison's novel is cast in epic form. Although he was influenced by several established writers, such as Herman Melville, James Joyce, Kenneth Burke, and William Faulkner, Ellison was one of a kind and his own man. In some ways Ellison's one-novel fame worked against him, because he was always being asked about his next novel. He was working on another novel, a much longer epic, in fact, but that novel was still in process when Ellison died in 1994. Ellison had worked on that second novel across many years and had completed all of its parts, but he had refused to release it for publication because he was not settled about how those parts should connect. The problem was one of disorder—lack of form. No matter how Ellison rearranged various sections, they still seemed out of context. His adding of characters and his endless improvising on their

---

[11] On this, see Alexander Wheelock Thayer's *Life of Beethoven*, rev. and ed. Elliot Forbes (Princeton: Princeton University Press, 1973) 351; Lewis Lockwood, *Beethoven: The Music and the Life* (New York: W. W. Norton & Co., 2003), esp. 292–93; Taub, *Playing the Beethovan Piano Sonatas*, 111; Charles Rosen, *Beethoven's Piano Sonatas: A Short Companion* (New Haven: Yale University Press, 2002) 136.

interaction had disrupted the form necessary for the novel's plot. That unfinished novel, with its lack of cohesion, remained a source of anxiety for Ralph Ellison until he died.[12]

I have offered considerable detail here about form in Beethoven's music and Ellison's novel writing, perhaps more detail than needed, but it has been shared to underscore the necessity to honor form and structure in shaping any composition, whether it be a symphony, sonata, novel, or sermon; and my statements about Beethoven and Ellison were to acknowledge the legitimacy of adapting a form or structure to make it better serve the "essential point" one seeks to share.

Sermon forms are many, viable, and valuable, but they should be chosen according to the function they are to serve. Choosing a form for an intended sermon sometimes exacts time. The time needed to choose that form can often be shortened, however, if one lets the text suggest the form its message should be given in the sermon. Fortunately, biblical texts can save us not only from having to search for a message, but also from having to fret or fuss over form. Those who do expository preaching know, and rejoice, that this is so.

3. A third essential required in composing sermons is *an honest concern for people.* Sermons are prepared for people—people involved in the details of living, people whose circumstances press and plague them, people who cry out for attention and help. Sermons must be composed with people in mind, people with ambitions and anxieties,

---

[12] See Arnold Rampersad, *Ralph Ellison: A Biography* (New York: Alfred A. Knopf, 2007), esp. 310–11. John F. Callahan, Ellison's literary executor after Ellison's death, stated that Ellison had worked on the second novel on and off for many years, trying to complete "his mythic saga of race and identity, language and kinship in the American experience. Sometimes revising, sometimes reconceiving, sometimes writing entirely new passages into an oft-reworked scene, he accumulated some two thousand pages of typescripts and printouts by the time of his death." See Callahan's introduction to Ralph Ellison in *Juneteenth: A Novel,* ed. John F. Callahan (New York: Random House, 1999) xiii–xiv.

likes and dislikes, emotions and complexes, fears and failures, interests and potential, people with wounds and remembered sins. Sermons must be composed in their interest, and by a preacher whose heart beats steadily with concern for them.

In the introduction to one of his books of sermons, Peter J. Gomes tells of being an avid sermon-taster from his boyhood, and of the powerful effect preaching has had on him across the years. Speaking of his boyhood, Gomes confessed, "I was moved not only by the language but also by the ideas that were generated; and in seeing how one man with a sustained effort could make words work, I cherished the thought that someday I might be able to do the same."[13]

But not all of the sermons Gomes heard in his youth and since were so enthralling. While a student at Bates College, Gomes had a job as organist at a local church whose preacher perhaps lacked the talent to create sermons or lacked awareness of their function, or perhaps both. Gomes remembered "one particularly awful Lenten sermon series" that pastor preached there, the theme of which was "The Complexion of the Crowd." As the sermon course proceeded, Gomes recoiled as that pastor preached about those in the crowd around Jesus who were "Blue with Loyalty," "Purple with Rage," "Green with Envy," or "Black with Treachery." Gomes lamented, "Lent was very long that year."[14]

That experience as a listener helped to sensitize Peter Gomes for the pulpit ministry that has been his in the years since. Speaking about his more than thirty years at Harvard's Memorial Church, Gomes stated that he has never preached a sermon there that he first preached elsewhere. "I resolved early on," he reported, "that my congregation would get the best of my first efforts. I would preach to their situation as I came to know it—not abstractly or generally—and

---

[13] Peter J. Gomes, *Strength for the Journey: Biblical Wisdom for Daily Living* (New York: HarperCollins, 2003) xii.

[14] Ibid.

I would always preach to them, especially the students, as I wish I had been preached to when I was in college."[15] He then added, "These convictions, together with my desire to make words work and my persuasion to connect the living faith with the living condition of honest, smart, but confused people, shaped my agenda as a preacher."[16] To "connect the living faith with the living condition of people"—that must be the consuming concern in composing a sermon to be preached.

It is concern that flavors a sermon, giving it that personal tone that preaching should convey. Concern invests the sermon with "soul," and "soul," that inmost mystery of yourself, gives utterance the winsomeness of music. Jesus taught and preached with "soul," which explains in part why "common people heard him gladly" (Mark 12:37b KJV). "Soul" is truth's ablest messenger, truth's most trusted herald.

"Soul" makes language passionate, and as Thomas Carlyle aptly pointed out, "all passionate language does of itself become musical."[17] He was right: "All in-most things, we may say, are melodious." "All deep things are Song. It seems somehow the very central essence of us, Song; as if all the rest were but wrappages and hulls!" "See deep enough, and you see musically."[18] So much lies in that word "song." It bespeaks a theme, a melodic theme on which any variations, verses, or movements are based. And the word "musical!" It speaks of personal expression, vision, meaning, form, accent, sharing, contagion, feeling, "soul," depth, access to the divine.

Sermons *can* sing! And they usually do when they have been personally composed, pointedly formed, and persuasively shared. Prayerfully conceived and composed, the sermon is a functional statement to "connect the living faith with the living condition of

---

[15] Ibid., xiii.
[16] Ibid.
[17] Carlyle, *On Heroes*, 95.
[18] Ibid.

people." Whether narratival in form, or given a four-point, three-point, two-point, or one-point structure, a sermon sings when life conditions demand it and love motivates its creation and delivery.

George W. Truett (1867–1944) had composed a singing sermon when he used Deuteronomy 33:25—"As thy days, so shall thy strength be"—to preach about "A Promise for Every Day."[19] Living conditions demanded it, and love motivated Truett to explain and remind, through that sermon, that "some days are little, and some days are large, and in all those days, commonplace and ordinary and routine days, Jesus says: 'I will be with you.' And then when come life's testing days—days big with meaning, with terror, with pain, with duty, with trial—Jesus stands there to fortify us as we go on clinging to him."[20]

The members at Concord Baptist Church in Brooklyn, New York, were hearing sacred song as Gardner C. Taylor, their pastor, was preaching from Jeremiah 8:22 about "A Balm in Gilead."[21] Greatly impressed by how his sainted father, Washington Taylor, had preached that subject and text years earlier, Gardner Taylor mentioned that he was using the outline his father had left him, but that the substance and application of the message were his own. That sermon had reached its third point, and its "high note," when Taylor stated that the balm tree's healing power was in its thick liquid, which came out only when the tree was cut and pierced, and that Jesus had to be wounded before the healing flow of his blood could work its wonders in our lives. Taylor concluded with this: "We know at levels deeper than reason that by His wounds we are healed, and in His abandonment the way is open for us to be won forever to God.

---

[19] George W. Truett, "A Promise for Every Day," vol. 8 of *20 Centuries of Great Preaching: An Encyclopedia of Preaching,* ed. Clyde E. Fant, Jr., and William M. Pinson, Jr. (Waco: Word Books, 1971) 144–52.

[20] Ibid.,149.

[21] See pages 71–80 of Gardner C. Taylor, *Chariots Aflame* (Nashville: Broadman Press, 1988).

Christ heals our soul's disease, and He is our Balm in Gilead."[22] That is the gospel message, and a personal experience of what that gospel means and grants can flavor any sermon about it to be heard as song.

Sacred song was in the air at Howard University's Rankin Chapel when Vernon Johns (1892–1963), Martin Luther King, Jr.'s, legendary predecessor at Dexter Avenue Baptist Church in Montgomery, Alabama, was preaching on "The Romance of Death." Johns died shortly afterward.[23] That singing sermon was his "swan song."

Speaking personally, my experience of a call to preach happened during an engaging sermon that grabbed and held my attention. I was at church, part of a large congregation at worship, but my attention was divided. The worship service was in progress, but I was paying more attention to a music score I had brought with me. A piano student at the time, I often carried some music score with me when away from home, using any available moments to study the notation and structure of some composition I wanted to memorize. That morning, I was engrossed in a Chopin waltz. But during a brief let-up in my concentration on that waltz, I found myself being captured by the spirit of the sermon being preached. As I opened myself to the meaning of that moment and to God, I felt caught up in an almost transfixed state of consciousness, and I heard a voice speaking within me: "I want you to preach!" The bidding I heard, though gentle, bore the unmistakable authority of a higher realm. I felt both disturbed and settled. I knew I would have to say yes—and I did.[24]

---

[22] Ibid., 80.

[23] See Taylor Branch, *Parting the Waters: America in the King Years 1954–63* (New York: Simon & Schuster, 1988) 902.

[24] For a fuller report about the inner struggle that ensued to give the pulpit priority over the piano, see James Earl Massey, *Aspects of My Pilgrimage: An Autobiography* (Anderson IN: Anderson University Press, 2002) 52–54. For a theological assessment of struggle as part of the "call" experience, see William H. Myers' *The Irresistible Urge to Preach: A Collection of African American "Call" Stories*

More than sixty years have transpired since that holy hour of call, but the meaning and momentum gained from listening to God, then and since, have kept me assured, directed, encouraged, and committed to preach. Since that call, I have known the work to which my head, heart, and hands were to be devoted, and my concern to preach has never dulled. If that concern ever leaves me, I want the day before that happens to be my last!

(Atlanta: Aaron Press, 1991) 230–32 and *God's Yes Was Louder Than My No: Rethinking the African American Call to Ministry* (Grand Rapids: Eerdmans, 1994), esp. 37–46. For a published interview that gives Gardner Taylor's report about his experience of call to ministry and the struggle that preceded and ensued, see Myers' *The Irresistible Urge to Preach*, 328–30, and *God's Yes Was Louder Than My No*, 38n, 124–25, 127–28.

MEASURING A PREACHER'S CREATIVITY WITH A BORROWED RULER

Joel C. Gregory

Creativity describes a concept that we recognize in the concrete, but it is also a definition that eludes us in the abstract. We may recognize a creative artist, author, architect, or preacher, yet the quality that defines creativity across disciplines we capture only with difficulty.

Psychologist Morris Stein attempts to present an orientation to this abstraction: "Creativity is a process that results in a novel work that is accepted as useful, tenable or satisfying by a significant group of people at some point in time."[1] The emphasis rests on novelty, satisfaction, and the nature of the persons accepting the work as creative. Yet these generalizations present a challenge in defining or measuring creativity in preaching.

This contribution explores aspects of creativity in preaching measured by some psychological research measurements of creativity. There are boundaries of creativity given the nature of divine revelation. Once those are established, this effort will look at five accepted research measurements of creativity as applied to examples of preaching, including those of Gardner C. Taylor: divergence, individual development, intrinsic motivation, community influences, and transpersonal/transcendent influences. The latter will be expanded to consider Carl Jung's theories of synchronicity as they relate to the preaching life. Finally, there will be a word about shepherding creative experiences with an example from the creative writer Anton Chekhov. This research represents the belief that all

---

[1] Morris I. Stein, *Individual Procedures*, vol. 1 of *Stimulating Creativity Series* (New York: Academic Press, 1974) xi.

creativity comes from God, no matter what the discipline may be. Inferences may be taken from any creative field to inform another.

Most agree that creative preaching is desirable. Still, the nature of creative preaching also defies abstract categorization. Creativity diverges across the diverse landscape of anything called *preaching* in the United States, not to mention globally. For pastors of some traditions, creative preaching would involve no more than finding another striking example of assonance from an online dictionary. The outer limits of such creativity might be expressed by moving through the parable of the prodigal son with a rhyming scheme that describes the prodigal's madness, his badness, and his gladness. For others, creativity would involve moving from a deductive, linear sermon to an inductive, nonlinear narrative. Riding the Lowry Loop would be for them a screaming roller coaster as they descend into the analysis of the "ugh."[2] For still others, that narrative creativity is already assumed, and creativity in preaching moves toward edgy conditions for "doing church." Lucy Rose once proposed a church at the round table in which a nonhierarchical community of peers preach to each other and the preachers are more like facilitators of the homiletic discussion.[3] In such an environment, all language about God is provisional, and the best a preacher can do is make a wager for which the congregation may make a counterwager. For Jana Childers, the creative moment comes out of the angst of two competing ideas wrestling for attention during preparation. This contest produces a creative spark, which gives birth to the sermon.[4]

These limited examples offer a wide variety of creative preaching with the choice of words, the selection of homiletic forms, the

---

[2] See Eugene L. Lowry, *The Homiletical Plot: The Sermon as Narrative Art Form*, rev. ed. (Louisville: Westminster John Knox Press, 2001) 39–52.

[3] See Lucy Atkinson Rose, *Sharing the Word: Preaching in the Roundtable Church* (Louisville: Westminster John Knox Press, 1997) 59–85.

[4] Jana Childers, "A Shameless Path," *Birthing the Sermon: Women Preachers on the Creative Process*, ed. Jana Childers (St. Louis: Chalice Press, 2001) 36.

environment within the church, or the private moment of sermon conception in preparation. Such diversity begs the question, "What common ground belongs to most creative sermons?"

The Limits of Creativity in Christian Preaching

Abraham Maslow describes the creative moment as an experience of losing self in a peak experience that transcends the past and future and lives only in the moment. This creative moment is described "as being naked in the situation, guileless, without *a priori* expectations, without 'should's' or 'ought's,' without fashions, fads, dogmas, habits or other pictures-in-the-head of what is proper, without surprise, shock, indignation, or denial," all of which he ascribes to a childlike state.[5] In this flow, inhibitions are lost, fear disappears, courage wards off ridicule, trust replaces striving, and the individual enters into a state of Taoistic receptivity in which the thing created becomes an end in itself.[6] We might agree that such a state befits a deaf Beethoven manically composing a symphony or an obsessed Jackson Pollock drizzling paint onto a canvas while sitting on the floor of a hut on Long Island. But does this state also describe the creativity of a preacher?

Creative preaching has boundaries for canonical Christians. One boundary is the canon itself. Although we may find Hertzberg's or Gopnik's latest ruminations in *The New Yorker* stunningly creative, they are not the psalms or 2 John. The preacher's creative muse works within the confines of a prescribed canon handed to him in that great *paradosis* that has a venerable history. We work with a given, in the same sense that a piano has eighty-eight keys for both the beginner and Van Cliburn. This defines an element of creativity in Christian preaching. We are creative within a given canonical perimeter. To be

---

[5] Abraham H. Maslow, "The Creative Attitude," *Explorations in Creativity*, ed. Ross L. Mooney and Taher A. Razik (New York: Harper & Row, 1967) 48.

[6] Ibid., 50–54.

specific, we may not next Sunday invent a "Quadrinity" rather than a Trinity in order to say something fresh.

A responsible discussion of Christian preaching embraces the larger boundaries of preaching itself. God is a speaking God, so we can name God in preaching. Immink posits against more evocative preaching in which "concepts like truth, objectivity, universality and reason are viewed with extreme suspicion." In an elegant and nuanced appeal, he calls for a return to some boundaries that define the act of preaching, including the suggestions that actual predications may be made about God rather than evoked from analogs in human experience.[7] Certainly, a review of Gardner C. Taylor's sermons has clearly reflected a preacher who believes predications can be made about God. While leaving room for mystery, Taylor has nevertheless exercised creativity within a boundary of the Protestant view of biblical preaching. He believes that God speaks, and that we can make predications about what God said.[8]

Fred B. Craddock also reminds us that the congregation does not crave boundless novelty. In fact, he insists that ninety percent of what

---

[7] F. Gerrit Immink, "Homiletics: The Current Debate," *International Journal of Practical Theology* 8/1 (April 2004): 104. Was accessed online and retrieved 10 July 2009 from Academic Search Premier database.

[8] Gardner C. Taylor, "The Preacher's Trinity of Needs: The Preacher's Authority," given at the Sprinkle Lectures, Atlantic Christian College, Wilson, North Carolina, 1983, in *Lectures, Essays, and Interviews*, vol. 5 of *The Words of Gardner Taylor*, comp. Edward L. Taylor (Valley Forge: Judson Press, 2001) 236. Referring to P. T. Forsyth, Taylor declares in agreement, "Preaching then is not the exploration, or exploitation, of an idea or of ideas but rather the placarding and announcement of a long, divine act which comes to the view of time in Eden, proceeds through individuals who are set upon and seized by the determined searching purpose of God.... This is the preaching the Bible brings to the preacher, and it is within these august considerations authentic pulpit work is ever to be done." Such expressions may be found throughout the Taylor sermons and lectures.

we say ought to have the ring of the familiar.[9] Folks really do want to hear the old, old story, and it really does seem sweeter to them than the first time they heard it. To use a very nonecclesial comparison, those attending a Willie Nelson concert may listen to his new stuff for two hours, but they will not leave until the ageless septuagenarian nasally intones "On the Road Again."[10] They really do want to hear some of the old stuff. Likewise, Christian preaching is not served by being totally novel. People in the pew do not want a better, postmodern substitute for the prodigal or the Good Shepherd looking for the lost sheep. In other words, the preacher might pause before changing that story into a modern example of someone looking for his lost iPhone among all of his other gadgets.

There is also the boundary of a given tradition. Thomas G. Long opines that all denominational traditions have a downside and an upside. The downside involves the blinders that our peculiar traditions put on all of us. Church doctrinal traditions all suffer myopia. Yet there is also no traction for preaching in having *no* tradition.[11] Preaching may be *said* from no known tradition, but it will not be widely *heard* from no known tradition. Creativity that blows away all tradition in the name of novelty creates shock, and shock ends communication. Emil Durkheim insisted that tradition builds community. If creativity pushes ecclesial tradition over the edge, you have no community.

The necessity for other boundaries could be expanded. For example, some creative moves work with one preacher's personality but not with that of another's. Tony Campolo can say things that

---

[9] Fred B. Craddock, *Preaching* (Nashville: Abingdon Press, 1985) 46, 160.

[10] Willie Nelson, "On the Road Again." "On the Road Again" was released in November 1980 and became one of Nelson's most recognizable tunes throughout America and the world. It was Nelson's ninth number one hit, and it reached number twenty on the Billboard Hot 100.

[11] Thomas G. Long, *The Witness of Preaching* (Louisville: Westminster John Knox Press, 1989) 53.

would get me thrown out or possibly knocked out, but he is applauded because his preaching style fits him. This involves the boundary of personality. Introverted preachers cannot become pulpit clowns in order to be creative. The difference between a river and a flood is a boundary. For creativity to flow, it must flow within some defined boundaries, Maslow notwithstanding.

Boundaries for creativity may belong to the venue, the aesthetics, the accepted liturgical tradition and any variety or combination of things that could push a congregation over the edge and create shock, which stops communication. You may be as creative as you wish, but if you do not communicate at all you are singing a solo with no one listening.

Within some canonical and ecclesial boundaries, can creativity in preaching be defined using generally accepted academic canons for creativity? If so, what canons apply?

Measurement and Description of Creativity

Is there any basis for measuring creativity other than sheer subjectivity, such as "I know art when I see it"? Before discussing the narrower measurement or description of creativity in preaching, we may consider generally accepted approaches to creativity in any discipline. Marquee names in psychology have studied creativity for the last twenty-five years. The *cognitive* school bases its research in a mechanistic view that creativity "is merely a fascinating puzzle or problem to be solved, not a mystery."[12] In the mid-twentieth century, psychometrician Joy P. Guilford proposed the design of creativity tests, similar to IQ tests. When given a puzzle to solve, creative people demonstrate *divergent thinking*, which uses unique ways to

---

[12] Melvin E. Miller, "Introduction" in *Creativity, Spirituality and Transcendence,* ed. Melvin E. Miller and Susanne R. Cook-Greuter (Stamford CT: Ablex Publishing Corporation, 2000) xxi.

solve the problem by drawing outside the line, or idiosyncratic personal approaches to arrive at the solution.[13]

In contrast, Gruber approached the study of creativity through individual case studies of creative persons who show that they "engage in a wide and broadly connected network of enterprises; exhibit a sense of purpose or will that permeates their entire network, giving direction to their daily and yearly activities; favor the creation of exploitation of images of wide scope...and display a close and continuing affective tie to the elements, problems or phenomena that are being studied."[14]

Other models of creativity deal with personality and motivation. Freud famously lodged creativity in sublimation of libidinal energy. Behaviorists find motivation for creativity in material rewards. Others find that creativity best flows from intrinsic motivation, the sheer joy of engaging in a creative endeavor as a thing in itself.[15] Mihaly Csikszentmihalyi points to intrinsic motivation as a shared characteristic of creative people, while at the same time emphasizing personal, cultural, and historical contexts that inform the concept.[16] These intrinsically motivated creators reach their zenith in the flow experience—that highly honored peak experience in which all else disappears except the thing being created and the experience of creation. Gardner went further in the direction of Gruber in a magisterial study of Freud, Einstein, Picasso, Stravinsky, T. S. Eliot, Martha Graham (dancer), and Gandhi to determine the commonalities and divergent aspects of these acclaimed creative individuals.

---

[13] Howard Gardner, *Creating Minds: An Anatomy of Creativity Seen through the Lives of Freud, Einstein, Picasso, Stravinsky, Eliot, Graham and Gandhi* (New York: Basic Books, 1993) 20.

[14] Ibid., 22–23.

[15] Ibid., 24–26.

[16] Miller, *Creativity, Spirituality and Transcendence*, xxii–xxiii.

Joel Funk, a psychologist at Plymouth State College, represents a relatively newer departure for explaining creativity—that of the transpersonal or transcendent approach. Along with Wilber, Alexander, and Washburn, Funk argues for a "paradigm shift in one's conception of mind and reality...a transcendent mode of consciousness or a 'Ground of Being' that is ontologically prior to and qualitatively different from the ordinary egoic consciousness studied by mainstream psychologists."[17] He even goes so far as to assert, "If we are 'made in the image of God,' then human creativity mirrors divine creativity. If the microcosm reflects the macrocosm, as esotericism maintains, then we as human beings must embody, to some extent, the characteristics of the divine as well."[18]

That the *imago dei* is defined by or includes creativity is not an original concept with Funk. Theologian James Leo Garrett, Jr., summarizes historic and systematic theologians' views on the *imago dei*. A number of them approach defining this concept as creativity. Philip Edgcumbe Hughes, for example, identified a constellation of capacities, including creativity, as stamps of the *imago*.[19] If indeed, as believers confess, there is a transcendent source for creativity, psychology and theology may have a *tertium comparationis* in the creativity discussion.

These measurements or descriptions of creativity may provide some new angles of vision on creativity in preaching. Creative preachers seem to formulate their sermons through *divergent thinking*, the capacity measured by Guilford in her creativity tests. There is no "preacher creativity score" psychometric test. Anecdotal evidence for divergent thinking in preaching, however, is accessible. The creative preacher/pastor Ralph Douglas West, Sr., for example, once preached

---

[17] Joel Funk, "Inspired Creativity," in *Creativity, Spirituality and Transcendence*, Miller and Cook-Greuter, eds., 58.

[18] Ibid., 60.

[19] James Leo Garrett, Jr., vol. 1 of *Systematic Theology: Biblical, Historical and Evangelical*, 2d ed. (North Richland Hills TX: Bibal Press, 2000) 464.

a series of messages with a divergent view of the evangelical pop-culture book *Left Behind*. His series addressed those "left behind" at critical junctures in the biblical narrative: the two servants who waited while Abraham took Isaac to the mountain (Genesis 22:3–5), the servant left at Beersheba when Elijah escaped to the wilderness (1 Kings 19:3–4), and the powerless disciples at the bottom of the Mount of Transfiguration (Matthew 17:14–18). Rather than looking at the passages from the traditional frontal aspect, West addressed the scenes from the point of view of those left alone as their master/mentor disappeared. The two with Abraham and Isaac waited within an atmosphere of sheer mystery. The servant of Elijah waited while a mentor left him alone at the edge of the wilderness. The disciples were left powerless in the outer circle while Jesus and the inner circle were above them on a mountaintop. Such experiences seem appealingly more relevant to the congregation than other popular riffs on being left behind.

Such preaching may be compared to an anamorphic painting, one that may best be seen in perspective by looking at it from the side. Perspectival anamorphoses in painting began at least by the fifteenth century (Hans Holbein used it). An object is inserted into a painting that can be seen only from another angle of perspective, usually from an oblique angle. You cannot see the object from a straightforward perspective.[20] Anamorphic preaching takes a sidelong

---

[20] Fred Leeman, *Hidden Images: Games of Perception, Anamorphic Art, Illusion from the Renaissance to the Present,* trans. Ellyn Childs Allison and Margaret L. Kaplan (New York: Harry N. Abrams, Inc., 1975) 9: "The system of central perspective not only rationalizes the relationship between objects in a picture, but also establishes a relationship between the viewer and the represented images. Anamorphoses are an extreme example of this subjectivization of the viewing process. The observer is first deceived by a barely recognizable image, and is then directed to a viewpoint dictated by the formal construction of the painting." That is, the observer sees the anamorphic image from an oblique angle. See Susan Foister, ed., *Holbein in England* (London: Tate Publishing, 2006) 12. The painting there presented may be the most famous anamorphosis: *The Ambassadors.* Beneath

view at texts to discover characters, situations, and concepts that may be seen best from an unusual angle of vision.

Randall O'Brien exemplifies an anamorphic creative approach to the Jacob, Leah, and Rachel cycle. Typically, preachers look at the threesome as a triad in a tableaux that quickly dismisses Leah, and the congregation typically rejoices that Jacob finally stays on eHarmony long enough to get Rachel and live happily ever after. O'Brien takes an anamorphic look, a divergent but faithful way to look at the passage. He asks, "What is it like to *get* Leah?" He explores living with life's second choices. Then he does another anamorphosis: What is it like to *be* Leah? How do you live when you know that you are the second choice in anything? He demonstrates how this unwinds in holy history. This change of perspective lights up a familiar narrative with light coming from another window that we have not seen before.

Taylor's sermons abound in anamorphic approaches to texts, demonstrating divergent creativity. In his sermon "Balm in Gilead" (Jeremiah 8:22), Taylor looks at the familiar phrase from the anamorphic viewpoint of the location, unimpressive nature, and medicinal use of the plant. The plant comes from *outside* Israel. Likewise, we need help from beyond ourselves. Moreover, just as the plant is not a majestic tree but a mere unsightly bush, there was nothing humanly impressive about the Christ who saves us. The plant yields its medicinal power not from its leaves or roots, but from being cut; only when it is cut does it bleed forth its healing balm. In the wounds of Jesus we find redemption.[21]

---

the feet of two gentlemen is an object indecipherable from a frontal view. From an oblique angle, it is a skull. The skull sits beneath a table strewn with objects of human achievement in music, arts, and exploration. The insinuation is subtle: the presence of mortality lurks beneath all human achievement and may only be seen from an angle.

[21] Gardner C. Taylor, *Quintessential Classics, 1980–Present*, vol. 3 of *The Words of Gardner Taylor*, comp. Edward L. Taylor (Valley Forge: Judson Press, 2000) 29–34.

In "Wide Visions from a Narrow Window" (Job 19:25–27), Taylor brilliantly uses the device of a narrowing window as Job's harrowing trials multiply. Here is the anamorphic device of using a concrete object—a window—as a metaphor with an extended *tertium* throughout the text. Early in the message Taylor proclaims, "The window has narrowed out of which he looks upon the landscape of life. Once, there had been the homes of children and fruitful fields and grazing cattle and bleating sheep. But now the window has narrowed."[22] Later, in the midst of Job's awful cries, Taylor preaches, "Here is where the window narrows to a slit."[23] Finally, at the triumphant conclusion, Taylor rhetorically throws the window open with Job's proclamation of indomitable faith. One can almost feel the air come in.

In the message "It Takes All Kinds" (Matthew 22:31–32), Taylor takes an oblique angle with the divine statement, "I am the God of Abraham, Isaac, and Jacob." He does a character study of each patriarch by portraying his respective strengths and deficiencies. Abraham towers as a giant. Isaac becomes a disappointing non-entity. Jacob is the twisted deceiver. Yet God is the God of them all. Taylor takes an oblique angle on this passage related to the resurrection of the dead by offering a word of encouragement for the living: we can all be in God's family.[24]

When applied to preaching, the criterion of creativity suggests that we look not only at sermons, but rather at underlying principles

---

[22] Ibid., 65.

[23] Ibid., 66.

[24] Gardner C. Taylor, *50 Years of Timeless Treasures*, vol. 6 of *The Words of Gardner Taylor*, comp. Edward L. Taylor (Valley Forge: Judson Press, 2002) 11–15. Other sermons in volume 6 demonstrating anamorphoses are "The Word Moses Could Not Say" (Exodus 32:32) 73–77; "Why Murder in Church?" (Mark 12:4–9) 90–95, a sermon delivered on the occasion of the tragic murder of Mrs. Martin Luther King, Sr., while sitting behind the church organ; and "Down Payment and Will Call" (Ephesians 1:11–14) 221–28.

that motivate a creative preacher over a lifetime of preaching. Reinhold Niebuhr's anthropology motivated him to rail against Henry Ford from his Detroit pulpit, and that same anthropology motivated him to assail racial injustice and diplomatic myopia. The creative element of Niebuhr's preaching came not from any one sermon, but from a larger gestalt—a constant from Christian anthropology that informed all of his preaching. He exemplifies a preacher whose creativity may best be explored by taking it in as a whole. No one sermon embraces the creative impact of his lifetime, from Detroit to Union Seminary.[25]

An in-depth study of Taylor's lifetime pulpit achievements reveals a whole that is more than the sum of its parts. A profound empathy for the human condition, a sometimes stinging call for social justice, and a personal piety exist together in an atmosphere laced with the mystery of God.[26] The legacy of Taylor may be measured in a way similar to the *oeuvre* of a great artist whose similar themes play throughout a lifetime.

How may we measure the creativity of the intrinsically motivated preacher—the preacher who does the thing for the sheer joy of doing it? This raises other questions that go to the heart of preaching itself. Is the act of preaching a thing to be committed to for the unadulterated joy of doing it creatively? Is the pulpit a self-gratifying exhibition of rhetoric for the intrinsically motivated preacher? If so,

---

[25] See the bibliographical data on Niebuhr in Clyde E. Fant, Jr., and William M. Pinson, Jr., eds., vol. 10 of *20 Centuries of Great Preaching: An Encyclopedia of Preaching* (Waco: Word Books, 1971) 342–56.

[26] When the observation was made that the major theme in Taylor's preaching was the combination of social justice and warm Christian devotion, Taylor responded, "I hope that has been true. And if my preaching has drawn any attention, more than the regular run of things, it has been due, I think, to that attempt to bring the Gospel then, and the Gospel now, together in the belief that what God has joined together, no man ought to seek to put asunder." Gardner C. Taylor, interviewed by Joel C. Gregory, 17 March 2008, interview 3, transcript, Baylor University Institute for Oral History, Baylor University, Waco TX, 15.

where did the congregation go during this peak experience, this "going with the flow"? Is the preacher driven to create sermons in the same way Michelangelo and Picasso were driven to create art? It is challenging to find a biblical model for preaching that is as intrinsically motivated as artists motivated by the thing itself, without regard for the public perception of the thing. The prophets spoke of the "burden of the Lord." An assessment of Paul's preaching would not leave you with the impression that he enjoyed the sheer aesthetic pleasure of composing and delivering sermons, certainly not the Paul who wrote, "Knowing the fear of the Lord, we persuade men" (2 Corinthians 5:11), nor the Paul who was stoned at Lystra but still showed up the next day preaching at Derbe (Acts 14:19–21).

The history of preaching surely has known preachers who may have been in love with their own rhetorical skills. Henry Ward Beecher of Plymouth Church in Brooklyn or Joseph Parker of City Temple in London belonged to a league of preachers who seemed conscious of their ability to turn a phrase. They gave some the impression that they were preachers who would have enjoyed listening to themselves even if no one showed up.[27] Of Beecher, O. C. Edwards, Jr., writes, "So effective was his communication that his preaching came to be regarded as one of the tourist attractions of the metropolitan area that every visitor from this country or abroad had to experience."[28]

---

[27] See Debby Applegate, *The Most Famous Man in America: The Biography of Henry Ward Beecher* (New York: Doubleday, 2006) 173. Joseph Parker in *A Preacher's Life: An Autobiography and an Album* (Boston: T. Y. Crowell, 1899) 251, brags in his own autobiography of the electrifying effect of his response in a theological debate, claiming direct inspiration of the Holy Spirit for his repartee. This would be no surprise to those familiar with his ministry.

[28] O. C. Edwards, Jr., *A History of Preaching* (Nashville: Abingdon Press, 2004) 636.

In comparison, I do not find a trace of such rhetorical swagger in Taylor's sermons. In his first Lyman Beecher lecture, Taylor speaks of the audacity of preaching at all:

> Measured by almost any gauge, preaching is a presumptuous business. If the undertaking does not have some sanctions beyond human reckoning, then it is indeed rash and audacious for one person to dare to stand up before or among other people and declare that he or she brings from the eternal God a message for those who listen which involves issues nothing less than those of life and death.[29]

The overall tone of this lecture, as well as all of Taylor's comments about ministry, does not betray someone who preaches for the intrinsic joy of creating a rhetorical masterpiece. Although a rhetorical giant, Taylor displays an attitude toward preaching that is more like one of an ambulance attendant trying to get humanity some urgent help than someone who enjoys polishing the ambulance and blowing the siren.

The Significance of a Creative Community

A fourth psychological measurement of creativity investigates the environment of the creator. Creativity in preaching depends on various environmental factors. One congregation criticized its pastor for dull sermons. He responded that he would preach less dull sermons when he had a less dull congregation. It is a Sisyphean task for a pastor to preach creative sermons to a decidedly uncreative congregation. As Craddock pointed out, the congregation has a role in preaching. The work does not all belong to the preacher at any

---

[29] Gardner C. Taylor, "Recognizing and Removing the Presumptuousness of Preaching" [Lyman Beecher Lectures, Yale University, 1976] in *Lectures, Essays and Interviews*, vol. 5 of *The Words of Gardner Taylor*, comp. Edward L. Taylor (Valley Forge: Judson Press, 2001) 147.

point in preaching, certainly not in the creative process.[30] A stimulating congregation will produce a stimulated preacher.

In Howard Gardner's study of creativity based on seven creative geniuses, he discovered that each of them had an individual or community of support that fostered creativity. Sigmund Freud had Wilhelm Fliess, who served both as a partner in dialogue about Freud's unprecedented ideas in psychology as well as a personal confidant and nurturing figure in non-professional areas of Freud's life.[31] Georges Braque, although different in striking ways from Picasso, became the artist's inseparable companion for six years before World War I, undoubtedly providing the stimulus that helped him work out the torqued and twisted figures of cubism. Gardner states, "Without question, the particular form cubism took and its speed in transforming the artistic world resulted from the unusually intense and productive collaboration between these two artists, still not thirty years of age."[32] Gardner also demonstrates a similar collaborative stimulation of creativity between Louis Horst and Martha Graham in dance, Ezra Pound and T.S. Eliot in literature, as well as the Diaghilev circle and its influence on Igor Stravinsky.[33]

Mauzy and Harriman note that environment continues to be a fundamental part of creativity: "Climate has an overwhelming influence on the success of creativity. Creativity does not occur in a vacuum; it needs a sympathetic environment." They go on to insist that "persons need to build a defense system against the hostility or apathy that creativity faces from the larger environment."[34] Similarly, in his clinical psychological work on creativity, Morris Stein has observed, "Environmental factors also play a critical role in blocking

---

[30] Craddock, *Preaching*, 25–26.

[31] Gardner, *Creating Minds*, 62.

[32] Ibid., 160–61.

[33] Ibid., 384.

[34] Jeff Mauzy and Richard Harriman, *Creativity, Inc.: Building an Inventive Organization* (Boston: Harvard Business School Press, 2003) 7.

or facilitating the creative process. It is possible that some individuals would manifest more creativity if they were in environments that valued and supported creativity."[35]

Regarding his creativity in preaching, Taylor pays tribute to factors in his own environment. His family experience, the African-American experience as a whole, and the community of preachers with whom he labored and spoke during the golden era for preaching in New York City formed a constellation of influences. Concerning the early influences in his life, Dr. Taylor recalls,

> I heard a lot of preachers, black preachers, in Louisiana. And I profited from them. Sometimes their language was very crude, and sometimes their reasoning was coarse. But they were wrestling with something. It was what theologians—theologs—call *theodicy*, the ways of God with people. And I recall, long before the liberationist theologians came along, these men in their own way were trying to figure out what was the reason and logic and divine purpose in the black presence in America.[36]

Another influence on Taylor was his father, a preacher who did not finish high school and who died by the time Taylor was thirteen: "I remember his preaching, and he was talking about the battle of Thermopylae and Wolsey and the London Tower. Oh, it got into me. And somehow he was relating it to his Gospel so that I have never had a problem relating what is happening to what God has done."[37]

When Taylor went to the Concord Missionary Baptist Church in Brooklyn for his magisterial ministry, there he was, surrounded by a constellation of great preachers. He points to the influence of his conversations with Sandy Ray, Paul Scherer, William Sloane Coffin,

---

[35] Stein, *Individual Procedures*, 9.

[36] Gardner C. Taylor, interviewed by Joel C. Gregory, 22 January 2007, interview 1, transcript, Baylor University Institute for Oral History, Baylor University, Waco, TX, 3–4.

[37] Ibid., 4–5.

Harry Emerson Fosdick, Robert McCracken, George Buttrick, Norman Vincent Peale, and Adam Clayton Powell. Today, Taylor pays eloquent tribute to the chemistry among this coterie of pulpit giants that pushed him into his own creativity.[38]

The cultural context of preaching surely contributes to creativity. Taylor has repeatedly emphasized the reality of vivid narrative imagination in oppressed cultures, such as the African-American experience. The suffocation of freedom by oppression on the one hand may produce an explosion of creativity on the other. The creative impulse may be such that the oppression of persons—like the compression of air in a pneumatic tool—will find an outlet. The striking narrative creativity in Taylor's sermons underscores this. In the maturity of his latter years, Taylor identifies environmental influences that, from the beginning, have fertilized his creative preaching.

Even brief exposure to creative communities boosts creative insights. Both cognitive and affective communities may stimulate creativity in preaching. Over a four-year period, I have conducted thirty-three four-day, small-group seminars for preaching pastors in association with a program sponsored by Georgetown College in Georgetown, Kentucky. Some 211 preachers have participated in fifteen locations throughout the United States and at Regents Park College in Oxford. This model utilizes one sermon text per day in a group reading of the text and related analytical exegetical commentaries. The group works through the text together, with each member contributing insights to the exegetical and homiletic task. The cumulative impact of this approach of working five hours daily for four days has demonstrated the cognitive aspect of group exegesis and discussion. Over the same four-day session, affective relationships have also developed among the preachers, which contribute to a

---

[38] Gardner C. Taylor, interviewed by Joel C. Gregory, 17 March 2008, interview 2, transcript, Baylor University Institute for Oral History, Waco, TX, 6–12.

community of both empathy and support for the challenging task of creating biblical sermons with authenticity and integrity. Post-seminar evaluations across four years with groups of disparate locations, widely varied educational backgrounds, and different tenures in ministry have yielded a consistent evaluation of enhanced creativity. This multiplication of perspectives, combined with the polyvalent nature of texts, has enriched the experience. This micro-environment of mutual encouragement has heightened creativity through both cognitive and affective interaction.

Creativity from Other Disciplines and Transcendent
Sources for Creativity

Creativity begets creativity. There may be some credence to the "Mozart Effect."[39] Preachers who regularly expose themselves to other creative circles may find themselves thinking creatively.

Leonard Sweet practices what he calls "randomizing rituals." That is, he seizes things to read randomly that have nothing to do with preaching or theology. While running through an airport, he may pick up a copy of a sewing magazine. At another venue, he might clutch something else. This randomized approach to reading fertilizes his imagination in ways he cannot anticipate. All of this feeds his specialty: semiotics.[40] His preaching shows evidence of metaphors flowing from multiple sources.

The preaching life indeed may manifest synchronicity, a concept defined by Carl Jung, in the creation of sermons. Synchronous events

---

[39] Edward F. Zigler, Matia Finn-Stevenson, and Nancy W. Hall, *The First Three Years & Beyond: Brain Development and Social Policy* (New Haven: Yale University Press, 2002) 139. The authors point out, not approvingly, the oft-quoted but empirically unproved relationship between listening to Mozart and cognitive enhancement.

[40] Leonard Sweet, untitled lecture at George W. Truett Theological Seminary's 5th Annual Conference for Pastors and Laity (sound recording, digital CD), MA 0564, February 5–7, 2007.

appear to be random, but upon further reflection of experience, they seem not to be random at all. Events, people, and circumstances that superficially appear to be unrelated and disconnected turn out to be significantly related. This is Jung's own definition: "I chose this term because the simultaneous occurrence of two meaningfully but not causally connected events seemed to me an essential criterion.... Synchronicity therefore means the simultaneous occurrence of a certain psychic state with one or more external events which appear as meaningful parallels to the momentary subjective state."[41]

Jung gives both empirical and anecdotal evidence in his essay. In one twenty-four-hour period in 1949, Jung personally encountered no less than six independent references involving a fish: fish for lunch on 1 April; a proverb about fish; a Latin reference to *piscis*; a patient who showed him impressive pictures of a fish she had painted; an embroidery with fish-like sea monsters he observed that evening; and, on the following morning, a patient with a dream about a fish that swam straight toward her. All of this occurred while Jung was studying the archetypical significance of the fish symbol in all literature. On top of all that, at the very moment he was writing the work cited, he walked to a lakeshore and found a dead fish that was one foot long and apparently uninjured. This completed a seven-fold experience in twenty-four hours, with each instance and person completely separate and unknown to the other.[42] He further gives remarkable instances of synchronicity in empirical studies, anecdotal events, and his own experience.

I suggest that creative preaching lives with the expectation of the synchronous. That is, something in the lived experience of the preacher will touch the lived experience of the author remembered in the biblical text. To live the preaching life is to be surprised by bus

---

[41] C. G. Jung, "Synchronicity: An Acausal Connecting Principle," trans. R.F.C. Hull, *The Interpretation of Nature and the Psyche*, vol. 51 of *The Bolingen Series* (New York: Pantheon Books, 1955) 36.

[42] Ibid., 14–15.

bench signs, billboards, tattered magazines in the waiting room, program notes for an opera, bumper stickers, art museums, short stories, and snippets from Garrison Keillor. One of Jung's corollaries of synchronicity simply stated is this: "The more you look for it the more you see it." If you expect synchronicity, it happens. He arrived at this conclusion based on empirical evidence from actual trials.

Likewise, any preacher with an intentional, planned program of preaching may know the focus of messages ahead. A preacher whose sermon plan includes subjects such as greed, isolation, singleness, a need for guidance, or theodicy will have creative lived experience stalk him. An embarrassment of riches awaits the preacher who is simply aware. Then, synchronicity happens. There can be a flow of preaching preparation in which horizons fuse—now and then merging—and creative insight into the text tackles the preacher from behind.

Taylor certainly lived with a sense of this kind of transcendence in his preaching. Although he may not have used the term *synchronicity*, his preaching and life provide overwhelming evidence for his belief in a Providence that brings together apparently acausal events and random sequences to give them a special meaning.[43]

---

[43] Gardner C. Taylor, interviewed by Joel C. Gregory, 22 January 2007, interview 1, transcript, Baylor University Institute for Oral History, Baylor University, Waco, TX, 12–13. Taylor has often referred to the event that led him to drop the pursuit of law and surrender to ministry. He was driving the car belonging to the president of Leland College, a 1934 Dodge sedan, when he struck a Model T Ford that cut in front of him. One man died on the spot. The accident was witnessed by two whites, whose testimony exonerated him at the inquest. This was so unlikely in the Jim Crow South that he considered their random presence at the event to be an act of God, which later thrust him into ministry. His ministry was born in synchronicity.

Shepherding Lived Experience

The corpus of Taylor's sermons demonstrates another motif. He seems to ripen experiences before taking them to the pulpit. There is no sense of hurry, rush, prematurity, or pragmatism in the lived experiences he uses. Mellowed with the robustness of aged reflection, they have then been woven into his sermons. One also senses that he has not lived life to collect stories for sermons, but rather the stories in his sermons have come from a life really lived.

Some experiences must not be imported into the sermon next Sunday. They may be an aesthetic experience of value in their own right. Indeed, the preacher may not be best served by the immediate import of every creative experience into a sermon. In Chekhov's play *The Seagull*, the troubled writer Tregorin complains bitterly to Nina, a young woman of means and sensitivity, that he cannot experience life because he uses his experiences up in his art:

> Every moment I keep thinking about the story I haven't finished. I notice a cloud, which looks like a grand piano, and I think: I must mention somewhere in a story that a cloud floats by looking like a grand piano. There is a smell of heliotrope. I make a quick mental note: sickly-sweet, widow's deep purple, I must remember this when I describe a summer evening.... I have no rest from myself. I feel that I am cannibalizing my own life. For the honey I send off to the great unknown, I gather the pollen from my favorite flowers and then tear up their petals and trample on their roots.[44]

Indeed, Chekhov himself suggested shepherding experiences and ripening them but not delivering them to print prematurely.[45] The preacher could well learn from both Chekhov's character Tregorin and the dramatist's literary experience itself. Tragedy, triumph, art,

---

[44] Anton Chekhov, *The Seagull*, trans. Nicholas Saunders and Frank Dwyer, *Great Translations for Actors Series* (Newbury VT: Smith and Kraus, 1994) 36.

[45] D. S. Mirsky, "Chekhov," *Anton Chekhov's Short Stories*, ed. Ralph E. Matlaw, Norton Critical Edition (New York: W. W. Norton & Co., 1979) 296.

music, reading, and travel are worthy experiences in and of themselves, rather than merely events to be used at a later time. In fact, that attitude stunts creativity in preaching. The preacher need not be a "lived experience harvesting machine" that must sift through every encounter and observation until it fits a sermon. The creative preacher can live in the moment, not planning the next sermon story.

Gardner Calvin Taylor has lived *lives*, not just *a life*. He has preached to presidents. He called John F. Kennedy, Robert Kennedy, and Jackie Robinson by their first names. He vacationed with Martin Luther King, Jr. Yet none of these experiences with icons of history cheaply permeates his sermons. He has lived life to the brim, and, like ripened fruit, some of it falls naturally into his creative homiletic art.

THE MAGIC OF MUSIC AND METAPHOR: PREACHING AND THE ARTS

Donald E. Demaray

"'And what is the use of a book,' thought Alice, 'without pictures or conversations?'"
—Lewis Carroll[1]

"Bach gave us God's Word;
Mozart gave us God's laughter;
Beethoven gave us God's fire;
God gave us music that we
    might pray without words."[2]
—From a German opera house

The Magic of Metaphor

Reverend Charles Lutwidge Dodgson lived nearly a half-century at Christ Church College, Oxford University, where he taught mathematics. He seemed to have an uncommon fondness for Christ Church, his *alma mater*. His pen name was Lewis Carroll (Lewis from the Latin for Lutwidge and Carroll from the Latin for Charles), author of *Alice in Wonderland*. Deaf in one ear and afflicted with a stammer, he nonetheless taught university classes for decades. Though ordained, he seldom preached. During a social evening, he might have said very little, even nothing. Shyness, no doubt enhanced by his handicaps, robbed him of normal conversation.

---

[1] Lewis Carroll, *The Annotated Alice: Alice's Adventure in Wonderland & Through the Looking Glass* (New York: Bramhall House, 1960).

[2] Anonymous. Found on a wall in a German Opera House.

When with children, his spirit often found release. Children loved him. Though appearing rather austere, he stood tall and neatly dressed. The professor was full of fun. He played games, did magic, invented puzzles with words and numbers, and seemed never to tire of entertaining young people.

His favorite little girl, Alice Liddell, daughter of the dean of Christ Church College, may have become Alice in Wonderland. The relationship, rather like niece and especially loved uncle, created joyful rapport.

The Interplay of Left and Right Brains

Imagine—an Oxford professor of mathematics *and* the author of children's stories! What appears a contradictory pair of behaviors is actually quite common: the left and right brains co-mingling and feeding each other.

(1) Thomas Jefferson while writing the Declaration of Independence, sometimes stumbled over finding just the right word; playing his violin teased out of his brain just the right words to put on paper. Someone called Jefferson the Jascha Heifetz of his generation.

(2) His teachers thought schoolboy Albert Einstein stupid. Refusing this diagnosis, his parents bought their son a violin. Albert became one of the seminal mathematicians of all time. In adulthood, Einstein played with a string group for fun, relaxation, and no doubt cognitive enhancement.

(3) J. S. Bach knew musical theory and mathematics—else he could not have composed his magnificent fugues. Listening to any of Bach's compositions (He created over 1,100 of them!), one is aware of his left-brain prowess, as well as his ability to translate cognitive material into enormously esthetic music.

(4) Architect Frank Lloyd Wright described Beethoven as a master architect of tones.

(5) Any of us can think of professionals whose left and right brain works in concert.[3] I think of a university president who writes poetry; of a female doctor who does ballet; of a research physiologist who builds and finishes furniture; of a concert violinist who does French cooking; of two professional musicians who majored in mathematics before going into music (music and mathematics are, of course, intimately related).

Great preaching has always related knowledge (left brain) to beauty of expression (right brain). An aesthetically appealing story liberates listeners to understand hard facts. An apt metaphor shows, often immediately, the truth of an event or doctrine.

Take, for example, the old story of the lad who, from his hillside cottage, looked across the valley to see windows in a house light up like fire at sunset. The people occupying that dwelling, he thought to himself, must enjoy great happiness. One day he packed a lunch, went down the hill, through the valley, and up the other side until he came to the house where the windows blazed with light. The family welcomed him, fed him, and even invited him to stay the night because of the distance back to his home. Early the next morning, he looked across the ravine to see his own house—he gasped as his cottage windows caught fire in the morning sun. This story ends with a triplicate from T. S. Eliot: "And the end of all our exploring / will be to arrive where we started / and know the place for the first time."[4]

Great preaching brings together knowledge and beauty of expression.

---

[3] For further information on right/left brain, see on the web "Music and the Brain" by Laurence O'Donnell III, http://www.cerebromente.org.br/n15/musica. html accessed online 07/10/09. For more reading on this subject see Mihaly Csikszentmihalyi, *Flow: The Psychology of Optimal Experience* (New York: HarperCollins, 1991) and Douglas R. Hofstadter, *Gödel, Escher, Bach: an Eternal Golden Braid* (New York: Basic Books 1979).

[4] *Celtic Daily Prayer: Prayers and Readings from the Northumbria Community* (New York: HarperCollins, 2002) 445–46.

The Power of Pictures

Three boys grew up in a home with a memorable painting of a ship. They saw the picture every day. In manhood each son joined the navy, quite to everyone's surprise since the family lived landlocked, away from ocean, lakes, or rivers. The mother and father discovered that the ship on the wall made its everlasting impression on the developing minds of their sons.[5]

Pictures communicate, especially today with presentation software programs, movies galore, computer screens, slick magazines, and an abundance of photographs in our newspapers. Eugene Peterson, very much aware of our picture-oriented age, builds his writing on that principle. Listen to his rendering of this pair of verses followed by commentary: "As high as heaven is over the earth, / So strong is his love to those who fear him. / And as far as sunrise is from sunset, / He has separated us from our sins" (Psalm 102:11–12, *The Message*).[6]

Peterson's comment goes like this: "What God has done for us far exceeds anything we have done for or against Him. The summary word for this excessive, undeserved, unexpected act of God is 'salvation.' Prayer explores the country of salvation, tramping the contours, smelling the flowers, touching the outcroppings. There is more to do than recognize the sheer fact of salvation and witness to it; there are unnumbered details of grace, of mercy, of blessing to be appreciated and savored. Prayer is the means by which we do this."[7]

Actually, our Western culture could not survive without pictures, without metaphors. We use them all the time in everyday conversation, classroom lectures, news broadcasts, sitcoms, and, of

---

[5] Ibid.

[6] Eugene H. Peterson, *The Message: The Bible in Contemporary Language* [New Testament with Psalms and Proverbs] (Colorado Springs: NavPress, 2007) Ps. 102:11-12.

[7] Andrea Wells Miller, ed., *The Eternal Present: Daily Readings from Today's Most Inspiring Christian Writers* (New York: Crossroads, 2003) 205.

course, sermons. Metaphor is part of the staple diet of our native speech. George Lakoff, linguistics professor at the University of California Berkeley, and Mark Johnson, Southern Illinois University professor of philosophy, make this point very well when they observe that "our ordinary conceptual system, in terms of which we both think and act, is fundamentally metaphorical in nature." John Koessler tells us why: "Metaphors help us to understand one thing by pointing to something else and saying, 'This is that.'"[8] Much of this unbreakable habit stems from the King James Version of the Bible ("Be thou a rock of refuge for me, a strong fortress to save me!" Psalm 31:2b) and Shakespeare's Othello ("There are many events in the womb of time which will be delivered"),[9] not to mention children's literature, which conditions us from our early years (recall Aesop's "The Hare and the Tortoise").[10]

Great preaching brings together knowledge and beauty of expression.

Choosing the Right Words

As everyone knows, Alice in Wonderland follows the rabbit down a hole. Thinking she has fallen 4,000 miles, she wonders about Latitude and Longitude: "Alice had not the slightest idea what Latitude was, or Longitude either, but she thought they were nice grand words to say."[11] On her trip downward, she thinks about

---

[8] Haddon Robinson and Craig Brian Larson, eds., *The Art & Craft of Biblical Preaching: A Comprehensive Resource for Today's Communicators* (Grand Rapids: Zondervan, 2005) 125. See index under "artistic elements," "imagination," "metaphor," "parables," and "storytelling."

[9] *Othello* is one of William Shakespeare's famous plays.

[10] For further reading, see David Levine, *The Fables of Aesop* (New York: Macmillan, 1964). This book is the adaptation of eighty-two of Aesop's best-known fables, including "The Hare and the Tortoise," along with a brief history of each fable.

[11] Carroll, *The Annotated Alice,* 27.

coming out the other end of the earth and seeing the "Antipathies"—
"she was rather glad there was no one listening, this time, as it didn't
sound at all the right word."[12]

Carroll knows not only how to bring gentle satire to our cultural
penchant for using wrong words, but he also knows how to pick and
choose right words. He pictures Alice seeing "the loveliest garden"
with "beds of bright flowers and those cool fountains."[13] A few pages
later, Carroll tells us in the most delightful and metaphorical way to
choose our words carefully: "'Speak English!' said the Eaglet. 'I don't
know the meaning of half those long words, and what's more, I don't
believe you do either!' And the Eaglet bent down its head to hide a
smile: some of the other birds tittered audibly."[14]

I tell my students to use simple words, reminding them of John
Wesley's admonition to read First John as a model of simplicity. Big
words tend to put people off, and often we can express ourselves far
better with common language. To parade our knowledge with high-
sounding words exposes our ignorance, often linguistic ignorance,
and surely ignorance about communication.

Yet sometimes a big word—its sound and rhythm and place in a
sentence—does the job. *Reader's Digest* deliberately includes
unfamiliar words here and there not to discourage readers, but as an
educative method (see, for instance, the monthly vocabulary test).
Inside us lives an etymologist. We like new words, their origins, their
exact meanings. We respect words.

The Bible respects language and models word choice. Right
words perform with penetrating accuracy. In the Hebrew mind,
words are like stones, palpable, making sounds when they land on
listening ears, stinging when they hit someone. Psalm 12 relates to
the good and bad uses of language and ends with this set of lines:

---

[12] Ibid., 28.
[13] Ibid., 30.
[14] Ibid., 47.

God's words are pure words,
Pure silver words refined seven times
In the fires of his word-kiln,
Pure on earth as well as in heaven.
GOD, keep us safe from their lies,
From the wicked who stalk us with lies,
From the wicked who collect honors
For their wonderful lies (*The Message*).[15]

John's Gospel provides the supreme illustration of the biblical way of viewing words; in his prologue to the Fourth Gospel, John sees Jesus, the Son of God, as the *Logos*—the Word.

Have we lost the power of words in our culture? Not quite, someone says, for we treasure grand address like Ronald Reagan's Berlin speech in which he used the memorable expression, "Mr. Gorbachev, tear down this wall." The complete paragraph in which that sentence occurs reads: "General Secretary Gorbachev, if you seek peace, if you seek prosperity for the Soviet Union and Eastern Europe, if you seek liberalization: Come here to this gate! Mr. Gorbachev, open this gate! Mr. Gorbachev, tear down this wall."

This address, delivered 12 June 1987 to the people of West Berlin,[16] was audible on the east side of the Berlin wall. It consisted of 2,703 well-chosen words. (Part of the genius of the above paragraph lies in its parallelism—a classic rhetorical device.)

Yet we do throw words around. We dishonor language by fillers and posturing and phrases empty of substance. The true preacher is a

---

[15] Peterson, *The Message*, Ps. 12:6.

[16] Ronald Reagan's speech on 12 June 1987 to Germany and the world at the Brandenburg Gate, protected by a Plexiglas shield from possible gunfire from beyond the wall. For more details, see Patti Davis, "Back to the Wall," *Parade*, 11 June 2007, http://www.parade.com/features/touchstones/070612-ronald-reagan.html (accessed 17 October 2008).

wordsmith. He or she looks for just the right term because the right one is the telling word and often suggests moral implications as in the above illustrations from Psalms and President Reagan.

Great preaching brings together knowledge and beauty of expression.

Comic Relief and How to Get Serious

A preacher friend says, "If you want people to get serious, make them laugh." Humor opens minds to serious thinking about the gospel. Exposing the incongruities of life serves as sandpaper to remove the varnish that protects us from facing truth. Mind you, my friend had no thought of using satire to embarrass people; rather, he wanted to let humor say what otherwise may not get through to listeners.

Humor, like all components of communication, lies shrouded in mystery, yet it penetrates even to the recesses of the heart. No wonder one theologian says angels break through to us when wholesome laughter abounds. In genuine mirth we experience God's grace.

In fact, humor possesses the capacity to brighten the hard demands the gospel makes on us Christians. The Way, not easy despite what some assert, requires focus and serious attention. Discipline too. Biblical preachers project that hard truth. Yet if both preacher and listener live out the requirements of the gospel, balance must characterize lifestyle, perspective must refresh the soul. A good laugh helps.

One of the fascinating scientific findings of our time we can put into one word, the term used for humor studies: *gelatology* (from the Greek word for laugh). Research documents hormonal changes when we laugh, often resulting in clear perspective and therapy in our depths.

All the arts engage in humor, often in subtle ways. Haydn wrote the Joke Quartet (the String Quartet in E flat); Mozart did the divertimento in F for two horns and strings, a parody exposing the lesser composers of his day; Beethoven, despite the tragedies of his life, could engage in a musical joke. The musical expression *scherzo* comes from the Italian literally meaning "joke."

Likewise, pulpit people, possessed of a memory bank full of incongruities and surprises, know how to mix the mortar that holds the sermonic bricks together with delight and substance.

Great preaching brings together knowledge and beauty of expression.

The Poetic Touch

Eugene Peterson believes poets guard the language. Yes, true poetry shows careful selection of words, puts them in commanding places, alerting the mind. Good poetry captures attention and speaks to the deeper places of the human heart. Eugene H. Peterson's recent trilogy of books models respect for words.[17]

Great preaching has about it the touch of poetry. Space and pace, pause and tone, rhythm and words—all open the access door to truth. The vehicle called poetry communicates, in words yes, but also in the silence between the words. C. S. Lewis captured this function of verse in a single sentence: "Doubtless it is a rule in poetry that if you do your own work well, you will find you have done also work you never dreamed of."[18] Lewis explains further when he observes that poetry "is a little incarnation, giving body to what had been before invisible and inaudible."[19]

---

[17] See Peterson's *Christ Plays in Ten Thousand Places*; *Eat This Book: A Conversation in the Art of Spiritual Reading* (Grand Rapids: Eerdmans, 2006); *The Jesus Way: A Conversation on the Ways That Jesus Is the Way* (Grand Rapids: Eerdmans, 2007).

[18] C. S. Lewis, *The Allegory of Love* (London: Oxford University Press, 1938) 221. For further reading, see Wayne Martindale and Jerry Root, eds., *The Quotable Lewis: An Encyclopedic Selection of Quotes from the Complete Published Works of C. S. Lewis* (Wheaton IL: Tyndale, 1996).

[19] C. S. Lewis, *Reflections on the Psalms* (New York: Harcourt, Brace and World, 1958) 5.

So poetic expression gets at the mystery of life, doing so through the grand gift of imagination. Directive prose may prove fruitless not only because the human ego defends itself against "being told things," but also because we have precious little access to the resources for precise definition. We do have memory banks capable of responding to melody, rhythm, silence, and words that bring together reflections that in turn erupt into insight, into *aha* moments that say, "Ah, that's the secret"; "Oh, that's the meaning of my existence"; "That's the clue to relationships"; "That points to God." All of this is robed in a mix of emotion and mind, metaphor and story. Take, for example, three quick sentences from Hildegard of Bingen: "Glance at the sun, see the moon and stars. / Gaze at the beauty of earth's greenings. / Now, think."[20]

Great preaching brings together knowledge and beauty of expression.

The Unity of the Arts

We often observe that "the arts are one"—poetry, painting, music, dance, architecture, and the others. John Ruskin showed the commonalities of the arts by listing its laws, focus, repetition, continuity, contrast, etc., all of which we use in any artistic expression.[21] We put the arts-are-one principle into practice in our churches. In a typical service of worship, we read the poetry of the psalms, sing the psalms and lyrics to classical and contemporary tunes, hear the sermon, all marching together to communicate the profound and ultimately inexplicable truths of the gospel and life. The arts are so fully one in worship that the singing is preaching, the preaching is melody, the poetry is a sermon, and the sermon is poetic.

---

[20] Quoted by Ruth Rejnis in *The Everything Saints Book* (Avon MS: Adams Media Corporation, 2001) 178.

[21] See Howard Tillman Kuist's *These Words upon My Heart: Scripture and the Christian Response* (Richmond VA: John Knox Press, 1947).

Take, for example, the following component: repetition. John Ruskin, London-born art critic, sage writer, social critic, author, poet, and writer, distinguished between repetition and continuity, the former when one item is simply repeated (identical twins in a family photograph), the latter in a succession of similar items such as a colonnade.[22] Continuity, replete with power, points to the center of a work of art and adds to the sense of beauty, as in a Rembrandt biblical painting where lines of light point to Christ. The columns in a great cathedral carry the eye forward to the altar and enhance beauty. So in a symphony (Beethoven's Fifth, with its well-known dot, dot, dot, dash motif), continuity makes sense of the whole, as does a motif in a sermon such as Gardner Taylor's "His Own Clothes," the phrase heard over and again highlighting Christ and the cross. Continuity creates a sense of unity to establish focus.

Great preaching brings together knowledge and beauty of expression.

The Storyteller's Trance

Rhythm, pace, pause, and interaction between storyteller and audience factor into moments of spellbinding listening. In the context of focused attention, truth often penetrates to the very soul of the hearers. Professional storytellers call this phenomenon "the storyteller's trance." The dance of teller and listener not only documents the spirit's work and the preparation of the speaker, but also determines the narrator's tempo, tone, and style, for the storyteller gathers up audience clues and incorporates them into delivery.

The trance works two ways, from the audience and from the storyteller. Once the narrator absorbs himself or herself in the tale

---

[22] For more reading, in John Ruskin (1819–1900), *The Complete Works of John Ruskin,* ed. Sir Edward Tyas Cook and Alexander D. O. Wedderburn (London: George Allen; New York: Longmans, Green, 1903-1912).

and gets on a roll, the psychologist's "flow" kicks in. Just there, say the psychologists, the subliminal depths of the speaker come to the surface, helping to shape the substance and character of the story, even revealing the tale's words beyond the words. When Tony Snow, late White House press secretary, played the flute (yes, he was an instrumentalist as well as a news analyst), he got into the music so thoroughly that, it was said, he "flowed."[23]

The vehicle called trance opens ears to hear and eyes to see—ears to hear the joys and sorrows of life, eyes to see the Creator's work and the evil of sin. This deep musing also opens hearts to our humanity. Narrative, often a species of metaphor, identifies us as the human beings we are, capable of great achievement, also of enormous harm. Direct statement may not communicate; it may, in fact, close ears and eyes. The "indirection" of a tale may, by its very subtlety, penetrate the soul.

Great preaching brings together knowledge and beauty of expression.

The Magic of Music

Franz Joseph Haydn, when asked about the source of his joy, famously replied, "I cannot make it otherwise. I write according to the thoughts I feel. When I think upon my God, my heart is so full of joy that the notes dance and leap from my pen, and since God has given me a cheerful heart, it will be pardoned me that I serve Him with a cheerful spirit." When Haydn composed and listened to his music, his heart "leapt for joy," and he experienced "uncontrollable gladness."[24]

Plato observed that the fastest route to the soul is music. The Romans made music the center of the wheel of learning, knowing

---

[23] For more information on psychological flow, see Mihaly Csikszentmihalyi. *Flow: The Psychology of Optimal Experience* (New York: HarperCollins, 1991).

[24] See Patrick Kavanaugh, *The Spiritual Lives of Great Composers* (Grand Rapids: Zondervan, 1996) chap. 3.

that melody and song transport knowledge to the mind. We know little of what music sounded like before 800 or 1000 AD; we do have manuscripts to show us the power of melody or harmony. George Frideric Handel put the musical potential principle into action in the *Messiah*.[25] The Wesleys understood music's drawing power more than most in their day; this explains why they brought together sermon and song.

Listen to a Mozart piano concerto (#5, e.g.), and experience the carrying power, indeed the pulling capability, of his delicate traceries that lift us to heaven. The sheer playfulness of his moving harmonies makes one's spirit dance with enormous joy. No wonder Karl Barth wished first to see Mozart before Thomas Aquinas or Augustine in heaven! Barth believed God and Mozart had a special relationship.[26]

Music, like poetry and indeed all the arts, evokes feelings of joy, of loneliness, nostalgia, evil, and redemption. Barth hears in Mozart a dialog between heaven and earth, good and evil. In short, music is a vehicle of both renewal and insight.

Richard Lischer captures the musical quality of Gardner Taylor's voice in these descriptive words:

> The Taylor style relies on a voice like a pipe organ; its stunning vocal range produces an equally impressive emotional range but one that never degenerates into posturing or histrionics. Taylor is able to achieve profound emotional contact through his natural timbre; he can soar in a disciplined tremolo, use his resonators to toy with

---

[25] By 1740, George Frideric Handel had completed *Messiah*, which was first performed in Ireland. *Messiah* includes the "Hallelujah Chorus," which caused the king to fill with emotion and rise to his feet when he first heard it during the inaugural performance, a tradition that continues today. Further reading on the Internet may be found through a search at URL: http://gfhandel.org/messiah.htm. Accessed 09/22/09 Also, see Donald Burrows, *Handel, Messiah* (New York: Cambridge University Press, 1991).

[26] See the reprint of Karl Barth, *Wolfgang Amadeus Mozart* (Eugene OR: Wipf & Stock, 2003) 16.

sounds, and he can gravel, when provoked, like Louis Armstrong. In comparison with the most acclaimed preachers, Taylor's high baritone is purer, his low more richly resonant, and the mastery of his vocal instrument more complete.[27]

Lischer follows these comments with an example: "On one occasion, as he read some of the proper names in Luke 3—Tiberius, Ituraea, Trachonitis—members of the congregation were heard to respond, 'My Lord, My Lord!'"[28]

The preacher, like a violinist, enjoys a great tonal range, even to semi-tones. J. S. Bach, that creative and knowledgeable innovator, inherited a scale different from ours. Prior to Bach, C-sharp and D-flat were not the same. With his mathematical genius, Bach did away with tones between the two; he did the same for all the black keys.[29] A sensitive ear like Jascha Heifetz could hear tones between C-sharp and D-flat, and indeed could play them. So it is with a master preacher whose voice can nuance his or her tonality to communicate just what needs saying.

Take note A on the piano. The piano tuner, using his tuning fork, adjusts A to 440 vibrations per second. But he can tune A to 444. Heifetz could indeed distinguish the difference as many of us could not. By the same token, a great voice like Gardner Taylor's can be used to profit mini-tones and does.

However, "in-tuneness" is a much larger concept in fact, it relates not only to accuracy of pitch but quality of tone. How do you

---

[27] Richard Lischer, "Gardner C. Taylor," in *Concise Encyclopedia of Preaching*, ed. William H. Willimon and Richard Lischer (Louisville: Westminster John Knox Press, 1995) 466.

[28] Ibid.

[29] See "Bach and Mathematics" on the internet through Google: "Music, Mathematics, and Bach." Rahul Siddharthan, "Music, Mathematics, and Bach (1.Layers of Melody)" in *Resonance*, 4/3 (March, 1999) 8-15. Published in Springer India, in co-publication with Indian Academy of Sciences, Indian Institute of Science, Bangalore, India. General Article 10.1007/BF0283719.

explain one's tears while looking at a Monet lily pond? Or choking up while hearing Bach's *Mass in B Minor*? Or weeping during a sermon? Art moves us. It also hides in mystery, rather like the contrasting truth about God revealing, yet concealing, himself. Revealing and concealing, intermingled, make defining God an impossibility. Yet we hear, know, sense, and experience God.

Haydn, composing music for the mass on the text "Lamb of God, who takes away the sins of the world," exclaimed that an "uncontrollable gladness" seized him. He wrote for God and believed God inspired his compositions. No wonder he, like Bach before him, often wrote *In Nomine Jesu* at the top of his score sheets and *Soli Deo Gloria* at the close of his score sheets.[30] Haydn went to a performance of his *Creation* shortly before he died. While the audience applauded, he uttered with lifted hands, "Not from me—from there, above, comes everything."[31]

Great preaching brings together knowledge and beauty of expression.

Pictures, Yes; Also Conversation

For gospel preachers, metaphors, in whatever form they come—hymn lyrics, allegory, analogy, story—serve as vehicles for carrying the revelation, truth. The arts must both convey and stimulate conversation about Jesus, the center of Christian faith, the cross and resurrection, the promise of salvation. Method and content are inseparable. Method without substance may entertain; substance minus pleasing vehicles robs the dialog of beauty and communicability.

The subject of the conversation, the substantive test of preaching, lies in *kerygma*, the content of the gospel, and in *didache*, the application of the faith. Given this pair of homiletical factors, alongside the artistic components, full-orbed preaching takes place.

---

[30] Kavanaugh, *The Spiritual Lives of Great Composers*, 22.
[31] Ibid., 23.

C. H. Dodd did a pioneer work on the *kerygma* in his little book *The Apostolic Preaching and Its Development.*[32] Subsequently, scholars have commented on the common denominators of New Testament preaching, often with particular reference to the earliest sermons in the Acts of the Apostles. Robert H. Mounce, in *The Essential Nature of New Testament Preaching,* summarizes *kerygma* in nine parts:

A proclamation of the
1. Death,
2. Resurrection, and
3. Exaltation of our Lord,
4. All seen as the fulfillment of prophecy and
5. Involving our responsibility.
The resultant evaluation of Jesus as both
6. Lord and
7. Christ.
On this basis hearers of the gospel must
8. Repent and
9. Receive forgiveness of sins.[33]

Notice the intimately scriptural character of this kerygmatic outline. Gardner Taylor says, "One finds it difficult to lay enough stress upon the necessity for the preacher to open his whole being before the Scriptures."[34] One must see Christ and his relation to the totality of scripture, then apply the grand truths.

Just there, at the point of applying the truths, the preacher comes face to face with *didache.* Gospel preaching relates not only to the mental grasp of revelation; pulpit endeavor goes a significant step

---

[32] C. H. Dodd, *The Apostolic Preaching and Its Development* (London: Hodder, 1950). Reprint by Baker, 1960.

[33] Further reading by Robert H. Mounce in *The Essential Nature of New Testament Preaching* (Grand Rapids: Eerdmans, 1960).

[34] Gardner C. Taylor, *How Shall They Preach: The Lyman Beecher Lectures and Five Lenten Sermons* (Elgin IL: Progressive Baptist Publishing House, 1977) 60.

further—articulating the ethical implications of the gospel. Repent. Yes! But repentance is no easy believism. Often it is hard work, involving forgiveness for some dishonesty, paying back money stolen, putting one's IRS report right. And, yes, even the preacher must walk the walk as well as talk the talk—thus, Pastor Taylor's admonition to open oneself, one's "whole being," to the mirror called scripture.

Interestingly, churches that emphasize doctrine (*kerygma*) to the minimalization of application (*didache*), suffer stunted social growth. A gospel primarily in the head issues in minimal acts of kindness and social betterment. On the contrary, a church that focuses mostly on social outreach (*didache*) robs its people of the theological anchoring that fosters healthy Christian security. Interestingly, the history of the church tells us that those most attuned to scriptural belief are also those most active in ethical and social application.[35]

The bottom line: powerful preaching brings together both *kerygma* and *didache*. In fact, scripture associates the two so closely that the scholars tell us we cannot separate them, that a good term for Bible-based homiletics is didactic-kerygma.

Great preaching brings together knowledge and beauty of expression!

---

[35] See, with its extensive documentation, Timothy L. Smith, *Revivalism and Social Reform: American Protestantism on the Eve of the Civil War* (Baltimore: The Johns Hopkins University Press, 1980).

DOCTRINE THAT FLIES:
USING STORY TO COMMUNICATE TRUTH

Michael Duduit

To hear some cultural observers in the church, we are living in a postmodern age in which doctrine does not matter. Doctrine is considered to be one of those things we slip into our sermons occasionally—like a mother slips the medicine in with a spoonful of sugar—or else it is ignored altogether.

Is there still a place today for preaching doctrine? Does it really matter what you believe?

I heard John MacArthur tell a story that came from what I am sure is one of your favorite magazines, *Feathers*, the publication of the California poultry association. No doubt you have a copy of *Feathers* right there on the desk next to your issue of *Preaching* magazine.

According to the article's author, the FAA tests windshields on big jets with a specially equipped gun that shoots dead chickens. When they are testing the jets, they shoot a dead chicken out of this gun at the exact speed the jet would be flying, and that tells them if the windshield is strong enough to withstand the impact of a bird flying into the jet at a high speed.

Evidently, the British wanted to test the windshield on a brand-new, high-speed train, so they got in touch with the FAA and borrowed their special chicken gun. They lined it up in front of the train, adjusted the settings, and shot the dead chicken at the train. It crashed through the windshield, went right through the engineer's chair, and embedded itself in the control board behind the chair. They contacted the FAA to see what they might have done wrong. The FAA looked over the test results and reported back just one suggestion: first, thaw the chicken.

There is a right way to do things and a wrong way to do things, and if you do things the wrong way you will not get the right results. Likewise, there is a right way to understand truth and a wrong way to understand truth, and if you do not look at things the right way you will not find real truth. In other words, it *does* matter what you believe.

What we believe about God and God's work is called doctrine, and that means doctrine does matter. What we believe about doctrinal issues can make a difference in our eternal destiny and the destiny of those we love and serve. Doctrine matters—and that means the way we *communicate* doctrine matters. How we share the truth of God and God's work with humanity can be the key factor in whether or not people understand the truth of God and God's work among us, which is what doctrine is all about.

Let me offer an example. Have you ever flown a kite? Think of how a kite moves with the wind yet is linked to the ground by a string. You might think that if you cut the string, the kite would soar even higher, but that is not what happens. If you cut the string, the kite will soon tumble down and land in the trees or crash to the ground. Preaching is a bit like that kite—its methods adapt as the culture changes, but it must stay linked to the Word of God. If preaching ever becomes disconnected from the Word, it soon comes crashing to earth.

I believe that preaching doctrine can be like flying a kite if we do it effectively—the truths of God's Word take flight and grab the attention of all who see. And one of the most effective ways to make doctrine fly as we preach is through the use of story.

You may be saying to yourself, "Doctrine and story? Those do not go together. When you preach doctrine, you have to use explanation and definition, argument and logic. What part does story have to play in preaching doctrine?" As a matter of fact, there may not be more valuable tools in preaching doctrine than the use of story and narrative.

In an interview for *Preaching* magazine, Haddon Robinson talked about how his own views of exposition had developed over the twenty years since he first published his book *Biblical Preaching*. One of the major shifts was in his view of the importance of narrative in preaching. He said, "Behind the biblical narratives there is theology. There's a tendency to think that God gave us those stories so that we would have something to tell our kids before they went to bed. But the stories are a way of telling us about God. So as we look at the story and see it in its context and then its broader context, I have to ask, 'How does this writer through the dialogue, through the action of these characters, get across his idea?'"[1]

Do not overlook that reality: there is an underlying theological foundation that informs biblical stories. Yet that is not only true of the stories drawn from the pages of scripture; there needs to be a theological undergirding to any stories we use in preaching. Stories are not used for their own sake; they are used to express biblical truth in a unique and powerful way.

There certainly is no better model of such preaching through story than Jesus. His favorite method of preaching seems to have been the use of stories and parables. If there was anyone who could have adequately explained the kingdom of God in a logical argument, Jesus would fit the qualifications. Yet, instead, he told stories. Jesus told about lost coins and lost sons, about farmers sowing seeds and workers in a vineyard, about the power implicit in a tiny seed or in a speck of yeast. In these stories and more, the Lord helps us grasp and identify with theological truths in a way that would be nearly impossible if presented through any other medium. In fact, Jesus knew that some truths are far too vital to be left to mere explanation—they can only be truly captured through the power of story.

---

[1] Haddon Robinson, "Expository Preaching in a Narrative World," in *Preaching with Power*, ed. Michael Duduit (Grand Rapids: Baker Books, 2006) 154.

Why Are Stories Such Effective Tools in Sharing Doctrine?

We are a story-based culture. All too often, I have heard preachers say, "My people do not remember what I preached last Sunday; all they remember are the stories!"[2] Ever felt that way? Does that not tell you something about how people learn and remember truth? Instead of lamenting that they *only* remember the stories, the effective preacher will take that to heart and use stories strategically to communicate biblical truth in a way that will be heard, understood, and retained.

Bruce Seymour says that "we need stories the way a fish needs water. We live and move immersed in stories. Stories help us make sense of the world. Stories help us pass our understanding on to others. Stories shape us. In a sense, stories mark us as human. Milton Dawes, a research scientist, suggests that stories are so intrinsic to humanity that 'one way to describe our species is that we constitute a storytelling form of life.'"[3]

One reason we tell and remember stories is because we were born that way; we were created to enjoy story. Do you think it is a coincidence that when the Creator gave us the Word, over half of it was in the form of story and narrative? The one who made us built in a love for story.

As long as there is recorded human history, there is story. The people would gather and sit by the fire for hours as the tribal storyteller would tell the stories of the people's past. Millennia later, it is more of the same, though now the tribal storyteller is more likely to have a forty-two-inch plasma screen. Look around you, and you will see that we are a story-consumed culture—in movies and TV, music and books. We do not want to be away from our stories too long, so now we download them into a little electronic device we can carry in our pockets.

---

[2] Author recalls from no specific preacher.

[3] D. Bruce Seymour, *Creating Stories That Connect* (Grand Rapids: Kregel Publishing, 2007) 9.

Every four years we find ourselves caught up in the pageantry and action of the summer Olympic Games. It was not too many years ago that network officials were concerned that TV ratings for the games were not as strong as needed, and were mostly drawn from male viewers. They came up with an idea: film some "up close and personal" stories about the athletes and their families, their backgrounds, their special challenges. These stories caused ratings to skyrocket. Now, almost all sports programming is story-driven; there may be a play-by-play analyst telling you what just happened on the field, but the color commentator is there to weave a series of stories about the game, the coaches, the players, and their families. It works because we are drawn to stories.

Not only do we live in a story-based culture, but we share a story-based faith. As Wayne McDill wrote, stories are…

> inherent to the revelation of God in Scripture. Ours is a historical faith. What we believe has been made known in history in particular events, specific places, the lives and sayings of real people who have encountered God. Our faith has not come to us in philosophical pronouncements, mysteries, secrets, or theological formulas. God has rather revealed Himself through the experiences of ordinary people made extraordinary by His special involvement in their lives.
>
> Our faith comes to us in their stories. God speaks in the language of human experience. In the stories and scenes of their lives, we learn who He is and what He is doing. We meet Him ourselves in their stories as He awakens our understanding to the meaning of what happened there.…
>
> If the revelation of God comes to us in scenes and stories, the preaching of that revelation should be given to the audience in the same form. This does not mean, of course, that the preacher is a storyteller only. He is an interpreter as well. He must not only draw the pictures and tell the stories. He must interpret their meaning for

his audience. And he must tell new stories and draw new pictures for this generation.[4]

We are, indeed, a story-based culture. And that is true, in large part, because stories engage the imagination. There is not a preacher who has not had this experience—you are preaching on some topic, carefully and precisely explaining the concepts that are so important, when one look at the congregation tells you they are zoning out. Then you start to share a story to illustrate the concept, and suddenly people miraculously begin to rise from the dead. Their eyes grow brighter, they sit up straight, some edging forward in their seats as if they are afraid they might miss something. That is the power of story to engage the imagination.

Stories are powerful teaching tools that can engage listeners in significant ways. As Henry Ward Beecher said more than a century ago, "He who would hold the ear of the people must either tell stories or paint pictures."[5]

Think about how biblical stories have influenced what we think about God: David and Goliath, the story of Joseph, the good Samaritan, the prodigal son, and so on. Again and again, Jesus told stories—to help us understand what God is like and what the kingdom of God is all about. That is because stories engage us and help us understand things in a way that more abstract language may not.

Chip Heath and his brother Dan are authors of a fascinating book called *Made to Stick*, which analyzes why some ideas stay with us (or "stick") while others have so little shelf life. One of the most compelling techniques for creating a sticky idea, they argue, is the use of story.

---

[4] Wayne McDill, *The 12 Essential Skills for Great Preaching* (Nashville: Broadman & Holman, 1994) 223.

[5] Ibid., 242–43.

In his class at Stanford University on "Making Ideas Stick,"[6] Chip Heath leads his students through an exercise. Each student is given some information from some government report on crime patterns in the United States. Half are asked to make a one-minute speech on why crime is a problem; the other half makes a speech on why it is not a problem. Stanford students are smart, and they give good speeches. After each speech, the class rates the presentations, and the best speakers get the top rankings.

At that point, Chip does something else—perhaps plays a film clip to distract the students. Then, ten minutes later, he has the students pull out a sheet of paper and write down every single idea they remember for each speaker they have just heard. Students cannot believe how little they remember, even from a one-minute speech. What is interesting is that, of the speakers, most have used several statistics and only one in ten has told a story. But when asked to remember, sixty-three percent recall the story, and only five percent can remember any specific statistic. Another interesting observation is that the top speakers are not necessarily the ones that are remembered. As Chip says, "The stars of stickiness are the students who made their case by telling stories."[7]

Stories engage our imagination because they connect with our emotions—no wonder even we preachers remember them long after the sermon outline has been lost in the mists of memory. And if we remember the stories better than the rest, what do you think the people remember best?

Because stories engage our imaginations, they are able to do something else: to help us identify with a truth. Fred Craddock says,

---

[6] Chip Heath and Dan Heath, *Made to Stick: Why Some Ideas Survive and Others Die* (New York: Random House, 2007) 206. Chip Heath is a professor of organizational behavior in the Graduate School of Business at Stanford University, Palo Alto, CA.

[7] Ibid., 206.

"The greatest single power of story is the power of identification."[8] As we identify with the characters in a story, we become open to change.

In the book *Made to Stick*, authors Dan Heath and Chip Heath assert that "a credible idea makes people believe. An emotional idea makes people care. And...the right stories make people act."[9] That may well be because, as researchers are learning, when we hear a good story, we create a kind of simulation in our own minds. Although much of listening is a passive experience, when a story begins, we become active participants—we imagine, we empathize, we identify. Stories put knowledge into a framework that is more like our own day-to-day experience.

If you have small children, you see that all the time. They love to hear the same stories again and again, in part because the familiarity allows them to picture the narrative in their minds and to identify with the characters. After watching or hearing a story, children will often try to recreate it themselves, handing out the characters and playing the roles.

But that does not stop with adulthood. Even as adults, most people tend to be visual learners. We think through an idea by creating a mental picture of it. And, frankly, it is typically easier to create those mental pictures while we are hearing a story than while someone is explaining a concept. Why do people remember the preacher's stories better than the main points? Perhaps it is because they can hold onto those mental pictures that stories encourage.

That does not mean stories are to be used to the exclusion of propositional truth. Even though stories are vital, we still need concepts. In fact, one of the mistakes some preachers make is in failing to link the story to a key truth in the message. As Alan Nelson points out, "They fail to link the story to a message theme or to draw

---

[8] Fred Craddock, "Preaching as Storytelling," in *The Art & Craft of Biblical Preaching: A Comprehensive Resource for Today's Communicators*, ed. Haddon Robinson and Craig Brian Larson (Grand Rapids: Zondervan, 2005) 490–91.

[9] Heath and Heath, *Made to Stick*, 206.

a conclusion that hooks the receiver. Listeners think, 'Cute story, but what in the world did that have to do with anything?'"[10] Stories are powerful tools, but we have to make sure we use stories that are relevant to the key biblical truth we are preaching.

Stories help us to identify with a truth; no wonder, then, that stories can persuade. I am convinced one of the reasons Jesus used story so much is that it is one of the most persuasive tools available. Remember what the Heath brothers observed: While ideas may make people believe, "the right stories make people act."[11]

Years ago a state legislator was trying to push through an increased appropriation to expand the public health agency, but it was clear the bill didn't have the votes. Despite all the hours of testimony from doctors and public health officials, despite the reams of statistics and data, the bill was going to fail. So two hours before the vote, the legislative sponsor handed every member of the legislature an index card that contained this little story:

> A widowed mother of three small children received a routine chest x-ray and was told she had tuberculosis. She could not get treatment without giving up her job and if she did that, her children would be without support. She requested help from state health agencies, but was told they had no funds. So Mrs. Robinson went home to die, determined to care for Robert and Norman and Sarah as long as she could lift her tired hands.
>
> That same day, a farmer in her county noticed signs of cholera in his brood sow. He sent a telegram to a state official. Next day, a veterinarian made a trip to his farm, gave the hog treatment and cured it.
>
> Moral: Be a hog!

---

[10] Alan Nelson, *Creating Messages That Connect* (Loveland CO: Group Publishing, 2004) 84.

[11] Heath and Heath, *Made to Stick*, 206.

Two hours after receiving and reading that little story, the state legislature voted to increase funding for the state health agency. What testimony and statistics could not do, a story did, because it touched the legislators' emotions and persuaded them to respond.[12]

In a postmodern culture, where tolerance of other views is the most revered value, it can be particularly challenging to share biblical truth in traditional forms of argumentation and reasoning. What we consider a logical and well-presented idea is often simply ignored by postmoderns who reject the very concept of absolute truth. They say, "Your truth is your truth, my truth is my truth, and you have no right to try to make your truth my truth." In such a challenging environment, story becomes the secret weapon of Christian apologetics, because it sneaks truth into their minds riding on the back of narrative.

For example, before we recognize our own need for Christ, we must realize there is something wrong. Yet concepts like "sin" or "evil" are virtually rejected as out of place in a pluralistic society. But Chuck Colson tells a story that reminds us of the reality that bad choices can lead to devastating results. That was the case on the morning of 27 August 2006, as Comair flight 5191 tried to take off from Bluegrass Airport in Lexington, Kentucky:

> There was one operator in the control tower that morning. It was still dark. And as flight 5191 taxied out, the controller instructed its pilots to go to Runway 22. There was construction on the main runway, which knocked out its distance-remaining lights and caused confusion. The usual taxiway to the main runway was also closed. The pilots should have received Notices to Airmen about both these developments through prerecorded messages from the control tower. But these were not available. As a result, James Polehinke, the copilot, taxied on Runway 26 instead of Runway 22. Runway 26 was only 3,500 feet long, not enough for a...CRJ–100 to take off.

---

[12] Garrison B. Webb, *Creative Imagination in Preaching* (Nashville: Abingdon Press, 1960) 24.

According to investigators, Polehinke and the senior pilot, Captain Jeffrey Clay, failed to do a compass verification of the direction of the takeoff, which would have alerted them that they were on the wrong runway. Their flight manual required them to do this, and to verify it with the controller. A series of human errors committed, the plane raced down the short runway, smashed through the airport's perimeter fence, and into trees on the neighboring farm. Forty-nine people died in the ensuing crash.

Captain Polehinke was the sole survivor. He remained in a coma for more than ten days (and eventually had a leg amputated). When he regained consciousness, his first words were, "Why did God do this to me?"

This was a tragedy of immense proportions and a terrible burden that James Polehinke will have to live with. But should a person who got wrong instructions from the control tower, and then failed to verify his heading, blame God?[13]

Or, as I recently told my eight-year-old son, "We have to live with the results of the choices we make." A story can help us understand and act on that doctrinal truth.

And then there is the greatest story of all: of a God who loved his people despite their sin and, through the incarnation, sent his Son to earth to live among us. What a life that Son lived, and yet on a terrible day that we remember as Good Friday, he took our sins upon himself and died on our behalf on a Roman cross, paying the price of our sin. In fact, he willingly paid for the results of the choices you and I have made. He died and was buried in a borrowed tomb, but that was not the end of the story. On the third day, he reversed the natural order of things, bursting from death back into life, and rose victorious to show all of us that death is not the victor and that there is hope for new life for all of us in Christ. Now that's a story!

Millions upon millions of people in developing nations have seen the Jesus film, and tens of millions have come to faith in Christ as a

---

[13] Charles Colson, *The Faith* (Grand Rapids: Zondervan, 2008) 74–75.

result. Is it that a movie has such power? No, it is the story—the story of Jesus, the story of sin defeated and death conquered and hope reborn! People see the story of Jesus, many for the first time, and they are drawn to him. The story persuades them that he is the one God sent for them! God has sent us life and hope...through a story!

Preaching Doctrine with Story

So how do we preach doctrine more effectively? We use stories. In his sermon on John 10:9 (KJV), Gardner C. Taylor used a personal story to help his listeners think about the nature of the salvation Christ offers. He said,

> There are doors where for one reason or another we cannot enter because we are outsiders. I remember well a preaching engagement some years ago in the stately city of Adelaide in South Australia. Staying at the Grosvenor Hotel, I would walk over each evening to the Flinders Street Baptist Church, where the services were held. The passing of nearly twenty years has not erased from memory a particular evening of homesickness at being ten thousand miles from home and family, which came over me like a physical ache.
>
> The time of evening was that strangely touching hour when day turns quietly to night and all the family have come, from here and there, to gather in the light, warmth and joy of home. I looked at such a house, a lamp burning in what I took to be the living room with the family gathered there. It was not my family, nor my home, and the door was closed to me. I thought of home and kin, and a sickness almost physical settled for a moment over me as I walked on through the cool evening darkness to the church.
>
> Thank God, Jesus says that the fold, the gathering for which he is the entranceway, is open to one and all.[14]

---

[14] Gardner C. Taylor, *Quintessential Classics, 1980–Present*, vol. 3 of *The Words of Gardner Taylor*, comp. Edward L. Taylor (Valley Forge: Judson Press, 2000) 111–12.

Sometimes we need to help our people understand theological concepts, such as the notion of repentance, which is often misunderstood. No matter how many times we have explained the Greek term *metanoia*, some folks still do not grasp it! So Stuart Briscoe explains why he used a story to teach repentance, saying, "I want people to understand that repentance might be a simple step rather than a big leap, but it nonetheless needs to be ventured."[15] A woman wanted her pastor to pray with her because she no longer felt Christ's presence. When he asked about her problem, she said, "I don't want to talk about it. Just pray for me. That's all I want of you." He probed gently anyway, and eventually she began to cry: "I'm living with my boyfriend, and I really have no intention of moving out." She wanted to sense Christ's presence while she lived in disobedience. She needed to repent and end the disobedience if she were to feel close to God again.[16]

The doctrine of God's providential care is another theological concept where story helps us. Max Lucado is a wonderful weaver of meaningful stories, and he tells a story about a fly he saw in an airplane. He wondered, "Why does a fly in a plane fly in a plane?" So he interviewed the fly, asking, "Why don't you settle down?" The fly responded, "Because I'm holding this whole thing up!" Then, Lucado shares the application: "We don't have to spend our lives frantically waving our wings. God's holding us up. We can sit down and rest in Him and trust Him to carry us."[17]

Another great story about God's presence and provision comes from Jill Briscoe, who knew Corrie Ten Boom, the Dutch woman whose family helped rescue Jews in the Netherlands after the Nazi takeover. Corrie said that as a little girl, she had heard stories about people who confessed Christ even at the cost of their lives. She told

---

[15] Bill Hybels, D. Stuart Briscoe, and Haddon W. Robinson, *Mastering Contemporary Preaching* (Portland: Multnomah, 1990) 90.

[16] Ibid.

[17] Dave Stone, *Refining Your Style* (Loveland CO: Group Publishing, 2004) 23.

her father that she did not think she could be courageous enough to do that. The next day, her father walked her to the bus stop as usual so she could go to school. As the bus rounded the corner at the end of the road, her father took the fare out of his pocket.

"Corrie," he said.

"Yes, father?" she replied.

"When do I give you the money for the ride?"

"When I get on the bus, father," she replied.

"Corrie, if you are ever called to suffer for Jesus, remember that your heavenly Father, like your earthly father, will give you the penny as you get on the bus."

Brisco goes on:

> Corrie remembered his words as the Nazis came to take her and her family away to the concentration camps. If you have read her story, you will know that God gave Corrie many pennies—pennies representing the divine provision of courage each time it is needed— for many rather hellish bus rides before she escaped the dreaded death camps. Don't worry that you won't make a good confession of faith if your life is on the line.... God will give you the penny when and if you need it.[18]

In preaching about the presence of God in our lives, I love to share the story of the preacher's young son who slipped out of the church pew to go to the bathroom. When he returned to the service, he had his pants down around his ankles. Hearing his father's voice, he toddled on up to the pulpit area to get his dad's help. The pastor, seeing his son in this condition, kneeled down and said, "Son, how can I help you?" to which the boy replied, "My shoes are untied."

Isn't that often the way it is with us? We come to God without truly recognizing our real need, but the Father knows what we need, and responds.

---

[18] Jill Briscoe, *Spiritual Arts* (Grand Rapids: Zondervan, 2007) 32.

How do you tell stories well? That master storyteller Fred Craddock suggests several characteristics of good storytelling:[19]

(1) The storyteller is not speaking to people, but speaking for them. Craddock notes, "The mark of a good story is that when it's over people say, 'As you were talking I was thinking about when…' Good storytelling speaks for the congregation and evokes their own stories."

(2) Stories must be realistic: "[They] must have the smell and sound and taste of life. When you tell a real story, everybody is relaxed. It's not confrontation time. It's not challenge time. 'Once upon a time…' Everybody relax. And in that relaxation you're drawn into the story, and identification begins to take place. The great single power in storytelling is the power of identification. And things that have long been in the head, known, begin to move toward the heart, and that's when life is changed."

(3) Stories create an experience. "Preaching is not just transferring information. It's creating the experience of that information," Craddock notes. "The way you put the words together creates it." In other words, help us see the scene, smell it, touch it: "Do not rush to the destination. Take the trip."

(4) The fit of a story is important. Make sure the story is appropriate to the sermon. Often, stories are wasted because we get excited about them and want to use them right away, but end up trying to stuff a square peg into a round hole. Save the story for the right moment in the right message.

Allow me to add some additional suggestions to the ones Craddock provides. For instance, seek illustrations that will connect with a contemporary listener. The best illustrations are drawn from the world in which our listeners live. Although we all turn to outside references for illustrations from time to time, the strongest ones you use will come out of experiences in your own life, or the lives of your

---

[19] Craddock, "Preaching as Storytelling," 490–91.

people, or from the newspapers they read, the TV shows and movies they watch—the world in which they live. Find illustrations to which listeners can relate.

Also, good stories stand on their own. A good rule of thumb is that if you have to spend too much time explaining the story and why it illustrates your point, leave it out. If illustrations do not clarify and connect, then they are not doing the job they were meant to do. A good story will leave you positioned as a communicator to drive home the truth—not to have to explain the story.

Use detail to add interest and credibility to illustrations. Another thing that helps illustrations connect with listeners is the use of appropriate detail. Listen to a great storyteller, and you will observe the use of detail—not so much as to bore, but just enough to create interest and credibility. Words can be used to create images in the minds of the listener.

Similarly, be specific rather than general. As Craig Brian Larson notes, "Being specific—means saying *Luger* rather than *weapon*; '89 *Taurus* rather than *vehicle*; *adultery* rather than a *sin*; *the nails through Christ's palms* rather than *Christ's sufferings*; *Bob, the 45-year-old overweight Chicago detective with the scar on the back of his hand* rather than *the officer*. The gunpowder is in the specifics—the more precise the better."[20]

Even as we use story in preaching, there are some cautions to keep in mind. First, don't turn the focus of your sermon into amusing the crowd. If you are a good storyteller, people will enjoy listening to your stories, and you'll enjoy telling them. It is possible to lose your bearings in such a situation and let the sermon become a time of entertainment rather than a time when you bring biblical truth to bear on the lives of people. It is not bad to entertain people along the way—that keeps them focused and attentive—but the

---

[20] Craig Brian Larson, "Preaching Pyrotechnics" in *The Art and Craft of Biblical Preaching*, ed. Haddon Robinson and Craig Brian Larson, eds. (Grand Rapids: Zondervan, 2005) 487.

entertainment must always be a strategic tool, not the purpose. Your purpose in preaching must always be to communicate biblical truth in order to set the stage for life change.

One way to keep your focus is to make sure your stories really illustrate biblical truth and accomplish a strategic purpose in the sermon. Even a great story has no place in the sermon if it is not going to help you drive home the biblical "big idea" of that particular message. In fact, one of the mistakes we preachers are prone to make is to come across a great story and try to wedge it into our next sermon, whether it fits or not. The result is a wasted story and a less effective sermon. If you find a great story, write it down and save it for the message where it will best do its work.

Another caution: Do not take stories from others' lives and retell them as if they were your own. First, it is dishonest and deceptive, two qualities that have no place in a God-anointed message. Second, it is dangerous, because someone will eventually realize that you stole someone else's story and pretended it was yours; from that point forward, your integrity is suspect. Pastors have been fired from their churches for doing precisely that.

Bryan Chapell tells about the preacher who had gained a reputation as one whose messages were easily understood and well received. Other pastors wondered what it was that made this preacher so effective, so they invited him to come and teach them his "technique." But instead of explaining how to preach better, he simply talked about Jesus and the parables he shared. Finally, one pastor said, "Brother, you and I were in seminary together, and I know you to be a man of great learning. Yet it seems to me you are not being true to your own gifts when you spend so much time telling stories. Why not simply say what Scripture says—why not present truth as truth?"

The speaker thought for a moment and then responded,

To answer, let me tell you a story. One day, Bare Truth came walking into town. What he had to say was very important, but he looked very intimidating with bulging muscles and hard knuckles. Some people remembered when he had hurt them before. As a result, most people went into their houses to wait for Bare Truth to finish his business. Only the strongest of the townspeople did not mind Bare Truth's visits.

The next day Parable came to town. He looked just like most of the town's people and dressed in ordinary clothes, but he told of all the places he had been and the sights he had seen. All the people loved to visit with Parable. They came out to greet him and invited him into their homes. "Come in and have a cup of coffee and a piece of pie," many offered.

Bare Truth was upset that Parable got a reception so unlike his own. He went to the other town visitor and said, "Tell me, Parable, why do people greet you with such warmth when I am Truth they should hear?"

Instead of answering, Parable took off his hat and jacket and put them on Bare Truth. Truth was transformed. He was no less strong. He was no less Truth. But the people saw him in an entirely different light. When he put on Parable's clothes, Truth showed he really was concerned that the people hear him. When the people recognized that Truth cared enough about them to find out what he needed to do to have them listen to him, they listened all the more intently. The very people who had invited Parable for coffee and donuts now invited Truth, too.

And to this day, when Truth has business in town, he puts on Parable's clothes so that the people will hear him and deal with him.[21]

---

[21] Bryan Chapell, *Using Illustrations to Preach with Power* (Grand Rapids: Zondervan, 1992) 188–89.

Truth in story form is still truth. One final story: Once upon a time, most of the religious leaders spent their days thinking of lots of little rules by which they could make it less and less likely that people would possibly break any of the big rules. The people were used to preachers wagging their bony fingers at them and reminding them of all the different rules they just might possibly break, thereby delaying the coming of the Messiah. And the people wondered if there was any hope.

But then came another, different preacher. Where the other preachers frowned, this one laughed a lot. Where the other preachers shooed the children away so they would not interrupt an important sermon, this preacher invited the children to gather around him while he preached. And while the other preachers warned the people about all the things they should *not* do, this new preacher told them about the great big things they *could* do, and in the process of doing them they would be showing their love for God.

And while all the other preachers argued about the fine points of the law, this new preacher was different, because he told stories. He told them about a foreigner who rescued one of the home folk, and in the process they learned that they might have neighbors they'd never acknowledged before. He told about lost coins, lost sheep, a lost son, and in the process the people learned that God loved them more than they ever realized.

And he told them about a kingdom—a special, remarkable kingdom that was unlike the petty kingdoms and provinces of their world. He told them about a kingdom that seemed so small and yet would ultimately be greater than they could imagine. He told them about a King whose invitations to the wedding banquet were snubbed, so he invited others to come in their place. And he told about a rich man and a poor man whose eternal destinies were reversed.

He told stories that helped the people know that God loved them more than they could imagine. He told stories that helped them enter a kingdom not of this world. And he told stories that help us to know that preaching can really, truly fly.

PREACHING DOCTRINE, SERMON GENRE, AND GARDNER C. TAYLOR'S SENSE OF PROVIDENCE

Thomas G. Long

Sermons and Genre

Keen observers of American preaching recognize that sermons, like ties and hemlines, change style from time to time. Expository preaching, all the rage one season, gives way in the next season to storytelling sermons, or first-person sermons, or dialogue sermons, or sermons with presentations and video clips, or put-your-coffee-cup-down-on-the-pulpit-and-chat conversations. Even strong ethnic minority churches (Korean-American, African-American, and others)—that have firmly set inner gyroscopes that have kept them on a constant course in regard to preaching style despite cultural crosswinds—are beginning to change trajectories, especially as some members of those traditions become more affluent.[1]

How could it be any different? In a nation some wryly dub "the United States of Advertising," where images jump at us like popcorn kernels every waking minute, and electric-hot, rapidly evolving communication is our cultural adrenalin, preachers feel pressed to somehow keep up. After all, how are you going to preach to a congregation where you know that some of the folks out there are checking messages or surfing the web on their iPhones as you speak?

---

[1] See, for example, the fascinating analysis of T. D. Jakes not simply as a preacher, but as a symbol of social and thus homiletical change in the African-American church, in Shayne Lee, *T. D. Jakes: America's New Preacher* (New York: New York University Press, 2007).

Preachers, like teenagers at the mall, are on the prowl for the next new thing, something to connect with their ever-fickle listeners.

What is less frequently observed is that underneath these surface changes in preaching style, there are more important, and more fundamental, shifts not in style but in *genre*. Genre is a slippery word, but when it comes to sermons, I mean something that runs deeper than whether the preacher is animated or subdued, walks around the chancel or stays in the pulpit, uses images or not, quotes romantic poetry or speaks colloquially. I mean instead how a preacher employs a set of rhetorical conventions and strategies that work together in a certain context to achieve a certain purpose. I am close here to Carolyn Miller's claim that genre is a form of social action, that when it comes to spoken discourse (e.g., sermons), genre best focuses "not on the form of discourse but of the action it is used to accomplish."[2] For Miller, "a genre is a rhetorical means for mediating private intentions and social exigence."[3] To put it another way, when a preacher discerns that a congregation needs something (this is the "private intentions" part)—for example, to be taught a truth, to feel joy, or to get busy working against domestic violence—and then pulls together the best words said in the right way given this cultural moment (this is the "social exigence" part), to get that accomplished (this is the "rhetorical means" part), the preacher has summoned a preaching genre.

To better understand this (and to move away from sermons for a moment), consider other examples of communication: letters of reference, kidnapping ransom notes, and political stump speeches. In each case, these expressions may be flowery and ornate or straight and direct; they may be grammatically correct or syntactically mangled (or, in the case of the ransom note, a series of words cut from newspaper headlines crudely pasted on a sheet of paper); they may be

---

[2] Carolyn R. Miller, "Genre as Social Action," *Quarterly Journal of Speech* 70/2 (May 1984): 151.

[3] Ibid., 163.

unctuous or threatening; they may even be true or false. But one can identify them generically by the kind of action they seek to achieve. This is deeper than style. An employer may get something very formal—"Dear Mr. Bixley: I am writing herewith to recommend Margaret J. Jones for your position of finance manager"—or a note scribbled on a golf scorecard—"Hi, Bix. About your finance job. Marg Jones is a winner!" Both are recognizable as letters of recommendation because they share the same goal: to get the job for Margaret Jones.

Construed this way, the importance of genre to American preaching has deep historical roots. When the first English-speaking preachers in the New World, the Puritans, showed up on the bleak shores of New England, they brought with them a very clear and precise understanding of sermon genre. They were profoundly shaped by the brilliant, if eccentric, French Protestant logician Peter Ramus, whose controversial views of rhetoric and pedagogy kept him skittering across Europe from one teaching post to the next, a step or two ahead of the tar-and-feather mob. Ramus nevertheless made good sense to the Calvinists on the continent, and thus to the New England-bound Pilgrims. The result was that the sermons they preached in the colony were built strictly along Ramist lines, which meant that they were divided into three crisp divisions: doctrine, reason, and use.

While the American Puritans were busy scratching out a living and actually trying to preach these sermons in Massachusetts, the English Puritans back home in London were busily helping to draft the *Westminster Directory for Worship* (1644), which gave them a wonderful opportunity, when they got around to speaking of sermons, to put their stamp on what form a sermon should take. The Westminster divines deftly outlined the Ramist method of rhetoric about as well as can be done in a succinct description. The sermon, they said, was to have the three familiar sections: doctrine, reason, and use. In the doctrine section, the preacher ought to draw out "in plain terms" the theological claims and ideas found in the biblical text, explaining them if necessary. In the reason section, the preacher should show why these biblical doctrines can make sense to contemporary minds and should provide illustrations that "convey the truth into the Hearer's heart with spirituall delight." In the use section, the preacher brings it home, showing the practical implication, "which is a consequence of His doctrine."[4]

The language is antiquated, but what the Puritans did, in essence, was to set the GPS coordinates for American preaching for the next nearly four centuries. In short, what Westminster advocated and the Puritans put into practice were sermons not only in three parts, but sermons in three different *genres.* The preacher who is trying to teach something, namely a doctrine, is going to employ different literary patterns and strategies than a preacher who is trying to move people by making a theological idea somehow reasonable and clear to the listener's mind and heart. The form of the discourse must understandably shift when a preacher is in the more practical voice of helping the hearers figure out experiential issues in life.

The Puritans wanted to do it all and thought every sermon should embrace all three genres. It should teach true doctrine, connect to the reasonable capacities of hearers, and bring home the practical bacon every time. Not to touch all the bases was to fail to deliver a solid preachment. In fact, in the middle of the eighteenth century, when British evangelist George Whitefield, with his dramatic, impassioned, largely extemporaneous sermons, hit the American scene like the Beatles' invasion, turning heads, moving hearers to tears and repentance, and—no small thing here— threatening the accepted Puritan way of preaching, the faculty at Harvard got up on its back legs and snarled at the traveling evangelist and his ilk. Their big complaint was that Whitefield and the

---

[4] Quotations are from *A Directory for the Publique Worship of God throughout the Three Kingdoms of England, Scotland, and Ireland,* London, 1644, Speer Library, Princeton Theological Seminary, Princeton, New Jersey.

preachers who were trying to imitate him were messing with the method, that their sermons did not adequately address doctrine, reason, and use. They were thin doctrinally, inadequate in terms of reason, and especially mangled in the use, or application, section. They always closed their sermons in the same, predictable way (no surprise in this; evangelists before and since tend to have a standard "closing argument"). The Harvard academics griped that these "*extempore* Preachers give us almost always the same Things in the applicatory Part of their Sermons, so that [it] is very little akin to their Text, which is just open'd in a cursory, and not seldom perverted manner, and then comes the same kind of Harangue, which they have often used before, as an *Application*."[5]

This is interesting because, instead of accusing Whitefield outright of bad faith and crummy theology, the Harvard scholars took the relatively safest route of criticizing him for goofing up the genres—not enough doctrine, disconnected reason, and way-too-predictable use.

Shifting Genres and Neglected Doctrine

The Puritan preachers may have tried to do it all, but circumstances have changed. Attention spans have grown shorter, the culture drawn more inward spiritually, and preaching has adjusted, and, in the process, mostly downsized. What we have witnessed in the shifting patterns of American sermonizing since the Puritan divines held forth with their twenty-six-point sermons, all clicking in sequence from doctrine to reason to use, is that subsequent preaching has tended to pick one of these genres and to focus on it. We have seen a shifting back and forth among the genres—doctrinal sermons being in fashion for a while, then reason and experience gaining the

---

[5] Harvard faculty statement as quoted by Harry S. Stout in *The New England Soul: Preaching and Religious Culture in Colonial New England* (New York: Oxford University Press, 1986) 202.

upper hand, then practical "lessons for living" moving into the lead. In the last seventy-five years, for example, we have seen pulpit style go from the 1940s and 1950s teaching of key Christian ideas (doctrine) to the fascination, beginning in the 1970s, with narrative preaching (a kind of reason and illustration, with its stories that "convey the truth into the Hearer's heart with spiritual delight"), and then to the bullet points of more recent preachers who are concerned to spell out how to put the Christian faith to practical living (use).

The Puritans would be horrified, of course. For them, everything keyed off "doctrine," God's truth. A sermon that skipped right to "reason" would be hopelessly humanistic, and a sermon that began and ended with "use," not drawn explicitly out of biblical doctrine, could be nothing more than moralism. (The fact that the Puritans would have been right about this and that their fears have been borne out in recent homiletical practice is not only a long and complicated story, but also one of those irritating facts of church history that is perhaps best left for some later time when the word "Puritan" doesn't come across as the rough equivalent of "Taliban.").

As American preachers, based on their sense of what is most needed in a given cultural moment, bounce from doctrine, to reason, to use—from teaching, to experiencing, to practicing—ironically the genre that is increasingly the odd one out is doctrine. For example, the current genre that has prevailed in many "mainstream" pulpits for a half-century, namely narrative preaching (a form of storied "reason"), is under attack from many directions.[6] But this does not mean that doctrine will make a comeback. In fact, what appears to be elbowing narrative preaching out of the way is a certain new form of "use" preaching, with bullet-point presentations essentially aimed at practical wisdom for Christian living.

---

[6] See chap. 1, "A Likely Story: The Perils and Power of Narrative in Preaching," in Thomas G. Long, *Preaching from Memory to Hope* (Louisville: Westminster John Knox Press, 2009).

What happened to doctrinal preaching? Good, solid, here's-a-piece-of-theological-red-meat-to-chew-on preaching appears mostly neglected today, and in some ways it is no wonder. Americans hardly seem in the mood for meaty reflections on much of anything, from politics, to education, to public health, preferring instead a "get 'er done" pragmatism that does away with niceties like truth, ethical principles, and thinking things through carefully.

But in another sense, the ceding of the field to the other two genres, the stirring of hearts and practical living, seems strange. It is widely acknowledged among pastors that congregations today mostly lack biblical and theological knowledge and that one of the things most needed is the re-education of the church, the repairing of the breaches in terms of the average lay lack of knowledge about the fabric of the faith. So, why not the obvious answer? Why don't preachers step up to the plate and do more doctrinal preaching? Some good homiletical thinkers have recently urged just that and produced sturdy resources for getting the doctrinal job done.[7] Perhaps these resources will eventually begin to get traction in the pulpit, but for the most part preachers just keep on bemoaning their uninformed congregations while continuing to ignore their need to be taught.

Part of the reason, though, that I think preachers today are reluctant to head back into the thicket of doctrinal preaching is not because they do not perceive the need or because they lack encouraging resources, but because of a misunderstanding of genre, this time the genre that preachers *assume* is the only option for a "teaching

---

[7] See, for example, Ronald J. Allen, *Preaching Is Believing: The Sermon as Theological Reflection* (Louisville: Westminster John Knox, 2002) and, more recently, *Thinking Theologically: The Preacher as Theologian* (Minneapolis: Fortress Press, 2008); Robert G. Hughes and Robert Kysar, *Preaching Doctrine: For the Twenty-first Century* (Minneapolis: Augsburg Fortress, 1997); Burton Z. Cooper and John S. McClure, *Claiming Theology in the Pulpit* (Louisville: Westminster John Knox Press, 2003); and Robert Smith, Jr., *Doctrine That Dances: Bringing Doctrinal Preaching and Teaching to Life* (Nashville: B&H Academic, 2008).

sermon." What many practicing pastors think they must do if they are to preach Christian doctrine is to begin by saying, "Now the heart of our passage this morning is Doctrine X which is found as a 'clear teaching'[8] in many places in Scripture, and Doctrine X is absolutely true despite all manners of Anti-doctrine X thought in the culture. When we put this biblical witness together systematically, here is how the hip bone of Doctrine X fits into the thigh-bone of Doctrine Y and Z. If you want to be Christian (or Lutheran or Baptist or Methodist), this is what it is your duty to believe."

Preachers fear, with some justification, that such a sermon, under contemporary conditions of communication, would be hardly listenable. I do know congregations that gather respectable crowds weekly around just such propositional doctrinal preaching, but these congregations tend to be, like vegan restaurants, aimed at a niche clientele. Most congregations today have neither the appetite for systematic theology in the pulpit nor the skill to make sense of it. A number of years ago, I myself urged on preachers a stronger teaching

---

[8] Given the composite literary character of the scripture, the oft-used preaching phrase "the Bible clearly teaches" is a strange one indeed. If the Bible wished to "clearly teach" in that way, it would be a different literary type than it is; it would provide collections of propositional statements containing clear teachings, which is, of course, what the Bible does not do, or almost never does. The Bible tells so many stories, describes so many prophets and epistle writers doing their thing in social contexts that both are and are not like our own, and includes so many psalms and other poems that it is hermeneutically inescapable that hearing what God is saying to us in scripture is a matter not only of attending to the actual words of texts but of prayer and the exercise of faithful imagination. This is a good thing, actually, and is part of what enables the Bible to be a "classic" and to mediate God's Word to all kinds of circumstances across history. So usually what the preacher really means by "the Bible clearly teaches" is actually that this is a teaching the preacher "clearly" wants accepted.

voice in the pulpit, but perhaps without a sufficiently nuanced grasp of the genre challenges.[9]

Doctrine Revisited

In recent theological discussion, however, the whole issue for doctrine and genre has come up for reconsideration. A pioneering work, and one of the most influential in this regard, is George A. Lindbeck's *The Nature of Doctrine: Religion and Theology in a Postliberal Age*.[10] Lindbeck begins this study by noting an unusual feature of contemporary church life, namely that theologians and other participants in ecumenical dialogues frequently report at the end of the day that the partners in the dialogue have achieved basic agreement on some doctrinal issue like baptism or justification by faith. However, the people who supposedly have arrived at this theological consensus continue to swear their loyalties to traditional and denominational creedal affirmations that are logically incommensurate with each other. What gives? How can conversation partners claim to be in agreement when, technically speaking, they aren't? Are they telling the truth? Are they caught up in an ecumenical fantasy?

Lindbeck believes the mystery becomes a little less mysterious, if not solved, if we recognize that "doctrine" actually signifies more than one genre with more than one use. As is not fairly well known, Lindbeck proposes three such understandings of doctrine: cognitive, experiential-expressive, and cultural-linguistic (the approach that Lindbeck himself favors and develops).[11] Put simply, the cognitive approach sees doctrine as "truth claims about objective realities." So if A says that the only way to salvation is through believing in Jesus

---

[9] Thomas G. Long, "When the Preacher Is a Teacher," *Journal for Preachers* 16/1 (Decatur GA: Columbia Theological Seminary, [Lent] 1993): 21–27.

[10] George A. Lindbeck, *The Nature of Doctrine: Religion and Theology in a Postliberal Age* (Louisville: Westminster John Knox Press, 1984).

[11] Ibid., 16.

Christ as Lord, and B says, no, there are many paths to God, then the only way to go forward is to argue it through until one of them admits error, they arrive at a compromise, or they walk away from each other shaking their heads. The experiential-expressive approach sees doctrine as the way religious experience comes to language. In this view, A and B have had their religious experiences, which, when they get around to expressing them, use language that sounds incompatible. But if they get beneath the language to the experience, they may discover that they actually share a common core. The third approach, cultural-linguistic, sees doctrine more like a set of rules for life, something like "Drive on the left" or "Drive on the right." These are incompatible rules, so which is correct? Well, it depends on whether one is in Pittsburgh or Glasgow. Should you tackle the player on the opposing team or avoid bodily contact? Again, it depends. Are you playing football or basketball? So A and B, in conversation, may discover that each of them has a good doctrinal rule, but one that makes sense only when set down into a certain context. Thus, A and B may arrive at a mutual understanding—"Ah, I see; your doctrine makes good sense as a rule in your game and mine in mine, but we aren't playing the same game—without either one of them giving an inch on the adequacy of their own rules.

I have taken this sidetrip into Lindbeck's thought because it provides a way to connect doctrinal preaching with the notion of genre as a form of social action. I think most preachers have assumed that if they are going to do doctrinal preaching, then they are locked into something like Lindbeck's "cognitive" category, of suddenly being given the task of getting out the chalkboard in the pulpit and persuasively teaching the congregation *ideas* that are objective truth claims. But if the genre of the sermon is not a matter of stylistic features and internal structures as much as it is purpose and action, then other possibilities present themselves. What thoughtful preachers desire, after all, is not that their congregations master a load of theological information, but that they be theologically *formed*. The point is not to know the *right* theological answers, but to live the Christian faith as theologically formed people.

As a number of theologians are now beginning to argue, a congregation that is theologically formed is not necessarily one that can play Bible trivia but is something more like a troupe of improvisational actors. They know the basic script, and their roles, so well that they can "stay in character" whenever something new comes their way.[12] This is close to Lindbeck's cultural-linguistic understanding of doctrine, but with the added element of improvisation, it presses the creative edge of the cultural-linguistic scheme. The Christian life is less a recitation of theology and more an improvised performance of theology in ever-new, ever-unanticipated circumstances. The "truth claims" are still there, but they are not fixed rigidly in the lines and action; they are there as the underlying energy and direction of the performance. Living Christianly, then, becomes not like learning to speak Latin, a fixed, unchanging, historical language that one can use to communicate just fine as long as you are around other Latin speakers and aren't particularly interested in giving instructions for ordering a pizza, setting a digital video recorder, or doing anything else that requires a developing vocabulary. Living Christianly becomes, instead, much more like speaking a living, changing language—that is, observing correct grammar while at the same time coming up with new terms when circumstances demand them, like "road rage" or "garden burger."

The test of a church's understanding of the Holy Spirit, in other words, may not be its ability to explicate the intricacies of pneumatology, but in how it "speaks" the Spirit in its life, how it performs the doctrine of the Spirit in a church meeting or a church fight. Living together the performance of the gospel both expresses a community's theology and continues to form it. As theologian Shannon Craigo-Snell has observed,

---

[12] See Samuel Wells, *Improvisation: The Drama of Christian Ethics* (Grand Rapids: Brazos Press, 2004).

Acting out their relationship with Scripture, Christian communities shout and dance, they get happy and they mourn together, they bake casseroles and they sing hymns and comfort one another and open soup kitchens and raise money for the homeless. If Christian interpretation is really like theatrical performance interpretation, then these events and activities are not merely the results of an understanding that comes from interpretation: they are part of the interpretive process.[13]

What this means in terms of preaching is that the *genre* of doctrinal preaching is preaching that aims at forming the congregation theologically. The *means* for achieving this generic aim may vary. While the preacher may, on occasion, teach ideas, the preacher may also choose not to *explain* doctrine but to *perform* it.

Performing Providence

As an example of this possibility of performing doctrine, I want to explore briefly a sermon on the doctrine of providence preached by Gardner C. Taylor. The sermon, "Providence: The Control and Care of God," was published in 1981,[14] but an internal reference to racial "riots" signals that the sermon was perhaps first preached in the heat of the social upheavals in the mid-1960s. The sermon is a powerful statement about, as the title would indicate, the doctrine of providence.

Theologian Charles M. Wood points to the ecumenical Heidelberg Catechism for a definition of the classic doctrine of providence:

---

[13] Shannon Craigo-Snell, "Command Performance: Rethinking Performance Interpretation in the Context of Divine Discourse," *Modern Theology* 16/4 (October 2000): 481–82.

[14] Gardner C. Taylor, "Providence: The Control and Care of God," *The Scarlet Thread: Nineteen Sermons* (Elgin IL: Progressive Baptist Publishing House, 1981) 28–35.

Question 27. What do you understand by the providence of God?

Answer. The almighty and ever-present power of God whereby he still upholds, as it were by his own hand, heaven and earth together with all creatures, and rules in such a way that leaves and grass, rain and drought, fruitful and unfruitful years, food and drink, health and sickness, riches and poverty, and everything else, come to us not by chance but by his fatherly hand.

"This, or something very close to it," writes Wood, "has been widely accepted as the Christian doctrine of providence for a very long time. Whatever exists, exists because God wills to sustain it; and whatever happens, happens ultimately because God directs it. Whatever befalls us, whether it seems good or ill, is to be seen as 'provided' by God."[15]

Now to see this as a "cognitive" doctrine, to use Lindbeck's category, makes it difficult to preach for at least two reasons. First, to understand providence this way presents the language of the doctrine as an objective description of reality, something like, "It is forty-five degrees Fahrenheit outside and raining." That may work in a weather report, when people are looking for mere information, but to stand up in front of people in the twenty-first century and present theological truth as matter-of-fact objective information, to say, in effect, that it is a known, honest-to-God fact that the lightning strike that happened to hit *your* house and burn it down last night came "not by chance but by God's parentally loving hand," lacks a certain persuasive power, not to mention rhetorical appeal. Anyone who raised an objection, asking, "Hey, isn't it possible that maybe God doesn't aim each lightning bolt, that some of these things are just random?" would have to be silenced by a firm waggle of the teacher's

---

[15] Charles M. Wood, *The Question of Providence* (Louisville: Westminster John Knox Press, 2008) 1.

hand: "No, the doctrine clearly states that nothing is random. God controls all."

And that leads to the second problem with preaching the doctrine of providence cognitively: plausibility. To name one telling example, the young widow left with two small children whose husband was killed by a drunk driver is going to recognize immediately that the Heidelberg definition of providence, taken at face value, namely the idea that everything happens because God wills it, has for her monstrous implications about the character of God.

Theologian Lewis Smedes reports that when he was a young professor, his wife, Doris, "gave birth to a beautiful baby boy, who died before he had lived a whole day." Smedes and his wife had been trying for years, unsuccessfully, to have a child. "We had spent a decade," he said, "making love according to a schedule set by four different fertility clinics." Then, "after one summer night's lark on the sand dunes of Lake Michigan with no thought but love, Doris became a medically certified pregnant woman."[16] Two mornings after the baby was born, Smedes and a few friends gathered at the cemetery, and as their minister read "in the sure and certain hope of the resurrection," they buried the child that Doris never got to see.

Up to that point, Smedes had a serene, untroubled view of providence, but this experience changed him forever:

> Every good thing, every bad thing, every triumph, every tragedy, from the fall of every sparrow to the ascent of every rocket, everything was under God's silent, strange, and secretive control. But I could not believe that God was in control of our child's dying....
>
> I am no more able to believe that God micromanages the death of little children than I am able to believe that God was

---

[16] Lewis B. Smedes, "What's God Up To?: A Father Grieves the Loss of a Child," *Christian Century* 120/9 (May 2003): 38.

micromanaging Hitler's Holocaust.... I knew my portrait of God would have to be repainted.[17]

So what should the preacher do? Bounce around between sermons of reason and use, but stay clear of doctrine, especially the doctrine of providence? No, the doctrine of providence is essential to the gospel, and the church needs and deserves to be taught what is essential. What if, instead, the preacher understood the claims about providence from the great tradition, such as the statement in Heidelberg, not as cognitive, propositional texts, but more as scripts for "improv" theater, as plot synopses for a gospel drama in which all Christians are expected to learn and to play their parts? In regard to providence, this gospel drama is about a God who can be trusted and whose hand is guiding always and ultimately toward a benevolent end. A faithful character in this drama, then, leans outward, away from self-absorption, and moves in trust toward this loving God. A character in this drama does not spend time arguing about whether a leaf fell in the neighbor's yard rather than yours because "God willed it," but rather is one who "gets" the script, gets the idea that what is called for is climbing up there onto the stage and putting one foot in front of another, even in the dark, confident that God accompanies us along the way, that the ground underneath is solid, and that the path ahead can be trusted. As Wood says, "Learning *how* to believe means using the concepts which are ingredient in our belief as instruments through which we may perceive, understand, and respond to our world."[18]

This is, in my view, what Gardner Taylor's sermon on providence does. He does not exactly teach providence, nor does he argue providence, nor does he explain providence; rather, he *performs* providence.

---

[17] Ibid.

[18] Wood, *The Question of Providence*, 7.

The sermon begins with Taylor telling his congregation that he had intended to be preaching about another topic that morning but that he had gotten "waylaid" and that something else "got hold of me. And so here we are this morning talking about Providence."[19] For Taylor to bring up this shift of topic is not just confessing a late-breaking change of mind. It also intrigues the listener (what could have "got hold" of the preacher?) and subtly sets up the theme. Soon, Taylor will speak of providence as "God working out his plan and all our little schemes and aims are drawn into it." Without yet knowing it, the congregation has been treated to providence at work in the very choice of topic. The preacher is performing providence before even naming it.

Taylor swiftly tells his hearers that providence is an important part of Christian vocabulary and then gives not so much a definition, but a roadmap of the concept:

> Providence, [Tillich] said, is a quality which "drives" or "lures" us toward whatever it is that God has set out to do in our lives and beyond them. Providence means…that something is going on, so to speak, "behind the backs" of people in all their designs or plans. Joseph Parker spoke of Providence as God working out his plan and all our little schemes are drawn into it as "the whirlpool sucks all streams and currents"—and I might add, all debris, gum wrappers and driftwood "into its mighty and terrible sweep."[20]

The sermon now moves into a long central section in which Taylor gorgeously retells the story of Joseph, the son of Jacob who was nearly done in by his brothers, only to rise to the position of "Prime Minister of Egypt." Taylor is, in the best sense, a stage actor here, enacting a biblical story that has two levels: the human one that can be seen and the hidden one of divine providence. The note that keeps recurring in this retelling is that God was doing something

---

[19] Taylor, "Providence," 29.

[20] Ibid., 29.

"behind their backs," working the divine will in circumstances that seemed either utterly random or in human hands. The section ends in an engaging "run":

> If Joseph had not been sold into Egypt, he would not have been servant in Potiphar's house. If he had not been servant in Potiphar's house, he would not have been thrown in prison.... If Joseph had not been thrown in prison, he would not have met Pharaoh's butler.... If Joseph had not met the King's butler, he would not have been summoned to interpret Pharaoh's dream, and thus would not have become Prime Minister."

Taylor is moving toward the end now, and he allows Joseph's words to his brothers to sum up the theme of providence: "As for you, ye thought evil against me; but God meant it unto good." Taylor pauses a half-beat, admitting, "Something cynical in me does not want to believe that." Of course, by saying this Taylor identifies his hearers' skepticism about providence. The moment would seem to call for a vigorous defense of the logic of the doctrine. But that is not what Taylor does. He instead "stays in character." What happens in improv theater when someone in the audience stands up and challenges, "I find that hard to believe"? You step away from the exact script, while remaining faithful to the spirit of it. To the skepticism in himself and others, Taylor responds,"My experience says otherwise," and he goes on:

> There is a hand which guides our footsteps if we will but trust God, no matter what anybody may say or do. The world may try to hurt us, but God keeps our souls. Evil influences may try to block our way, but God tears down obstacles or makes us leap over them. The enemy may wound us, but God will heal our wounds. Strong winds may blow, but they speed us to port.
> Men may do what they will, but God is in charge. On a black Friday some men did crucify Jesus my Lord to death. Then they went to their weekends clucking their teeth and satisfied, but God acted and brought him from the dead. I rest me on that.... One day

we shall thank him for all that has happened in our lives—for every tear, every fear, every hurt, every opposition, every trial, every ache.[21]

That last sentence especially seems inspired, almost word for word, by the Heidelberg Catechism's definition of providence. But here the preacher does not speak as a creedalist but as a confessionalist, not as a teacher but as a believer, not in propositions or arguments but in the voice of doxology. Here is a preacher who "gets" the script, who understands the gospel story, and is up there on stage leaning in faith and trust toward the future and performing providence.

We see at the very least here a master preacher at work. If we look hard enough, we catch a glimpse of a way forward for doctrinal preaching.

---

[21] Ibid., 34–35.

PART TWO:

HONORING THE SCRIPTURES

WHAT SHALL THEY PREACH?

Marvin McMickle

During the third lecture he gave as the 1976 Lyman Beecher Lecture at Yale University Divinity School Gardner Taylor made an extemporaneous comment about sermon structure that has excited considerable attention. "How many points should there be in a sermon?" Taylor's answer, which was as provocative as it was humorous, was, "At least one!"[1] This question about how many points there should be in a sermon was raised against the commonly held belief that all sermons should involve the popular three points and a conclusion model. Should every sermon be based upon that familiar three-point approach, or is there some other principle around which our pulpit work should be organized?

When Taylor engages this question, he is raising a much deeper issue and pointing to a much more serious problem so far as preaching is concerned. How many points ought there be in a sermon? "At least one!" In making that comment, Taylor reminds his listeners and readers that rather than struggling with two or three different points, many sermons seem to have no discernible point at all. They just seem to drift from one random thought or text to the next without any logic or rationale. What Gardner Taylor was calling for was sermons that have at least one substantive point to make and at least one substantive claim to set forth for the benefit of those who

---

[1] This extemporaneous comment is only found in the original audio taped version of the lectures. Consult Gardner C. Taylor, *How Shall They Preach*, Lecture 3 original audio taped version, Berkeley Center communications: Visual Education Center, Yale Divinity School. The published version did not contain the extemporaneous comment.

have gathered to hear the sermon on any given day. "How many points ought there be in a sermon? At least one!"

A Sermon Should Have Only One Central Point

I lift Taylor's spoken comment to view because the question and his answer about how many points a sermon should have are the central focus of this essay. Since the title of his Beecher lecture was "*How* Shall They Preach?," then the title of this essay is "*What* Shall They Preach?" This essay will suggest not that every sermon should have *at least* one point. Instead, it will be argued that every sermon should have *only* one point. Preachers need not struggle to find multiple things of equal weight and worth to say in every sermon. Instead, preachers might do well to settle on one main point they would like to make in any given sermon, and then deliver that point with as much clarity and conviction as they can muster.

The search for multiple points in a sermon often leads to clever alliterations where the preacher tries to find as many things to say as possible, each point beginning with the same letter. It can lead to the use of words that rhyme or to an acronym where each letter in a word represents a different point in the sermon (e.g., L is for..., O is for..., V is for..., E is for...). This approach to preaching may be attractive to the ear, and it may win the preacher some points for creativity, but is it really possible that any congregation can hear and comprehend in one sermon three or more distinctly different points? More importantly, is it necessary that such clever devices be employed when declaring the gospel of Jesus Christ?

In those same Beecher lectures in 1976, he warned in another extemporaneous statement that in the sermon "the preacher can set out to prove that God is great or that the preacher is clever. However, you cannot do both in the same sermon."[2] Never is the risk of trying

---

[2] Ibid. Consult the same audio tape.

to be too clever greater than when preachers set out to make more than one solid point in their sermons.

In addition to this opening claim that sermons should be based upon one central theme or affirmation, it will also be argued here that the claim itself must be a matter of genuine importance and relevance in the lives of those who will hear that sermon. It will be further argued that the central claim should be rooted in a solid biblical foundation—whether the preacher starts with a biblical text and seeks to apply it to contemporary life or starts with some aspect of life and seeks to shed the light of scripture on that issue. Next, this essay will contend that the preacher should introduce the central claim of the sermon as early as possible so the listeners have some idea of where the message for that day is headed. Finally, this essay will seek to make preachers aware of the fact that they are working in an increasingly secular society that is dismissive of and/or openly contemptuous of preachers, the Bible, and the church. That fact notwithstanding, it remains the job of the preacher to declare the gospel of Jesus Christ as forcefully and persuasively as possible.

A Working Definition of Preaching

This essay will be governed by the following working definition of the task of the sermon: "Every sermon needs to make one clear, compelling, biblically centered and contextually relevant claim that sets some aspect of God's will and God's word before some specific segment of God's people. This is done with the hope that those people will be challenged, informed, corrected, or encouraged as a result of the word set before them that day."[3] This one central idea can be referred to as the sermonic claim. The phrase "sermonic claim" is meant to imply that a sermon should do one of the following things: (1) assert something that is significant; (2) ask for

---

[3] Marvin A. McMickle, *Shaping the Claim* (Minneapolis: Fortress Press, 2008) 6.

something that is substantial to the point, requiring personal or communal commitment; or (3) advocate for something that is sacred and deeply spiritual.[4] Plainly stated, the sermonic claim is the essence of what any sermon is about. It is the central truth or teaching of that sermon. It is a creative and engaging combination of what the biblical text says, how that message is communicated by the preacher, and some direction in regard to what the listeners are being asked to do as a result of hearing that sermon.

A word of clarification might be in order in regard to the difference between sermon content and sermon organization. The assertion that a sermon should have one clear and compelling point is not intended to limit the preacher in terms of how a sermon is to be structured. A sermon may employ a traditional three-point form of argument, but those three points should be directing the listeners to a single, central claim. The sermon may involve a dialectical approach of thesis/antithesis/synthesis, but that form of argument should still result in some consideration of a single sermon claim. The sermon may employ a narrative, biographical, or expository form, but preachers should exercise care in being sure that the sermon is only asking for one clear and compelling next step from the listeners.

The idea of what is being referred to here as the sermonic claim, or the central message of the sermon, has been discussed and/or defined by other teachers of homiletics as well as by leading preachers who have considered this idea of the sermon being focused on "one clear, compelling, biblically centered, and contextually relevant claim." Haddon Robinson says that every sermon should have "a main point or a big idea" around which the sermon is organized.[5] Samuel Proctor talks about the "proposition" or the "relevant

---

[4] Ibid.

[5] Haddon Robinson, *Biblical Preaching* (Grand Rapids: Baker Books, 1980).

question."[6] Thomas G. Long discusses this same issue in terms of the "focus" and "function" of the sermon.[7]

Fred Craddock is especially helpful when he refers to this idea of a sermon being based on one primary claim or one central point as "the theme" of the sermon, which the preacher should be able to state in one simple sentence. He reminds the preacher that in shaping a sermon, one is not only determining what will be said in that sermon, but one is also deciding what will *not* be said, at least not in that sermon. Craddock helpfully warns the preacher that the biblical text(s) we use for a sermon may hold more than one significant message that could be usefully explored and examined. It is rare that any one sermon can be shaped so that it allows all of that material and all of those possible insights to be covered.[8] That is where the central theme or message of the sermon comes in; it helps sort through all of the things that *could* be said in any one sermon and helps to narrow the preacher's focus down to what *should* and *will* be said in this particular sermon. As Craddock points out, there is a benefit for both the preacher and the congregation when the sermon has a single focus: "To aim at nothing is to miss everything, but to be specific and clear in one's presentation is to make direct contact with many whose ages, circumstances, and apparent needs are widely divergent. Listeners to sharply focused sermons have an amazing capacity to perceive that the sermon was prepared with them specifically in mind."[9] How many points ought there be in a sermon? Taylor humorously advised that there be "at least one." What is being argued here is that there be *only one* main point in every sermon,

---

[6] Samuel D. Proctor, *The Certain Sound of the Trumpet: Crafting a Sermon of Authority* (Valley Forge: Judson Press, 1994) 93–94.

[7] Thomas G. Long, *The Witness of Preaching* (Louisville: Westminster John Knox Press, 1989).

[8] Fred B. Craddock, *Preaching* (Nashville: Abingdon Press, 1985) 155.

[9] Ibid., 156.

illustrated, analyzed, and argued from as many angles as may be necessary to drive that point home.

Every sermon will undoubtedly have multiple parts or sections, such as an introduction, imagery, applications, and a conclusion. However, each of these components is important only insofar as they serve a common purpose, specifically helping listeners focus on the one central claim in that sermon. All of the parts of the sermon should be coordinated so that they all support, and in no way conflict with or obscure, that basic assertion.

The introduction should be interesting to the point of being intriguing, but its true value is as it sets the sermon in context for the major claim that is about to be stated. Imagery is not meant to be an anecdotal diversion from the main theme of the sermon. Rather, it should serve to bring clarity and a keener comprehension of the point set forth in the sermonic claim. Applications are the places in the sermon when the relevance of the sermonic claim is being made to those who are hearing the sermon. They demonstrate why it is important that people listen to and act upon what they are hearing in the sermon. Conclusions are not simply meant to bring the sermon to an end. Rather, the conclusion is meant to refocus attention on the central claim that has just been explored, and then hint at or clearly state what the preacher hopes the listeners will do as a result of having heard the sermon. All elements of the sermon should flow out of and be in service to the one central claim of the sermon.

Sermons Should Be Based upon Something Substantive

Not only should sermons be based upon one central claim or assertion, but that one major claim should address an issue or topic of real substance and importance. Sermons should spring up from and bear forth the great themes embedded in the scriptures—justice, grace, the sovereignty of God, the divinity of Christ, the sinful nature of humanity, discipleship, stewardship, the authority of scripture, and the work of missions and evangelism throughout the world. Sermons should emerge from the heart-wrenching questions and concerns that reside within the congregation and within the life of the preacher as well. Sermons should help people bridge the gap between the faith they hold dear and the troubling events they hear about in the news.

The one central point of the sermon must challenge people concerning things that are important both to their corporate faith and to their individual lives. It should not be based upon things that do not matter as people are attempting to navigate their way through life. It should not engage things that are irrelevant or inconsequential. Preachers should always try to deal with things that can make a serious, positive difference in the lives of those who hear the sermons, the church in which they gather, and the world in which they live.

When I was growing up in Chicago in the 1950s and 1960s, it was not uncommon to hear one person insult or criticize another with the phrase, "He/she ain't about nothing." There was no more dismissive or demeaning statement that one person could direct against another than to say those words. To say this meant that the person in question was not worthy of much attention and should not be expected to produce much in the way of accomplishment. The statement suggested that the person in question should not be taken seriously or expected to have anything significant to contribute to any discussion or the resolution of any problem.

Too many sermons on too many Sundays "ain't about nothing." Too many sermons are limited to superficial or simplistic considerations that make no real difference or have no substantive bearing on the great issues of life. This charge must be avoided by all those who stand to preach to the people of God. Sermons should be about things that are biblically and theologically compelling. Sermons should be about things that are intellectually challenging and engaging. Sermons should be about things that are contextually and personally relevant and applicable to the lives of those who hear the word on any given day.

It is unfortunate, for instance, that some preachers choose to waste time splashing around in the shallow water of positive thinking, prosperity theology, or narrowly defined "moral values" like arguments against homosexuality or abortion, while leaving completely unaddressed such justice issues as war and peace in Iraq, global climate change, the 45 million Americans who have no health insurance, and the conditions facing the 2 million Americans confined in prison—not to mention the 80 percent of those prisoners who would be better served by drug treatment that costs $5,000 annually than by incarceration that costs seven times that amount each year.

Surely preachers could find something to say about the stunning divorce rate that threatens one out of every two heterosexual marriages. People need to be encouraged and reassured in the face of the anxiety and hysteria associated with terrorism. Preachers could and should try to calm the fears of those in their congregation who are concerned about the outsourcing of jobs from America, as well as the steadily rising cost of living that is pushing more and more families into poverty. Sadly, the need still exists to address the continuing presence of racism and bigotry in our society that is increasingly taking the form of nooses being hung and swastikas being painted in public places.

Anyone who ever heard Gardner Taylor preach can attest to the fact that his sermons were *always* about something serious and substantive! All of us should strive to follow that example. Time is too precious to be wasted on pointless preaching. There are serious problems and agonizing concerns that confront people at the deepest emotional and existential levels every day. When they make the effort and invest the time to come out to worship on Sunday morning, many of them are coming with the words of Jeremiah 37:17 burning in their hearts: "Is there any word from the LORD?" When the sermon is over, those in the pew should have been moved in such a way that they can answer in the affirmative: "Yes, today there was a word from the Lord for me."

Haddon Robinson speaks to this approach to preaching when he says, "The expositor must also be aware of the currents swirling across his [sic] own times, for each generation develops out of its own history and culture and speaks its own language. A minister may stand before a congregation and deliver exegetically accurate sermons, scholarly and organized, but dead and powerless because they ignore the life-wrenching problems and questions of the hearers."[10] Sermons should be based upon a compelling central point that addresses some aspect of people's real, daily lives.

Sermons Should Be Rooted in Scripture

Since preachers aim to offer congregations a "biblically centered and contextually relevant" word, sermon preparation should most often begin with careful consideration of a biblical text. Preachers will never have to worry about finding a clear and compelling point for their sermons when they begin by giving consideration to the rich resources of biblical material. A reservoir of preaching that speaks to every imaginable aspect of human experience awaits any preacher who develops a systematic way of looking directly to the Bible for the claims and content of their sermons. Preachers should look and listen closely to the teachings, parables, doctrines, prophetic oracles, human encounters, miraculous moments, and character flaws and foibles so candidly and honestly revealed in the lives of characters recorded in the Bible.

There are lessons to be learned in the Bible about the divine/human encounter and about the struggle of living godly lives in a sinful world. The Bible talks about a God who can sustain and deliver people that are facing hopeless and desperate situations. It deals with issues of immigration and the mass movement of

---

[10] Robinson, *Biblical Preaching*, 77.

populations of people. One cannot read about the story of Israel, which begins with "a wandering Aramean" and continues with them being an essentially migrant or nomadic population, and not see the connection it establishes with the millions of people in our world today who have chosen to or been forced to become migrants.

The Bible addresses oppression and war and, as such, can speak to the personal, national, and international cost of such violence. The Bible does not shy away from issues of racial prejudice and, as such, has much to say to a society still deeply divided by race and ethnicity born out of hundreds of years of African slavery, the exploitation and destruction of Native Americans, and the recent rise of anti-Islamic sentiment.

A compelling sermon with a powerful central claim can emerge when a preacher looks and listens to the scriptures for questions and answers that mirror and shed light on twenty-first century concerns, issues, and events. Preachers would do well to look to scripture as the most regular and reliable source of preaching material. When the Bible is carefully studied and analyzed, the challenge will never be wondering what to preach. Instead, the preacher will be left wondering how to settle on that one main point out of all the ideas that can emerge out of the careful review of any passage of scripture.

While the movement for sermon preparation is usually from being "biblically centered" to being "culturally relevant," it can go in the opposite direction as well. Preachers can also begin with some issue that arises out of the heart-wrenching questions that reside within the life of the congregation, including the life of the preacher, and then look for a way to shed the light of scripture on that issue. The number of questions that could helpfully be addressed in a sermon is nearly unlimited: Is there really life after death? Why did I contract HIV, cancer, or some other life-threatening disease when I have been living a good, Christian life? How do I redefine my worth and my identity now that I have lost my job as a result of downsizing or corporate takeovers, or lost my breast as a result of a mastectomy?

If I get a divorce from an abusive spouse, can I remarry without being considered an adulterer? What should I do if my children do not choose to embrace this Christian faith that has meant so much to me?

While it is possible that questions such as these could be addressed when the preacher begins with the biblical text and looks for points of application, what is being suggested here is that sometimes the preacher can start with these emotional questions and concerns and then connect them to a biblical text that faithfully addresses them. Frankly, this is how most people who hear our sermons come to the scriptures; they are led there by their pain and their problems. There is some trial or trouble already at work in their lives, and they wonder if the Bible in particular and the Christian faith in general can provide them with any assistance or direction.

Whether the sermon emerges from a biblical text or from a heart-wrenching question drawn from the drama of human life, one thing remains the same—the sermon itself must be a message that is relevant to the lives and world of the listeners, but rooted and centered in the exegesis of some biblical text. It is the informed use of scripture as a source of authority in proclamation that distinguishes a sermon from the editorial page of a newspaper or a speech given by a policymaker. The editorial writer and the policymaker could speak at length about such issues as nuclear war, world hunger, race relations, or the implications of Thomas Friedman's observation that "the world is flat."[11] They could base their statements on their personal opinions, on public opinion polls, on a particular political ideology that governs the newspaper's editorial page, or the entity for which the policymaker is working. If that is all they did, no one would criticize them for how they went about their work.

That is not true for the preacher. It is not our personal opinion on any issue that is most important. It is not some well-informed update on the present status of any social or political issue that makes

---

[11] Thomas A. Friedman, *The World Is Flat* (New York: Farrar, Strauss, and Giroux, 2005).

for an effective sermon. It should not be the liberal or conservative slant of the congregation, or of the preacher for that matter, that determines the content of the sermon on any given day. Rather, the sermon should be based upon the truths that are being taught and the lessons that can be learned from the biblical text that has been chosen or assigned for that day.

The Central Point Must Be Set Forth as Quickly as Possible

Not only should sermons have one central point, and not only must that point involve something substantive, but preachers also need to understand that they must set forth that point as early in the sermon as possible so listeners have some idea of what is going to be discussed in that sermon and why that topic is of importance to their lives. Preachers need to be aware of the fact that from the moment we open our mouths in the pulpit, people in the pews are consciously and unconsciously asking themselves, "What's the point?" or "What does this have to do with me?" This is not an idle question. It is a question of great urgency to both the preacher and the listener. For the listeners, a sense that the sermon does indeed have something to do with their lives must come early in the sermon, or else their minds will begin to tune out the preacher and they will start thinking about other things.

In his classic communications book *Public Speaking—As Listeners Like It!*, Richard Borden names this dynamic "Ho Hum."[12] He describes Ho Hum in this way: "Do not picture your audience as waiting with eager eyes and bated breath to catch your message. Picture it, instead, as definitely bored—and distinctly suspicious that you are going to make this situation worse."[13]

---

[12] Richard Borden, *Public Speaking—As Listeners Like It!* (New York: Harper & Bros., 1935). I will discuss other items in the checklist in the following chapter.
[13] Ibid., 4.

What this means for preachers is that we must be aware that from the moment we stand up and begin to preach, the clock is ticking as to how long people will continue to pay close attention to what is being said. We must get the hearers emotionally engaged at the beginning of the sermon if we want them to stay with us until the end of the sermon. This is more likely to happen if there is one clear and compelling idea around which the whole sermon is being organized.

To use an athletic analogy, preachers should think of their work more like that of a sprinter in the hundred-meter dash rather than of a long-distance runner in the twenty-six-mile marathon. When the starting gun sounds for a marathon run, it is not required that the runners get off to an explosive start—they have miles to run and hours ahead of them before they approach the finish line. They can pace themselves and save most of their energy for the final miles of the race. Not so in the hundred-meter dash. In order to have any chance at all, the sprinter must explode out of the starting blocks and hit full stride within seconds. Success for a sprinter requires getting off to a good start. The same is true for preachers—success requires getting off to a good start. That means that the most important sentence in the sermon is the *first* sentence. The most important paragraph in the sermon is the *first* paragraph. The most important time frame is the *first* three to five minutes. Every effort must be made at the beginning of the sermon to make the case for why people should pay attention to what is going to follow.

As Borden puts it, "Your speech is not well organized unless you kindle a quick flame of spontaneous interest *in your first* sentence."[14] This is not simply an intellectual endeavor. It requires the use of a searching question, a compelling comment or observation, a riveting illustration, or an appeal to some current event that the preacher wants to review from a faith perspective. Early in the sermon, people

---

[14] Ibid., 3.

need to know what one central claim is coming, and they need to know that such a claim is interesting or relevant or essential for their development as Christians.

Claiming the congregation's emotional and existential engagement at the beginning of the sermon does not mean giving away all we plan to say from the outset. To sustain interest throughout the sermon, some things must be held back, some tension must be left that needs resolving, some questions must be raised that need answering. Preachers might want to consider a methodology described by Eugene Lowry, who talks about establishing a clear and quick connection with the congregation through the intersection of the "problematic itch," which is something of interest or curiosity for the audience, and the "solutional scratch," which is the answer or the way forward being offered by the sermon.[15]

Lowry encourages the preacher to begin the sermon with something that is, or can be made to be, of interest to the congregation, and then use the balance of the sermon to shed light on or to bring some resolution to that issue. This approach to preaching would work regardless of the sermon style or format that is being used. The preacher could move from the "problematic itch" to the "solutional scratch" when delivering a textual or expository sermon where the problem involves a hard-to-understand passage that can now be explained. It works if the preacher is delivering a topical sermon on a controversial issue or an urgent, current event that can be considered from a biblical and theological perspective. Whether the format is biblical storytelling, a doctrinal discussion, or even a biographical (first-person) sermon, Lowry offers a reliable way to establish an early, solid, emotionally engaged connection with the listeners.

---

[15] Eugene L. Lowry, *The Homiletical Plot: The Sermon as Narrative Art Form* (Atlanta: John Knox Press, 1980) 20.

The Central Point Should Be Made with Passion

On more than one occasion I have heard Gardner Taylor say that preaching is both a "matter" and a "manner." The "matter" involves what you say in your sermon (the central point). The "manner" involves the way in which that matter is delivered (passion and intensity). Good preaching is a solid balance of both matter and manner. Preaching should involve a clear and compelling central point that is delivered with enthusiasm, conviction, zeal, earnestness, urgency, or any other synonym that suggests that what is being said deserves to be heard because it is of the utmost importance.

As I have argued elsewhere, enthusiastic preaching was indeed part of the overarching biblical tradition:

> The prophets, Paul, and Jesus spoke with urgency, with conviction, and with a sense of purpose that was so compelling that they evoked an almost immediate response from those who heard them. Sometimes the response was conversion and faith in Christ. Sometimes the response was rejection and the need to flee the city to preserve their lives (Acts 19). But either way, it is easy to imagine that it was their obvious sense of conviction, of emotion, of passion (pathos) that moved the crowds who heard them. I sincerely doubt whether cold and dispassionate preaching would have resulted in "turning the world upside down" (Acts 17:6).[16]

Of course, we need not go all the way back to biblical times to find emotional expression being an essential element of proclamation. Passion in preaching is rooted in the history of American preaching. In many African-American churches, such words as celebration, intonation, musicality, whooping, and rhythm have served to describe not only the manner in which the sermonic conclusion is

---

[16] Marvin A. McMickle, *Living Water for Thirsty Souls: Unleashing the Power of Exegetical Preaching* (Valley Forge: Judson Press, 2001) 185.

presented, but also the way in which the preacher is emotionally invested throughout the sermon.[17]

Henry H. Mitchell notes that the use of passion or emotion in preaching may be the greatest point of divergence between black and white preaching in America today. He demonstrates, however, that this was not always the case. In his article "African American Preaching: The Future of a Rich Tradition," Mitchell notes that "the first Great Awakening burst forth with shouting…under no less worthy of a preacher than Jonathan Edwards…. The shouting really burst forth under Whitefield and the Tennents…. An ex-slave named Gustavus Vassa, in his autobiographical slave narrative tells how greatly he was impressed by the 'fervor and earnestness' of George Whitefield."[18] Part of what made preaching so effective during the Great Awakening was that it was forceful and compelling. Part of what makes so much preaching today so ineffective is that it is dull and is delivered without "fervor and earnestness."

Halford Luccock, who taught homiletics at Yale Divinity School for many years, made an observation about himself that might apply to many other preachers as well. In his book *Communicating the Gospel,* Luccock said, "Eugene Ormandy once dislocated his shoulder while leading the Philadelphia Orchestra. I do not know what they were playing, but he was giving all of himself to it. And I have asked myself sadly, did I ever dislocate anything while preaching, even a necktie?"[19]

---

[17] There is a wonderful treatment of the importance of emotion in preaching found in Evans E. Crawford and Thomas H. Troeger, *The Hum: Call and Response in African American Preaching* (Nashville: Abingdon Press, 1995) 21.

[18] Henry H. Mitchell, "African American Preaching: The Future of a Rich Tradition," *Interpretation* 51/4 (October 1997): 380–83.

[19] Halford Luccock, *Communicating the Gospel* (New York: Harper & Bros., 1954) 145.

Sermons Must Not Fear the Secularization of Society

Our sermons should help Christians think about their identity in Jesus Christ in a world that is increasingly secular on the one hand and increasingly diverse in religious expression on the other. How do Christians navigate the waters between those who insist that America is a "Christian nation" and the fact that America is home to an increasing number of citizens who are adherents to Judaism, Islam, and many other of the world's religions? The Bible can help shape sermons that can speak to those in this country who want to use the apparatus of organized religion in order to argue for certain public policy positions on issues ranging from abortion to same-sex marriage to prayer in public schools.

Given the rise of what is labeled postmodernity, some may even question the wisdom of the preacher focusing a sermon on "one clear, compelling, *biblically* centered and contextually relevant claim that sets some aspect of God's will and God's word before some specific segment of God's people." There are some people who challenge the authority of scripture in the twenty-first century. There are some who advocate for or practice a generalized, individualized spirituality instead of a biblically oriented, communal faith. Others argue that one path to God is as good as any other, so why should a person pay any more attention to what the Bible says than they do to what any other book or any other religious tradition has to say?

In some church circles various forms of communication, such as presentations, video clips, and small group discussions take the place of the sermon. Sanctuaries are being referred to as auditoriums that are designed not to include a cross or any other noticeable Christian symbols. The "pulpit" is being replaced by a "podium." Worship services are being replaced with classes, spiritual formation events, and motivational messages.

It cannot be doubted that we are living in an age where the authority of scripture and familiarity with the content of scripture can no longer be assumed by the preacher. We can also agree that we are living at a time when other religious traditions and approaches to spirituality are heard and seen everywhere we turn. That being said, those factors should not result in our sounding either retreat or surrender so far as our commitment to biblical preaching is concerned. Several helpful books have been written that assist preachers with going about their work in this postmodern context.[20]

As preachers, we should be conscious of the postmodern challenges that confront us if we want our sermons to be culturally relevant. This does not mean, however, that we should be intimidated or afraid to set forth a biblically based sermon. Some historical perspective is helpful. This is not the first time in history the biblical message has had to struggle in order to be heard. This postmodern world in which we preach is no more difficult a context for preaching than was the eighth-century BC world of Amos, the seventh-century BC world of Jeremiah, or the first-century AD world of Christ or Paul. All of them preached a biblical message in a world that was either unfamiliar with their scriptural authorities, unwilling to conform to them, or committed to other religious practices altogether. Our preaching predecessors were not put off by those realities. They simply preached whether it was "in season or out of season" (2 Timothy 4:2 ESV).

For instance, there is little doubt that Jeremiah faced a far more hostile and unwelcoming climate for his preaching than is the case for any of us today. His preaching about idolatry and corruption in the nation fell on deaf ears, but he continued to preach. His scrolls were cut up and contemptuously tossed into the fire by King Jehoiakim

---

[20] Some of these books include Robert Kysar and Joseph M. Webb, *Preaching to Postmoderns* (Peabody MA: Hendrickson, 2006); Graham Johnston, *Preaching to a Post-Modern World* (Grand Rapids: Baker Books, 2001); Ronald Allen, Barbara Shires Blaisdell, and Scott Black Johnston, *Theology of Preaching: Authority, Truth and Knowledge of God in a Postmodern Ethos* (Nashville: Abingdon Press, 1997); O. Wesley Allen, *The Homiletic of All Believers: A Conversational Approach* (Louisville: Westminster John Knox Press, 2005).

(Jeremiah 36:23–24, ESV); he was thrown into a cistern filled with mud as punishment for his unwelcome words (Jeremiah 38:1–10, ESV). Nevertheless, the prophet speaks words that give full expression to what every preacher in the postmodern world must feel from time to time: "O LORD, you have enticed me, and I was enticed; you have overpowered me and you have prevailed; I have become a laughingstock all day long; everyone mocks me. For whenever I speak, I must cry out. I must shout 'Violence and destruction!' For the word of the LORD has become for me a reproach and derision all day long" (Jer. 20:7-8, ESV). The words of Jeremiah could have been written with the preaching climate of the twenty-first century in mind. Preaching is lightly regarded, and the gospel is rarely heeded in a culture that prefers the opinions of scientists, pop music icons, and public policymakers over anything that comes wrapped in the phrase "Thus says the Lord."

That being said, we should not only identify with the challenges faced by Jeremiah in preaching the word of God in an unfriendly and unwelcoming world, but we should seek to match his determination to continue to preach a faithful, biblically centered message no matter how hostile or dismissive the environment may be for what we have to say. That is how Jeremiah continued to describe his preaching context: "If I say, 'I will not mention him or speak anymore in his name,' Then within me there is something like a burning fire shut up in my bones. I am weary of holding it in; and I cannot" (Jeremiah 20:9).

Paul experienced a similar problem of being heard by some but dismissed or denounced by others in his sermon in Athens in Acts 17:32-34. Surely Paul's attempt to preach about Christ, and especially about the resurrection of Christ in the presence of Stoics and Epicureans (Acts 17:17–18), corresponds to our challenge of preaching Christ in this postmodern world. Paul, challenging the superficial religiosity and the false gods he encountered at the Areopagus (Acts 17:22–31), reflects our challenge of preaching about

Christ in a culture that is content with private spirituality that views any path to God as being just as true and valid as any other. We can easily recognize the various responses to Paul's preaching—the same has happened to us. What is of greater importance and of far greater urgency is for all of us to be willing to identify with Paul's determination to preach Christ in a culture that is unfriendly, disinterested, or largely unfamiliar with our vocabulary and our values. There is no more uncompromising declaration of the gospel message than is found in Paul's sermon in Athens: "because he has fixed a day on which he will judge the world in righteousness by a man whom he has appointed, and of this he has given assurance to all by raising him from the dead" (Acts 17:31, ESV).

That is what we should be preaching, and that is the claim that our sermons should be setting forth—what God wants to say to the church and to the world, as that message is found in the scriptures. Our task as preachers is to delve into that message, select one portion of it that will be the basis for a particular sermon, and then preach that message in a way that is clear and compelling. Our task is to be an instrument through which a word of ultimate significance claims our congregations in a transformative manner. And it is our task to do this week after week, every time we step into the pulpit.

How many points ought there be in a sermon? There should be one central point, rooted in scripture, focused on a relevant concern, introduced as early as possible to the listeners, and delivered with passion.

A SENSE OF THE SCRIPTURES
IMPERATIVE

William E. Pannell

My search for that elusive quality in preaching, represented by Dr. Gardner C. Taylor's pulpit work, may have begun in the mid-1960s on the Wheaton College campus during a conversation with Joe Bayly, a friend of mine who was editor of *HIS* Magazine, the publication sponsored by InterVarsity Christian Fellowship. Joe was a person of keen sensibilities in matters pertaining to the gospel and good preaching. With obvious pleasure in his voice, he asked me if I had ever heard Dr. Gardner Taylor preach. I replied in the negative, and he commented, "Well, if he was a pastor anywhere near here I would join his church just to hear him preach."

Twenty-five years would pass before I met Gardner Taylor and heard him speak. The occasion was the annual day of celebrating the legacy of Dr. Martin Luther King, Jr. I had become a member of the faculty at Fuller Theological Seminary, and the sanctuary was filled with students and faculty and a large group of black pastors from the surrounding area, significant leaders in the church and community who, except for such an event, would scarcely appear on campus. Indeed the seminary had not distinguished itself by exposing its students to the sermonic offerings of African-American preachers. Most of the professors did not know who Gardner Taylor was, nor for that matter other blacks who would follow on similar occasions, such as Samuel DeWitt Proctor or the so-called "Harvard whooper," Charles Gilchrist Adams. That many in our school, a major evangelical seminary, had not been exposed to these black leaders testifies to the ongoing distance between white evangelicals and their counterparts in the African-American academic and ecclesiastical network. Lamentably, we live, even now, in different worlds.

Taking his text from Revelation 15, the man from Brooklyn began his sermon with a reading from the passage. Taylor read with a deep-throated cadence that caught the spirit of the passage. His interpretive reading sent a soft murmur among the congregants, especially the preachers gathered. Many of them had heard Taylor preach before, of course, and had come to know that in his reading of the scriptures the listeners could catch early suggestions of what would follow in the sermon itself by means of the cadence, the rhythm, the pauses, and the way words were so clearly articulated. As Taylor read the scripture, there was an unmistakable sense of anticipation; the text was alive with an energy waiting to be released.

Anyone who has heard the recording of Gardner Taylor reading from Luke 3:1–2 at Harvard University on the occasion of a sermon honoring the memory of Dr. King would not forget the drama generated by the articulated content of those two verses.[1] The scripture reading had been set up by a well-crafted introduction about the strange ways of God in dealing with the human race, the "awkward angles" by which the Spirit of God comes to humankind. But it was the way those verses were read that set the stage for one of the most memorable sermons in recent memory. There was a pregnant pause after Taylor's pronunciation of "Tiberias Caesar" and an articulate sounding of the place-name "Trachonitis." And the transition Taylor soon made to the power brokers in modern American life, both political and ecclesiastical, was electrifying.

Taylor's learned vocabulary was served by a rare vocal instrument, yet not for ostentatious display. Behind the vocabulary

---

[1] The compact disc format of that sermon on "The Strange Ways of God" is available in *Essential Taylor*, a two-disc set (Judson Press, 2000), disc 2. The printed sermon appears in Gardner C. Taylor, *Special Occasion and Expository Sermons*, vol. 4 of *The Words of Gardner Taylor*, comp. Edward L. Taylor (Valley Forge: Judson Press, 2000) 100–108.

was a fertile mind, a disciplined intellect that could pull words from a storehouse of learning when what had been written or memorized would not adequately convey a desired meaning. The sermon was carefully crafted in sentences that, taken together, paint the epic story of redemption. And the sermon was also about sound, and, in this case, a distinctive sound that melds an African-American texture from Louisiana modified by the dynamic of New York City. The sermon became an attempt to reveal the human condition from God's point of view, to uncover again its central theme that "God is out to take back what belongs to him." For this the preacher called upon the biblical record of that activity and an inner conviction that that record is reliable.

The preacher needs a text, a script if you will, a voice, sounds from above to inform, a "divine voice" as Stephen Webb calls it, that illumines, gives direction and authority to utterances.[2] Taylor is clear about this: "If a preacher is going to have the strength of the Word of God behind him, there must be a sense of scripture. All the moods, experiences, and thoughts of the human mind are contained in the scriptures. The Bible is full of life-and-blood people. It is frightfully honest."[3]

Living in the Scriptures

A "sense of scripture"—what does that mean? Is it the same thing as a conviction that the scriptures are the inspired word of God and, thus, the only rule for faith and practice? Probably not, although it does include that conviction. I suspect rather that this is an expression that grows out of Taylor's years of living with the scriptures, of gaining a sense of the mind of God concerning his

---

[2] See *The Divine Voice: Christian Proclamation and the Theology of Sound* (Grand Rapids: Brazos Press, 2004).

[3] Terry Muck and Paul Robbins, "The Sweet Torture of Sunday Morning: An Interview with Gardner C. Taylor," *Christianity Today Library*, 1 July 1981, http://www.ctlibrary.com/le/1981/summer/8l13016.html (accessed 20 October 2008).

desires for a relationship with humans and of "all the moods, experiences and thoughts" of humanity. And of course if the scriptures are not the authoritative word of God, then the preacher's feet are planted firmly only in midair in dealing with any human issues.

A sense of scripture would certainly probe the intentions of God for humankind. If the moods and thoughts of humans are discovered in scripture, so also are the thoughts and moods of a deity who cares about his creatures. This would allow a coming to terms with God's saving intentions as well as God's character. This would allow a coming to terms with the central theme of scripture, namely that the human race needs to be saved and that God has done something about that need, something so radical that human beings can now be reconciled to God, can know God, and can enjoy God forever.

One is reminded of Karl Barth's confession before fellow pastors, not all of whom were accepting of his theology. Barth admitted that a difference might exist between points of view in matters of theology, but that they shared a common standpoint as pastors, namely "the familiar standpoint of the man in the pulpit. Before him lies the Bible full of mystery, and before him are seated his more or less numerous hearers also full of mystery."[4] And Barth confessed his desire to take his place among fellow ministers in pursuit of an understanding and sympathy for "the situation every minister faces." And what was that? "To speak to the people in the infinite contradiction of their life, but to speak the no less infinite message of the Bible, which was as much a riddle as life."[5]

Barth's standpoint in the pulpit is a key to the strength of Protestant preaching. It is immediate and personal. It is God placing his finger on the end of David's nose and making an accusatory case for his transgression. It is prophetic as well, because God's servant

---

[4] Karl Barth, *The Word of God and the Word of Man*, trans. Douglas Horton (Gloucester MA: P. Smith, 1978) 104.
[5] Ibid., 101.

indicts a whole people for their faithlessness and idolatry. It is also evangelistic as the Word is heard as good news for the estranged and alienated. It is God extending the invitation to the prodigal to come home.

Sensing the Call

But a sense of scripture also references the interior life of the preacher, who as a mediator between God and people, must know how to discern the Spirit's mind regarding both parties. A sense of the scripture is about the disposition to commune with God, to refuse to emerge from God's presence without the assurance that God has spoken the word for the people. It is to possess an ear for God's voice in the text, a voice that informs the preacher of God's will and of God's understanding of what is really going on in God's relationship with humanity. For who has stood in the council of the Lord so as to see and to hear his word? How embarrassing it must have been, or should have been, to be "running" for God only to hear God say, "I didn't send you. You're on your own. Go ahead, tell your dreams, but know that your dreams are not my words."

But if preaching expresses the preacher's sense of the scriptures, does it not also reflect those rather awful strivings in one's own spirit when one realizes that the Holy Spirit has called one to preach? It is something of a summons, out of which comes what the Apostle Paul describes in 1 Corinthians 9:16 as a "necessity" laid upon him.

It is not unusual these days to face a class of seminarians whose curricular requirements lead to a course in homiletics. They will study, preach several times, heave a collective sigh when the quarter ends, and largely forget what it was about. This is understandable. Seminary students are usually pressed for time and energy, especially if they are married. Then, too, many of them come from congregations where preaching is marginalized in the name of "contemporary worship." These churches are growing in spite of preaching that is not only marginalized but oftentimes shallow of theological content. So if "effectiveness in ministry" is defined by growth—by "emerging" values—well, these students can add as well as subtract. In many contemporary churches there is no "pulpit"— just a see-through plastic stand carrying no hint of an ecclesiastical tradition.

The exceptions to all this are usually those few who entered seminary with a sense that God was calling them to a particular life of preaching. African-American students have tended to fall into this category more than their Anglo colleagues. Anglo students are called into the ministry, and within that calling they will preach. African-American students understand their call to ministry as mainly a call to preach. The church in the African-American community expects that the primary certification for a pastor is that she or he can preach. That is the certitude of a calling. This sense of God's hand upon those chosen to preach is not unique to African-American church tradition; however, it is a longstanding tradition in Protestant lore. One reads of the agonies of those who struggled with this inner conviction, or, in the case of others, a struggle until such a calling came. Among the latter there was a deep reluctance to entertain such a ministry without knowing that the hand of God lay heavily upon one's shoulder. In Euro-American tradition, one reads of this phenomenon in the writings of Latimer, Spurgeon, Wesley, Jowett, M'Cheyne, and so forth.

Accompanying this conviction of a call to preach was the preacher's felt need of a special gift of the Holy Spirit. I recall early teaching in my Bible college days when veteran faculty and chapel speakers would urge us to seek "the anointing" or the "unction" as a necessary and indispensable enduement for the preaching task. This was associated in most holiness circles with altar calls during revival meetings on campus and special days of prayer where tarrying for such an enduement was an integral part of the ritual. This "seeking" was often tied biblically to the experience of the apostles at Pentecost and throughout the story in Acts about the early church where the work of the Spirit of God is prominent: "Tarry...until you are endued with power from on high" (Luke 24:49, NKJV). Christian colleges and most seminaries are too sophisticated today to urge these experiences on their students. Or if this practice is still in vogue, I suspect that the language has changed. The practice of seeking the enduement of the Spirit does not feature prominently in the worship of these schools, nor is there much talk of it in most books written recently about preaching. I suspect that the difference may be that today's teachers have become more adept at the rationale in the service of some sort of apologetic approach to the ministry. Therefore, preparation for service is more likely to take the best from tradition, theology, and the social sciences and bring them to bear upon a student's inner life. This has much to commend it, of course, but still may not get to the observation made by Andrew Bonar when speaking about Robert Murray M'Cheyne: "From the first, he fed others by what he himself was feeding upon. His preaching was in a manner the development of his soul's experience. It was a giving out of the inward life."[6] Taylor might well have said the same thing to our students since he had long been convinced that the preacher, in order to be effective, is sustained in the long haul by the ability of the preacher to drink deeply from the well from which he or she preaches. "I tell [preachers]," Taylor reported, "not to neglect their own spiritual lives."[7] He added, "It's easy to get so engaged in the mechanics of preaching that one loses the vitality of it, the center." What results, then, is "nothing but a second-hand story, an arm's-length dealing with truth."[8] He went on to advise that "we must keep

---

[6] Andrew Bonar (1810–1892), *The Biography of Robert Murray M'Cheyne* (Grand Rapids: Zondervan, 1950). Originally published as chaps. 1–6 of *Memoirs and Remains of the Rev. Robert Murray M'Cheyne*, ed. Andrew A. Bonar (Edinburg: Banner of Truth, 1892).

[7] Taylor interview, "The Sweet Torture of Sunday Morning."

[8] Ibid.

ourselves full so we can empty ourselves in the pulpit."[9] It is this inner discipline that guarantees that one does not become a castaway after having preached to others about which 1 Corinthians 9:27 warns us.

Preaching and Human Need

A call to preach can also be triggered by an encounter with human need. In a mood-swing culture such as this one, it has not always been easy to define or understand what those needs may be. Philip Rieff argued that "it may not be possible to organize our culture again as an unwitting dynamic of moral demands claiming the prerogatives of truth, exercised through creedally authoritative institutions.... Trained to be incapable of sustaining sectarian satisfactions, psychological man cannot be susceptible to sectarian control. Religious man was born to be saved; psychological man is born to be pleased."[10] If this is so, then theology takes a back seat to psychology, and human need has to be defined more in terms of psychology than theology. Or that theology had to be understood in terms dictated by psychology. Added to that the growing momentum of social activity in the service of equality under law, and seminarians had to choose between counseling or action in the streets. Preaching tended to take a back seat in most mainline seminaries. It was this situation that caused the noted psychologist Karl Menninger to write his book *Whatever Became of Sin?*, in which he urged young people to rethink their views on the efficacy of preaching.[11] In those seminaries where preaching was still a centerpiece activity, the enterprise was largely evangelistic in nature or was devoted to confirming local congregations who were in their comfortable orthodoxies. The

---

[9] Ibid.

[10] Philip Rieff, *The Triumph of the Therapeutic: Uses of Faith after Freud* (Chicago: University of Chicago Press, 1966) 24–26.

[11] See Karl A. Menninger, *Whatever Became of Sin?* (New York: Hawthorn Books, 1973).

unanswered question in most of this preaching had to do with purpose: saved for what?

Writer Harry Golden is credited with arguing that the civil rights movement saved Christianity in America. If this is so, then it may well be that the same movement saved preaching in America, especially in so-called mainline groups. And it certainly added another depth to evangelical preaching by answering that troublesome "so what" question. The chief voice in this renaissance of preaching was Martin Luther King, Jr., who was soon aided and abetted by preachers in key pulpits in major urban centers. They had long discovered what Jesus knew about preaching, namely that to be authentic, it had to establish and maintain solidarity with people, especially those at the mercy of the powerful and the privileged. Jesus saw people scattered, defenseless, hungry, and shepherdless. Even though Jesus describes his ministry as one of preaching, teaching, and healing, all human suffering had a special call upon his life. According to Matthew 11:2–6, Jesus responded to the inquiry of John the Baptist by telling him that the blind were seeing, the lame were walking, the dead were being raised, and, even more striking, the poor were having the gospel preached unto them. If John had been tempted to question Jesus' commitment to "social concerns," or to doubt his commitment to rid the Jews of their Roman "benefactors," these words were calculated to comfort him and to set him straight. In stating his agenda in this manner, Jesus informed John the Baptizer that preaching, healing, and teaching the good news are more than mere words. These activities have a meaning far beyond the actual setting in which they are performed or the individuals affected. Taken together, these activities are symbolic of a divine solidarity with humankind in the exact sense of God's call to Moses that he speak to the powers in Egypt. Preaching is an action to assure an audience that "the I AM" is present—that God sees and hears and is moved and ready to act on their behalf.

Jesus was well aware of the politics of Palestine. He knew that politicians often behaved like foxes, and he knew well that the politics of religious leaders were equally crafty and deadly. One would do well to watch out for both groups because eventually the one group would be called upon to serve the other. Jesus knew how to exegete at ground level; he had eyes to see and ears to hear, and so he spent most of his time with "the folks." Today's preachers have little excuse for being ignorant of the charlatans that inhabit the community and parade as leaders. Now more than ever, the pulpit must be informed—must demonstrate a high degree of intellectual discipline. But it must also avoid the subtle seductions to which parishioners are prone. Here, one hears echoes of the Apostle's passionate yearning that "the Corinthians" not succumb to the seductions of the devil, lest they be led away from a single-minded devotion to Jesus Christ.

I recall Gardner Taylor being asked about what made him the preacher he had become. After introducing his wife, he gladly credited her with having introduced him to the arts, the theater, and great music. He stated that she was also instrumental in steering him away from being entrapped in too much political involvement. She had said to him at a crucial time that his preaching had become "very thin." It struck him very deeply, and he took it to heart. He trusted her, listened to her, respected her judgment—and returned to a deeper involvement with the scriptures.

The Grace-full Preacher

This sense of calling to preach is always accompanied by humility and gratitude—humility because the one chosen did not choose; the one called did not seek. The Apostle put it well in Acts 26:13–18 when he acknowledged that Jesus had appeared to him, giving his life new purpose as well as new direction. But nearing the end of a lustrous career, he joyfully confessed that it was by God's grace that he became who he was: "I was made a minister, according to the gift of the grace of God given unto me by the effectual working of His power" (Ephesians 3:7, KJV). Though a man of learning and erudition with many gifts for which he had become well known among his contemporaries, Paul boasted only about the grace of God and viewed himself as but the least among all the saints. Gardner Taylor confesses that there is tremendous power in accepting the verse, "By the grace of God I am what I am," for "when one has found that acceptance, that person has come into an incomparable authenticity."[12] It was this grace, he acknowledged, that was always at work in him and was the prime motivation for all his hard work for the gospel's sake and for the life of the church.

If preaching is anchored in a "sense of scripture," it is sustained by a deep sense of grace. Maybe it takes some years beyond formal education to appreciate the role of God's grace for ministry. Perhaps it is something akin to a marriage as it matures, allowing a couple to learn how blessed they have been for having been led to each other. Gratitude, after all, is a form of grace. It is an attitude of thanksgiving for having received the kindness and generosity of God.

Gratitude for God's grace also enables a preacher to be gracious to others, especially one's colleagues. A sense of the scriptures also encourages a sense of community with others who share the same commitment. Preachers have been known to harbor jealousies and a spirit of competitiveness. The Epistles record such incidences within the early church as various leaders seemed all too willing to depart from the lessons of the cross in order to gain ministerial emulation from their "fans." Ministers are not immune from the temptations often displayed in the broader culture, especially in entertainment, where the emphasis is on "show time," with plenty of bling-bling flashing about to impress the impressionable. And if the minister is placed on television, his or her integrity is further jeopardized. It is unseemly, but seems to work for many in the pulpit and in the pew. And yet it seems possible in such conflicting practices to rejoice that

---

[12] Taylor interview, 21.

in the midst of such shenanigans, Christ is preached. Armed with this spirit of grace, the preacher is content to let God keep score. Rick Bragg, Pulitzer Prize-winning author for *The New York Times*, admitted that a bad case of "prima donna fever" had gripped him in his early career: "I was too damn dumb to know that a swagger is a silly walk for a man with yet a long way to go."[13]

Management guru Max De Pree has commented that "we're seeing a movement in American corporate life toward more individualism, and to me, at least, that signifies less concern for the common good."[14] This trend means that many leaders are *less* concerned with developing a culture of trust and commitment within the organization and *more* interested in developing their own interests and ensuring large severance packages for themselves. It also means that corporations do not readily attract idealistic younger people interested in building a lasting culture where community values are cultivated and realized. Of course, a congregation is not a corporation, but it is nevertheless a community in need of sound leadership, models who know who they are and who know how to define for the community what their meaning is beyond church attendance and serving on countless committees. Church leaders are needed who can model a vital identity, who can model and explain what it means to be the people of God in the place where they live and lead. This requires being free from ego-centeredness, having a vision of who God's people are and can be, so as to honor God's agenda. This obviously calls for more than revival meetings, as useful as they may be, and it requires preachers to attend to a much deeper interior life than that which merely belonging to any ministerial alliance can provide.

---

[13] *All Over but the Shoutin'* (New York: Random House, 1997) 161.

[14] "The Leader's Legacy: A Conversation with Max De Pree," *Leader to Leader* 6 (Fall 1997).

Preachers learn from one another, especially from those with unusual gifts of exegesis, expression, or an imaginative approach to the text and its application to life. But not all preachers freely acknowledge their indebtedness to their sources, mentors, or colleagues. Taylor does, speaking often about the giants of the pulpit from whom he learned during his days as a pastor in New York: Ralph W. Sockman, Harry E. Fosdick, Sandy Ray, George Arthur Buttrick, and Adam Clayton Powell. Celebrating the grace of God for one's inclusion in a shared calling enlarges the capacity to receive the fruits of others' insights and even to employ those insights without stealing them to enhance one's own reputation.

Grace produces in the preacher a widened capacity for generosity and fairness in dealing with fellow servants of the gospel. Paul is again an exemplary model. In passage after passage, Paul praises his companions in the gospel, including the women who served with him. His writings are full of greetings to persons whom he knew personally, believers who had prayed for him and ministered to his needs, people who marched with him, if you will, across the empire to spread the gospel to *all* the world. No one lives to himself or dies to himself, as the saying goes. No one knows this better than a person alert to the demands of what it means to be called to preach.

A sense of the scriptures, with its reverence for God's word and the God of the word, reveals itself most prominently in the character of the preacher. I recall a colleague telling me of his experience in a church where he had just delivered an annual lecture. The series was held in honor of a previous pastor who had distinguished himself as one of the nation's premier preachers. He said that he made it his priority to seek an answer about why the man was so effective as a pastor/preacher. He was surprised to discover that with near total agreement the parishioners replied "his character." It was not that previous pastor's eloquence, nor his learning, nor his connections within the parent denomination, which could have brought notoriety to the congregation. It was that minister's character! Oscar Peterson, perhaps the greatest jazz pianist ever, paid a dear price in his personal quest to ensure that his public performances were as near perfect as possible. Peterson mastered the "text," intent to honor the intentions of the composer, and then in a style unique to his own immense gifts offered his rendition to his audience. He respected his audiences, but would not please the audience at the expense of the music. "A lot of artists have made that mistake," Peterson said, "but I look at people like Ellington, proving himself again and again, and the issue becomes quite simple. You have to be yourself and deliver an honest performance."[15] This kind of integrity creates an audience, a congregation, and those who value this kind of integrity tend to reproduce these values in their own lives.

Biblical Preaching and Finishing Well

Biblical preaching, an all-encompassing sense of the scriptures, then, is finally about the legacy of a preacher. Not that a preacher begins ministry with thoughts of a legacy, certainly not in terms that have come to prevail as indicators of success in ministry. A legacy is more than strategic planning, as necessary as that is. A legacy includes becoming part of a culture, or a community with a culture, and ensuring that this community is vital into future generations. It shares in the "moral purpose" of the community. It is highly unlikely that a committee charged with selecting a new pastor would ask the candidate about a concern to leave a legacy upon departing the church at tenure's end. To be sure, such a committee would have checked to see if there had been any scandal associated with the candidate, how the church had grown under his leadership, how many buildings had been erected, where he stood on key social issues of the day, etc., etc. In short, they would be concerned to delve into the person's "success" rate and the leadership skills that made his

---

[15] Alex Barris, *Oscar Peterson: A Musical Biography* (Toronto: HarperCollins, 2002) 184.

reputation. They would have listened to him or her preach several times. But questions about legacy?

The community of God needs preachers possessed with visions about God's people and their usefulness as God's agents who tend to God's agenda. Nothing could be more crucial than this, for if the culture has changed and will continue to devolve into further disarray, it will produce leaders with an even more toxic influence. This will be almost certain in a time when, as Matthew Arnold voiced it long ago, "the world…hath really neither joy, nor love, nor light, nor certitude, nor peace, nor help from pain; and we are here as on a darkling plain swept with confused alarms of struggle and flight, where ignorant armies clash by night."[16] In such a time, people seem to have an inordinate need for security, which, in turn, opens the door for would-be "heroes." Clergy as well as politicians, denominations as well as political parties vie for public acceptance based upon a promised resolution to these raging waves of discontent. So we welcome leaders whether they have character or not. A Spirit-anointed preacher will be an example, in the church and beyond, of godly living, of morality in personal and collegial relationships, of a willingness at the end of the day to allow God to keep the score.

And, in the end, it is fidelity to God and God's word that assures that the minister of the good news finishes well. This was always a concern with Jesus—not how a person begins, but how he or she finishes. So the Apostle Paul can write to his young colleague that at the end of his race, his body scarred and his soul weary from the battles waged, he could anticipate with certainty that God would not

---

[16] Matthew Arnold, 1822–1888, "Dover Beach," *English Poetry III: From Tennyson to Whitman, The Harvard Classics, 1909–1914,* http://www.bartleby.com/42/705.html (accessed 20 October 2008).

forget him when the awards ceremony took place. For the God of the scriptures is a righteous judge who has kept the score.

PREACHING AS EXPERIENCE OF THE GOSPEL: AN INSIGHT WITH ROOTS IN THE WISDOM OF GARDNER C. TAYLOR

Henry H. Mitchell

One never knows how great can be the impact of wisdom graciously shared and gratefully received. This was the case when my friend and contemporary, Dr. Gardner C. Taylor, invited me to preach at a Sunday evening service of the Concord Baptist Church of Christ in Brooklyn, where he was pastor. It was in the early 1950s, and I had been a student minister at Concord ten years before, so I was delighted to have a return visit during my trip from California, where I then served. Little did I dream how much I would receive, over and above the joyous renewal of friendships from my student days.

I preached in my usual manner, and the people warmly received me as a kind of son of this church. Gardner was warmly gracious, too, but he was kind enough to add some commentary later, in his office. It started with, "Henry, large bodies move slowly." He went on to criticize my rapid rate of delivery and how the hearers could not keep up with me, either in thoughts or in the deeper feelings that normally should have accompanied the ideas. In fact, it was primarily those feelings that he referred to when he suggested that "large bodies *move* slowly." He saw faith as an idea, abstract and lifeless, unless and until it came to slow, profound *movement* in a living soul.

I had not gotten similar impressions in Union Seminary classes of Dr. Harry Emerson Fosdick and President Henry Sloan Coffin. They were great souls, and I really admired and was moved, in a way, by their lectures and sermons. But I could recall no such descriptive emphasis on the response of feelings when these men lectured. I responded to their sermons and lectures as I always did to sheer greatness, but the often deeply moved quality of my response to these giants came largely from my own cultural habits, not those of the speakers.

Nor did I get my rapid rate of delivery from these instructors, or from the rapid pace of the then popular Billy Graham. In hindsight, I see my speed as the result of anxiety in the pulpit, which my wife, Ella, had already seen and complained about. I was slowly but not fully becoming aware of my inadequacy as a preacher in the African-American cultural community.

This, then, was the beginning of my awareness of my need, and of my search for an approach to preaching that was more effective in my culture. Such an approach would, in time and at its best, become the answer to the needs of the declining pulpits of congregations of *all* cultures. But I was neither thinking nor looking that far ahead at the time. A few years later, in 1959, I left my post as a regional missionary to accept a pastorate. Here, I was jarred into the realization that my previous popularity as a preacher had been based on the financial, legal, conflict-resolving, and building services I rendered. The many invitations to preach had been their sincere way of saying, "Thank you for all this critically needed assistance." It had little to do with my slowly emergent adjustments to my culture, as contrasted with the culture of my theological training.

My attention was now forcibly refocused and fixed on sermon preparation, rather than things like incorporation, blueprints, zoning, and arbitration. Even the call to that very congregation might have been partly a call to my grandfather, after whom I was named. He had served that Fresno church in the 1920s, and lots of people remembered him as quite a preacher.

My friend Gardner Taylor's words had been haunting me all along, but now they literally seized and directed my search. This effort was implemented by my focus of study for an M.A. in Linguistics, with my thesis on "The Genius of Negro Preaching." In research, I listened to some 200 sermons by great African-American preachers, looking for the "moving" to which Dr. Taylor had sensitized me. It was not exactly easy to find, using the alien tools of linguistic research, but it was a productive beginning.

The degree was awarded in 1966. Some of the chapters of my thesis became the heart of a book called *Black Preaching* (1970 and 1991), and I was appointed Martin Luther King, Jr., Professor of Black Church Studies at Colgate Rochester Divinity School (1969). Most importantly, the rest of my homiletical analysis up to the present has grown and is growing out of elaboration on the insights of that first advice from Dr. Gardner C. Taylor. This *festschrift* has triggered a long overdue awareness of just how pivotal that one conference of gracious advice has been for me. I see this understanding of preaching (as primarily experiential rather than cognitive) as the most important single insight necessary to the renewal of America's pulpits of *all* cultures and congregations.

Preaching: The Experience of the Gospel

The validation and implementation of this understanding requires far more than my case history. And, of course, much that I offer here has been said already in previous publications. However, the intensity of this single focus on the *experiential encounter* as such may be a new approach. If so, it will only seek to increase the still limited attention given to sermon design as art generating vicarious *experience*. It is popular now to supposedly deny cognitive emphasis in preaching, but this is only on the surface. The actual sermons reflect no such emphasis on experience when one stands to preach.

The actual preparation of most sermons is still virtually all cognitive. General professional enrichment is likewise nearly all cognitive, full of abstractions and generalizations. This is opposed to concrete imagery, such as was employed by Jesus himself in the parables. Many preachers would use more imagery if they had taken Jesus' example more seriously.

It is all too often assumed that actual spiritual experiences defy precise description. Thus, holistic impact, including lofty emotions, is all in the hands of God the Holy Spirit. We dare not enter into the process. It is only poetic justice that a piece honoring Dr. Gardner C. Taylor should emphasize the manifest experiential depths so evident in his preaching. The very fact that his utterance is so powerful and so devoid of dependence on notes suggests the easy recall of deep preparatory spiritual experience, as opposed to the rote memory of many books. It is thus from the heart, and only secondarily from the mind as channel, not source. The mental processes are indispensible, but only after they are given a meaningful *experience* to share.

Some years ago, I heard Dr. Taylor as he preached to a session of the Academy of Homiletics, the national guild of scholars and teachers of the craft of preaching. The sermon was delivered with what might be called orderly passion. It was not intentionally dramatic, but there were tears leaking out all across the audience. The text and theme were deeply theological, but the impact suggested that the faith communicated came from the *spirit* of a man of great intellect. It was only of natural necessity that this testimony of faith was sent through the mental processes and translated into words. I only regret that I, too, was so caught up that I failed to record the text and its impact for just such a sharing as this publication.

Let it be fully understood that Dr. Taylor's invariable theological depth was not an elective decoration of the gospel. His depth was, instead, at the very soul center of his messages, which leads me to insist that the emphasis here given to experiential encounter is not a means for dumbing down the good news. Quite to the contrary, it is a means of making real and reachable the most profound doctrinal affirmations of the biblical and ecclesiastical traditions. Theological depth is just plain essential to authentic experience of the Word. Anything less is a cheap imitation.

My point is that the experiential encounter of which I speak is with the *Living Word.* There are, surely, such things as empty, manipulated crowd experiences. But there is also an experiential Word of faith that literally comes alive and is used by the Spirit to *move* the hearer to a contagious response of faith. There are no complicated theological abstractions required, and the simplest of thinking minds can join in response, along with the learned members of the academy.

So how does all this come about? This peon of praise for the experiential would itself be futile and empty without some serious attention given to how a preacher is used by the Spirit to help generate these Word encounters.

Preaching: The Human Assignment

As far back as John Wesley, the emphasis on experiential encounters has been great, but without label, among Christians. And early African-American Christians have been noted for declaring things like, "If you ain't *felt* nothin' you ain't *got* nothin' (religion)." Whatever the race or particular denomination, there have been few, if indeed any, authorities willing to risk a "how-to" guideline for our participation in the way people are led to *feel* "good religion" to aid the Spirit's access to the experience-fed depths of human consciousness.

The technical name for these depths ("guts") is intuitive consciousness, and this is precisely where true faith is "stored" or retained. This version of the human psyche fits well with biblical understandings. We can take no work-credit or intellectual praise for the highest spiritual intuitions, or for salvation itself. We just receive these blessed experiences and insights and say, "Thank you, Lord." (We were not saved by works anyway; see Ephesians 2:8–9, KJV).[1]

---

[1] *The Holy Bible, King James Version* (Grand Rapids: Zondervan, 1962). Ephesians 2:8–9, author's interpretation. Text reads: 8: "For by grace are ye saved through faith; and that not of yourselves: *It is* the gift of God; 9: Not of works, lest any man should boast."

We were saved by faith, but faith is a gift (Ephesians 2:8), not the product of human intelligence. Obviously, millions have been saved and empowered without any reference whatever to this facet of human personality called "the intuitive." We were saved in spite of this oversight, not because of it. The Spirit uses *experiences* for vehicles of input into the intuitive, whether we know we have one or not. And all of this is relevant to preaching, because it is living experiences harnessed to the Word that the Spirit uses to make a sermon effective, even salvific.

We arrive now at the point where we must have a detailed explanation of a convincing and transforming experience of the Word. What, precisely, do we mean by this word *experience*, which could apply to so many things? What have we to offer that falls within the range of human capacity and yet can be employed by the Holy Spirit to save, sanctify, and empower other human beings?

The *experience* referred to is quite clearly not all direct; it is *vicarious* also. It is a consecration of the imagination of preacher and hearer by which people identify with characters, things, and situations as if they were there when this took place, as recorded in the Bible. It is not a matter of magic or mental games. This vicarious *identification* concentrates focus and impact on the intuition that is probably more intense than if the hearer had been there when it first "happened," whether in story or in actual life.

Jesus avoided abstractions like "compassion" and told a story of a hated Samaritan, with whom the hearers identified and were moved to imitate. Jesus didn't talk of a strange new doctrine called unconditional acceptance or grace. He told the story of a forgiving father, using concrete images of forgiveness to communicate the theology. Real-life prodigals identified with the son in the story and were moved themselves to return to relationship with God.

When a certain student saw all the ways this story paralleled modern life, he preached the parable in a youth revival in Los Angeles. Staying well within biblical bounds, he enhanced his youth audience's identification with the prodigal by avoiding put-downs. The younger son was just tired of no role of real recognition or responsibility, so he went out on his own. He thought of his riotous life as "public relations," a prelude to launching a business. He just "got took" and then was deserted. It was very effective among a group of youth who had insisted on living on campus and away from parental guidance. A student's refrigerator with only a sleeve of soda crackers and a bottle of faucet water really scored—to hear these stories told well provided powerful *vicarious experiences*.

These stories told by Jesus were not just to entertain the crowds. Of course, if the stories had not been interesting enough to hold attention, the crowds would have dispersed. The opposite of "entertaining" is "boring," not "educational." So Jesus' stories did entertain, but each had a primary purpose of transforming human behavior.

Every story, as a work of art (not a learned essay), had to have a central theme that held the story together. These themes, as used by Jesus, however, could perhaps be better described today as *behavioral purposes*. Every parable of Jesus had such a purpose, and this is what made the experiences so meaningful. Preachers today need to provide similar heroes and heroines of the Spirit (biblical and from human life), rather than simply to lay down doctrines and laws of what to do and not to do. The common people heard Jesus' images and stories gladly (Mark 12:37).

The principle of *identification*, of course, was at the heart of the effectiveness of these stories. But the parables of Jesus also included other venues than stories for this principle: metaphors and similes were the main ones. Thus, if he wished to motivate people's abstinence from judgmental put-downs, he painted word pictures of the similar appearance of the first growth of weeds and wheat. He knew they could not tell them apart, and their limits of insight were better pictured than codified into charges. The images of weeds gave them a frame of reference within which to gain holistic awareness of a basis for humility and kindness toward other people's limits.

Identification was greatly enhanced by familiarity, the similarity of situation between the predicament of the protagonist in the biblical or other story and the hearer in the congregation. The more familiar the person or situation, the more irresistibly was the hearer drawn into the influence of the experience, as if it happened to her or him. The Spirit used this mightily.

I had no notion of the epidemic prevalence of psychic depression until I preached "unprepared" in an emergency one Sunday, in Los Angeles, on Elijah's case. The unmistakable symptom of his seriously deep depression was Elijah's suicidal petition: "It is enough, O LORD, now take away my life, for I am no better than my fathers" (1 Kings 19:4, KJV). Elijah was fleeing for his life after Jezebel had "put out a contract" for his murder. In response to a realistic description of Elijah's depression, an amazing number from the audience came forward afterward to say it was their case to a tee; they had fully *identified* with this real need. They had come to offer unanimous and profound thanks for the spiritual solutions offered in the sermon. This experiential encounter had been surprisingly tailored by the Spirit to use familiarity that enhanced relevance to the depressions of these witnesses.

Nowhere is the necessity for this *relevance to need* in a spiritual encounter more apparent than in bereavement—the unspeakable grief brought on by the death of a loved one. Jesus himself affirmed being called "to heal the brokenhearted" (Luke 4:18, KJV). In my world, nobody anywhere is more sought after for masterful ministry to the heartbroken than Gardner C. Taylor, as seen in the many funerals across the nation for which he is asked to preach.

Dr. Taylor may never have heard of my rule of relevance to need, but he surely exemplifies what it demands. I have tried to figure out in further detail what his powerful secret might be, and I have cast it into a supplementary formula to the relevance rule, as applied to eulogies in funerals. I have sought to use it for my own permanent guidance:

(1) Affirm the acceptance of grief as the inescapable result of a loving relationship with a worthy soul. Within reasonable bounds, the expression of grief is physically, emotionally, and spiritually healthy.

(2) Take a text, and draw from it an experiential encounter in which there is movement from seeming sorrow, overwhelming handicap, and/or apparent defeat in life to ultimate fulfillment of life and victory in death.

(3) Celebrate the parallel victories in a biblical account and in the life of the deceased. Identification into the life stories of the Bible characters and the best of the life of the deceased may be used by the Spirit to move hearers to hopeful efforts toward their own victorious living and dying, as well as for their comfort in bereavement.

These suggestions were extrapolated from analysis of a memorial service eulogy honoring Martin Luther King, Jr. It was delivered in 1972 in the Harvard University Chapel. Dr. Taylor colorfully cited Luke's impressive list of the illustrious figures of the day: "Now in the fifteenth year of the reign of Tiberius Caesar, Pontius Pilate being governor of Judea, Herod being tetrarch of Galilee, and his brother Philip tetrarch of Ituraea and of the region,…and Lysanius,…Annas and Caiaphas being the high priests, the word of God came unto John the son of Zacharias in the wilderness" (Luke 3:1–2, KJV).[2]

---

[2] This passage, or major parts of it, is repeated three times in this sermon. It emphasizes experientially the irony of the erstwhile insignificance of the listed persons. This subtle humor serves in pastoral treatment of grief. The repeated publication wisely maintains the impact of the originally full delivery of the passage. Gardner C. Taylor, "The Strange Ways of God," *The African American Pulpit* 7/1 (Winter 2003–2004): 100–104.

In almost comic contrast, Dr. Taylor then used *twelve* whole verses to report John's word from God. Imagine all those names just to say when John preached in a *wilderness!* He may have had to eat the poor folks' menu of locusts and wild honey, but his mark on history was incalculably greater than that of those first mentioned. The comparison was seen and heard—*experienced*—as the preacher pompously recited those names and followed with his own high admiration for John. It was but a short distance mentally from that text to a despised black preacher from Georgia, who was Martin Luther King, Jr. There followed a review of some of Martin Luther King's prophetic utterances and a closing with celebration—an expression of irrepressible joy.

There is at least one more guideline for the design of relevant experiential encounters with the Word. It might be called a rule of the uncompromising, courageous address of sin. It may be in high places as well as among the lowly, applied to the powerful and entrenched as well as the powerless. This rule is applied in the fearless utterances of the God-driven and directed prophet. It may sound as if such a rule does not belong here with all these less confrontational encounters. However, the prophet Nathan did it before King David, and his story was used magnificently by the Spirit (2 Samuel 12:7–14, KJV). One could say that Nathan's sermon pre-figured Jesus' command to teach his followers "to observe *all things* whatsoever I have commanded you" (Matthew 28:20, KJV).

I once thought I had a valid exception to this rule. I declined to accept invitations to speak to white audiences on the race issue. I thought my prophetic address would be too much like begging and pleading for rights that God had already vouchsafed to me and my race. I had too much healthy pride and self-respect for that. At least, that was how I saw it at that particular time.

Imagine my horror, in 1954, when word reached me that my friend and mentor, Gardner C. Taylor, had accepted an invitation to preach at the Annual Session of the American Baptist Convention.

That was the year of the Supreme Court decision on the public schools, and the session he was to address was devoted to the topics of justice and *race!* He may not have used such a term as "focused experiential encounter," but that describes exactly what he did. And it surely was, then, the most awesome, memorable, and transforming worship experience of my entire life.

The early portion of Dr. Taylor's sermon has faded from memory, but the concluding celebration is eternally etched. He painted a vivid picture straight out of the book of Revelation (7:9 KJV), where it mentions every kindred and people and tongue. As 10,000 American Baptists (mostly white and not enthusiastic about civil rights) prepared for Holy Communion, a feast in heaven was portrayed, with all these ethnic and lingual identities. Jesus lovingly received every single person; nobody was denied. And it was easy to see that communion on this planet was to be governed likewise, in perpetuity, to the end of time.

Following the sermon, those whose throats would allow it joined in the spiritual "Let Us Break Bread Together." The rest just choked up and sobbed, but every eye of the 20,000 seemed moist with tears. The greatly distinguished Dr. C. Oscar Johnson (a white pastor from St. Louis) arose from his seat on the platform and lifted Dr. Gardner C. Taylor of Brooklyn from the floor with a powerful hug. Each being tall and large, it is hard to imagine a more powerful witness for justice and against racial discrimination. The majority of the hearing host may have been "conservative," content with the United States as it was, but nobody needed to be defensive, for none had been attacked. They had just been gently led to *experience* vicariously the very kingdom of God, and had yielded to it with spiritual joy and gladness. And surely none of them left as they came. The transformative influence of an *experiential encounter*, designed and delivered under the power of the Holy Spirit, is one of God's very best instruments for bringing in the kingdom. Amen!

PREACHING AS A CONTEMPLATIVE THEOLOGICAL TASK

Robert Smith, Jr.

While vacationing in Virginia Beach in summer 1992, I turned on the television, and to my surprise the renowned Dr. Gardner C. Taylor was being interviewed about his preaching career. The interviewer asked Dr. Taylor a question something like this: "With all of your preaching accomplishments, awards, and commendations, is there anything you could have done that would have made you a better preacher?" I remember to this day how Dr. Taylor closed his eyes, elevated his head, and rubbed his forehead for what seemed to be an eternity. After a long pause, he responded with what appeared to be a very mundane admission. Then he replied, "I could have been a better and more effective preacher if I had read the Bible more and prayed more."

To this day, I remember the incident so vividly because I was stunned by this simple remark from such a significant personality. I expected him to usher me into the realm of rarified eloquence. However, he chose to talk about such basic things as prayer and Bible reading. Suddenly, the mundane became majestic to me; the familiar yielded to the unfamiliar; the simple was transformed into the sublime. After bowing his head, closing his eyes, rubbing his forehead, and contemplating for a while, Dr. Taylor had produced such a profound statement with such common phraseology. In reflection, I realize that he was doing *contemplative theology* as a preacher. He was waiting for a thought bestowment within his spirit, an unction by the Spirit on his mind. He had not lost his thought; rather, he was waiting on a God-thought.

I was reminded of a sermon Gardner Taylor had preached nearly three decades before, titled "A Wide Vision from a Narrow Window." The sermon grew out of the experience of Job, who after losing health, wealth, family members, and friends, exclaimed, "I know that my redeemer lives and that at the latter day he shall stand upon the earth: And *though* after my skin *worms* destroy this *body*, yet in my flesh shall I see God: Whom I shall see for myself and mine eyes shall behold, and not another" (Job 19:25–27, KJV).[1] This moment cemented for me that the backbone of the preaching of Gardner C. Taylor is contemplative theology—preaching at the thought level. It is celebration, but it is also *cogitation*. Throughout his extensive preaching ministry, his preaching as contemplative theology has enabled him to be peerless in his proclamation, for out of texts that are common to all, he has been able to see a wide view from a narrow window that has been overlooked by many preachers.

Embarrassed and stripped of all clothing, forced to march to the gallows on 9 April 1945, Dietrich Bonhoeffer met his death. In recent times, he had become a riddle to himself and had experienced an internal civil war. This reality was brought to dramatic fashion by a moving poem he wrote from a prison cell. Through "Who Am I?" Bonhoeffer sought to identify clearly who he was, concluding this poignant poem with the admission, "They mock me, these lonely questions of mine. Whoever I am, thou knowest, O God, I am thine."[2]

Doing contemplative theology is literally taking the question mark of "Who am I?" and straightening it out until it becomes an exclamation point of, "Whoever I am, thou knowest, O God, I am thine," then lyrically pronouncing: "I am thine, O Lord. I have heard

---

[1] *The Holy Bible, King James Version* (Grand Rapids: Zondervan, 1962). Biblical verses quoted throughout this essay are from the KJV, NIV, and ESV and will be duly noted.

[2] Dietrich Bonhoeffer, *The Cost of Discipleship* (New York: Macmillan, 1959) 15.

thy voice and it told thy love to me, but I long to rise in the arms of faith and be closer drawn to thee. Draw me nearer, nearer, nearer blessed Lord to the cross where thou hast died. Draw me nearer, nearer, nearer blessed Lord, to thy precious bleeding side."[3] Ian Pitt-Watson, in his book *A Primer for Preachers*, gives preachers a much needed and refreshing word that calls for preaching as contemplative theology married with a graceful delivery of the message. Gardner C. Taylor's preaching is characterized by this union. Watson says:

> It comes to us when we get together truth thought, truth felt and truth done. We've got to know the Book; that comes first. And we've got to know what the Book says, follow in Christ's steps. But we can know truth and even do it and still be awkward, inadequate, graceless, until we get the feel of it. That is when we need to remember that it is not meant to be a solo dance. Christ wants us, his church, his clumsy bride, to try it with him. To begin with, we often feel more inadequate than ever when we do that, because we are so awkward and he is so full of grace. Then it happens, in our preaching as in our Christian living. We share in his grace. All the Book says comes alive and, when we preach it, what used to be contrived now becomes natural, what used to be labor now becomes spontaneous, what used to be a burden now becomes a blessing, what used to be law now becomes the gospel. Why? Because we are learning the meaning of grace; because now God's truth, thought, felt, and done, is embracing us in the dance—the Truth that stood before Pilate but that Pilate never recognized, because Pilate thought truth was a proposition not a person, a diagram not a dancer.[4]

While in the Greater Cincinnati/Northern Kentucky International Airport some time ago, I walked by an information booth

---

[3] "I am Thine, O Lord," *The Baptist Hymnal* (Nashville: Convention Press, 1991) 290. Words to the hymn were written by Fanny J. Crosby, 1820–1915; music by William H. Doane, 1832–1915.

[4] Ian Pitt-Watson, *A Primer for Preachers* (Grand Rapids: Baker Academic, 1999) 103.

where I saw a man who reminded me of Christopher Reeve.[5] He was a quadriplegic and had a specially built wheelchair. Leaning back as I walked past him, I heard him intoning a familiar song, "How Great Thou Art": "O Lord my God, when I in awesome wonder, consider all the worlds thy hands have made. I see the stars; I hear the rolling thunder, Thy power throughout the universe displayed. Then sings my soul, my Savior God to thee! How great thou art! How great thou art!"[6] No gesticulations, no gestures, and of course there was no moving of hands, no patting of the feet. As I looked at him, it appeared as if the booth where he was seated was the intersection where the celestial and the terrestrial met. It looked as if he was serenading the Savior as he was intoning the song.

Upon later reflection, I came to understand that there were five components of preaching as a contemplative theological task within that song: The first component is adoration, the idea of wonder: "O Lord my God, when I in awesome wonder."[7] It is what William Cowper expressed when he declared, "God moves in mysterious ways, his wonders to perform," and Robert J. Fryson, who passionately declared in the title of his song, "God Is a Wonder to My Soul." Rudolph Otto was thinking in this vein when he wrote about the *mysterium tremendum fascinosis*, translated from Latin as the deep mystery or the reality of God that brings us to God and leaves us transfixed with tremors. It is the idea of being before God and simultaneously experiencing trembling and adoration, adoring God while trembling before him.

---

[5] Actor Christopher Reeve, who was born 25 September 1952, played the hero role of Superman. Paralyzed after suffering a spinal cord injury when thrown from his horse in an equestrian competition accident in 1995 and confined to a wheelchair, he devoted the remainder of his life as an advocate for spinal cord research and died at age fifty-two on 11 October 2004.

[6] "How Great Thou Art," *The Baptist Hymnal*, 10. Words and music by Stuart K. Hine, 1927.

[7] Ibid.

Thomas experienced this wondrous reality when Jesus graciously invited him to come in faith and touch the nail prints in the Savior's hands and to thrust his hand through Jesus' side. The writer, John, never records that Thomas actually complied with Jesus' invitation to touch the external evidence of Jesus' crucified body, for when Thomas saw Jesus, his only response was, "My Lord and My God!"[8] This is the kind of experience that the disciples had when they were in the boat in a storm-tossed sea. They saw dust, but they also saw deity in dust, for they exclaimed, "What manner of man is this? Even the wind and waves obey him!" (Mark 4:41).

I have walked through Times Square in New York City. One can always tell the difference between tourists and the regular residents. The regular residents walk quickly and hurriedly, caught up in the hustle and bustle. They are not mesmerized and magnetized by the lights and the ambience there, never looking up, never breaking their gait or rhythm. Tourists walk at a much slower cadence, look around, and ask questions as if they are mesmerized by the ambience. What has happened to us as believers is that we have ceased to become tourists of God. We have become too familiar, too common with God that he is no longer majestic. To us he is no longer the great God of solemnity. We have lost our sense of wonder for God.

Maybe one of the reasons we have ceased to become as contemplative about God as we should be is because we have made God into our own image and after our own likeness. Is it really possible that we are guilty of theological idolatry? Do we worship the God who never was, the God who never will be, and the God who is not the God of the Bible? Is it possible that we have made God into a theological bellhop, an ecclesiastical red cap, and a Christological vending machine? Are we putting our prayer quarters in the Christological vending machine and making our selection? When we do not get what we want, do we start kicking on the machine out of

---

[8] John 20:28, *The Holy Bible, Today's New International Version,* Wide Margin Edition (Colorado Springs: Zondervan, 2005).

protest? Is this possibly why God is no longer looked upon as being the majestic God?

C. S. Lewis, in his very last work, *Letters to Malcolm: Chiefly on Prayer*, prays to God, "May it be the real I who speaks. May it be the real Thou that I speak to."[9] He was praying to be authentic, to worship God without any trappings. Is it possible for us to worship the wrong God? The Trappist monk Thomas Merton is often quoted as saying there are two kinds of selves: the real self and the projected self—the persona, the mask that we wear. The persona is not the real person; it is the self-created person that is created to satisfy the demands and the expectations of other people. God is telling us to unmask ourselves so that we can be the real self who prays to the real God.

I remember reading that Archbishop William Temple said that atheism is to be preferred to idolatry. Perhaps it is better to be an atheist than to be an idolater because as an idolater, one can be satisfied with the god who is thought to be the right god. Paul, in Acts 17 (KJV), encountered Athenians who were committed to the wrong God and, in an effort to be inclusive, even built a monument to the unknown god. Atheism means *no god*. One cannot even talk about atheism without talking about God because theism means God. One has to at least talk about atheism in the context of God. John O'Hare, Madeline O'Hare's son, moved from atheism to theism—from no god to God! The first component of preaching as a contemplative theological task is *adoration* or *wonder*—"O Lord my God! When I in awesome *wonder....*"[10]

The second component is cogitation (consideration): "Consider all the worlds thy hands hath made."[11] Preaching begins at the thought level. Jesus commanded, "Thou shalt love the Lord thy God

---

[9] C. S. Lewis, *Letters to Malcolm: Chiefly on Prayer* (New York: Harcourt, Brace & World, Inc., 1963) 82.

[10] "How Great Thou Art," *The Baptist Hymnal*, 10.

[11] Ibid.

with all thy heart, and with all thy soul, and with all thy mind" (Matthew 22:37, KJV). The mind is the point of contact between God and humans. This is definitely reflective thinking. Perhaps we have moved away from the famous dictum of René Descartes, *cogito ergo sum* (I think; therefore, I am), and moved toward German theologian and philosopher Friedrich Schleiermacher's well-known definition and description of religion as a feeling of absolute dependence—a kind of *sentio-ergo sum* (I feel; therefore, I am).[12] Maybe we are dangerously approaching the edge of becoming all feeling and non-thinking in our preaching—celebration without cogitation. Yes, we definitely feel, but there needs to be a foundation for feeling, and it has to be thought out. Without thought, there is no contemplative theological proclamation. The second component of preaching as a contemplative theological task is *cogitation/ consideration*: "Consider all the worlds thy hands have made."[13]

The third component is illumination: "I see the stars."[14] The hymnist prays, "Open my eyes that I may see glimpses of truth thou hast for me."[15] We can only preach effectively when we see the text through the eyes of faith. Like Ezekiel, we are asked, "Son of man, do you see what the people are doing in the dark?"[16] Our hearers are seeking for more than concepts about Jesus; they are seeking what Philip sought from Jesus. "Show us the Father and we will be satisfied" (John 14:8, KJV). In 2 Kings 6:17, Elisha prays that God would open the eyes of Elisha's frightened servant who saw the enemies but did not see chariots of fire of the army of God surrounding the hillside: "Lord, I pray thee, open his eyes that he

---

[12] Author's interpretation.

[13] "How Great Thou Art," *The Baptist Hymnal*, 10.

[14] Ibid.

[15] "Open My Eyes, That I May See," *Worship & Rejoice* (Carol Stream IL: Hope Publishing Company, 2001) 480. Words and music by Clara H. Scott, 1841–1897.

[16] Ezekiel 8:12, *The Holy Bible, King James Version* [author's interpretation].

may see." This is "depth seeing." John picks up "depth seeing" in John 1:1 (KJV) when he says, "In the beginning was the word." For John, it is *seeing into* instead of *looking at*. There was no way for John to see "the beginning of the beginning" (arche), so John begins his Gospel at the beginning of the beginning. This is where all Gospels start—in the mind of God before there were human beings. Therefore, preaching is a kind of seeing and engaging enterprise. The preacher stands on the wall as a watchman and sees in the distance what congregants may not be able to see. A preacher who is not willing to see with this kind of depth can never participate in the dynamic of "deep calleth unto deep."[17] The third component of preaching as a contemplative theological task is *illumination*: "I see the stars."[18]

Fourth comes aurality or hearing: "I hear the rolling thunder."[19] Faith must have ears. Seeing and hearing are tributaries that empty into the river of contemplation. As tributaries, they cross each other. What one hears makes an impression and gives one the desire to see what is heard and to speak what is seen. Paul asked the perennial preaching question, "How shall they hear without a preacher?" (Romans 10:14 NIV). Francis of Assisi is reputed to have said to preach the gospel everywhere you go and only use words when necessary. This is speechless evangelism. While this may be necessary during unique moments, most of our preaching will have to be done with words. If the heavens declare the glory of God, so must also the preacher. Speech must follow sight. If faith without works is dead, then sight without speech is incomplete. Isaac Watts, in his great rendition "We're Marching to Zion," lifts up this refrain: "Let those refuse to sing who never knew our God, but children of the heavenly

---

[17] Psalm 42:7, Ibid.

[18] "How Great Thou Art," *The Baptist Hymnal*, 10.

[19] Ibid.

King may speak their joys abroad."[20] In John 20, the author pictures the effect of *depth hearing*. The skeptical Thomas refused to believe the secondhand report he had heard from the disciples concerning the resurrected Jesus. It was only after he heard Jesus himself say to him, "Put your finger here; see my hands. Reach out your hand and put it into my side," that Thomas was able to respond in faith.[21] We need to move to the position of Peter and John in Acts 4:20 (KJV): "For we cannot but speak the things which we have seen and heard." If we have seen and heard a lot about what God has done, then we have a lot to say about who God is. "Let the redeemed of the LORD say so" (Psalm 107:2, KJV). The fourth component of preaching as a contemplative theological task is *aurality* or *hearing*. "I hear the rolling thunder."[22]

Fifth is singing: "Then sings my soul, my Savior God to thee, how great thou art, how great thou art."[23] Neil Postman, in his work *Amusing Ourselves to Death*, evokes author Aldous Huxley, who in *Brave New World* insists that people were not afflicted because they were laughing instead of thinking, but because they were laughing and did not know what they were laughing about or why they were no longer thinking.[24] We know why we sing. A songwriter declared, "Some folk may sing to pass the weary hours along. Some folk may sing to entertain a worldly throne. But I sing because I worship God in song, it's in my heart, it's in my heart. It's in my heart, a melody of love divine, it's in my heart that I am His and He is mine. It's in my

---

[20] "We're Marching to Zion," *The Baptist Hymnal*, 524. Words by Isaac Watts, 1674–1748; music by Robert Lowery, 1826–1899.

[21] John 20:27, *Holy Bible, Today's New International Version*.

[22] "How Great Thou Art," *The Baptist Hymnal*, 10.

[23] Ibid.

[24] For further reading, see Neil Postman, *Amusing Ourselves to Death: Public Discourse in the Age of Show Business* (New York: Viking, 1985).

heart, how can I help but to sing and shout, It's in my heart, it's in my heart."[25]

Contemplative theology is the cradle of doxology. It exists to praise God. When I was a boy, the very first song in our hymnal was "Holy, Holy, Holy." This opening selection in our hymnals introduced us to the fact that God is holy. The angels are very careful about how they exclaim and exult in God: They have two wings to cover their face, two wings to cover their feet, and two wings to fly away carrying God's message. The only song they sing is "Holy, Holy, Holy, Lord God Almighty; the whole earth is full of your glory."[26] The fifth component of preaching on a contemplative theological task is *singing*: "Then sings my soul, my Savior God to thee, how great thou art, how great thou art."[27]

When preachers theologize contemplatively, they do it in order to doxologize, to lift up and exult in God. Something ought to be summoned within us, evoked in us, when we think of God. Have you ever seen a magnificent sunset? Have you ever seen a majestic sunrise? Have you ever seen the ensuing afterglow? Something ought to be summoned up within us about the greatness and the majesty of God. In fact on 29 May 2006, I was watching television and saw Pope Benedict XVI speaking at the death camp in Auschwitz, Poland. While he was speaking, in the background a rainbow appeared. Some might have thought it was a coincidence, but I believe it was providence. It was as if God was reminding us of Genesis 9:11: "It will never happen again, here."[28]

---

[25] "It's in My Heart," *African American Heritage Hymnal*, 416. Lyrics by Arthur Slater; arranged by J. G. Boersma.

[26] "Holy, Holy, Holy," *The Baptist Hymnal*, 2. Words by Reginald Heber, 1783–1826; music by John B. Dykes, 1823–1876.

[27] "How Great Thou Art," *The Baptist Hymnal*, 10.

[28] Author's interpretation. Genesis 9:11 KJV reads, "And I will establish my covenant with you; neither shall all flesh be cut off any more by the waters of a flood; neither shall there anymore be a flood to destroy the earth."

Something ought to be summoned up when we think about God. Something ought to happen when we think about the text, when we think about God's word. In fact, when we think about God's word, when we take time, we become like theological, homiletical, and hermeneutical gemologists. The text is a gem. Preachers have to turn each facet, examine each angle, and let the light of revelation as it is refracted through the gemstone of the text bring them illumination.

Do we not understand as communicators of the word of God that texts are trying to catch up with us? They cannot catch up with us because we are not willing to be still, to be contemplative, to be reflective enough. Years ago, George Arthur Buttrick, after listening to one of his students preach, gave this piercing and penetrating critique: "If the text had smallpox, the sermon would not have caught it."[29] It takes time to turn the text and look at it. Then, God begins to show us things that we did not find in commentaries or any other books.

Turn to the text of Genesis 18:12 and carefully look at it. It says that "Sarah laughed." Sarah laughed because the angel had predicted that at the same time next year she was going to have a child. Sarah did not believe because she was post-menopausal and her husband was old. She laughed. But in Genesis 21:6, she laughed again; then, Sarah said, "They will laugh with me." It was as if God was saying, "The first time you laughed was because you had a *hermeneutic of suspicion*, but now you laugh because you have a *hermeneutic of assent*." God wanted to show Sarah that there were some things God was going to do that would seem humanly preposterous, ludicrous, ridiculous, and so illogical that the only response would be simply to laugh because there would be no human explanation. God would have to do it.

---

[29] Author listened to a cassette tape of this lecture containing the critique several years ago.

Keep turning the text, and focus your attention on Genesis 22. Turn every facet of the text. It will take time. God said to Abraham, "Abraham, take your son, your only son, Isaac, the one you love and go to the land of Moriah and offer him up as a *holocaust*, a burnt offering unto me. Abraham went home and after he got up that morning, he saddled his donkey, he took his servants, he took his son and headed out" (Genesis 22:1–3). In the very next verse, Abraham arrives at Mt. Moriah on the third day. Between verses 3 and 4, three days have transpired. What does one do in three days? One cannot *not* think in three days. What does one contemplate in three days? The three days were not for God. The three days were for Abraham. It took three days for Abraham to finally get to the place where Isaac had to die, not on the altar of Mt. Moriah, but on the altar of Abraham's heart. So by the time Abraham got to Mt. Moriah, Isaac was already dead. Abraham had made up his mind that it was better to trust the God of the promise even when it looked like the promise of God would not come to pass; for if it was necessary, God could allow Isaac to be killed, but God was able to raise him up from the dead in order to keep his word.

Keep turning the gem of the text to Genesis 32–33. In Genesis 32, Jacob is perhaps wrestling with a Christophany—that is, a Christ before Bethlehem—and he experiences two things: *transformation* and *dislocation*. Not only is his name changed, but his walk is changed. In Genesis 32:30, he sees the face of God, but in Genesis 33:10, the next day he sees his brother's face. Jacob was not ready to see his brother's face in chapter 33 until after he had seen the Lord's face in chapter 32.

Now, focus on Psalm 23:4. Notice that the rhythm of the text slows down. Don't be in a hurry to get past verse 4 and move to verse 5. When we come to verse 5 we notice, "You prepare a table before me in the presence of my enemies, You anoint my head with oil; my cup overflows."[30] Do we not know that we cannot get to verse 5, where a table is prepared before us in the presence of our enemies, until we have gone through the valley of the shadow of death in verse 4? God reminds us that the same One who prepares a table before us in the presence of our enemies is the One who is with us in the valley—the Lord.

Turn the textual gem one more time, and do not be in such a hurry. Allow the light of illumination to reveal precious truths of God from Ezekiel 37. Ezekiel had inherited a difficult situation. The valley was full of dry bones, but he kept on preaching until there was noise in the valley: the bones began to rattle. He continued to preach until there was unity in the valley: bone came to its connecting bone. He persevered in his preaching until there was a positive appearance in the valley. In fact, the bodies were covered with skin, sinews, and muscles. And then there was more noise in the valley. Listen attentively and acutely. We will hear something that precedes the blowing of the wind into the nostrils of these corpses. Up above our heads we will hear vultures in the air. Vultures! We admit that initially there were no vultures in the air above the valley of dry bones. Why? Because the bones were dry and had no flesh on them. In the very first verse there were dry bones. But now, in the wilderness, there are corpses, and vultures saw potential in the corpses—the bones now had flesh on them. We must be grateful for vultures. If we do not hear demonic vultures flying overhead, we must examine our ministry. We must thank God for demonic vultures because they indicate that we have moved from dry bones to great potential.

As gemologists, turn the text contemplatively and see the bigness of God in God's word. What is contemplative theology? It is being available to God, brooding over God, hovering over God and God's

---

[30] Psalm 23:5, *The Holy Bible, English Standard Version* (Wheaton IL: Crossway Bibles, Good News Publishers, 2002).

word, delighting in God. Or, as Dr. Mack King Carter talks about, "finding the divine delicious." It is being lost in the wonder of God. It is longing after God to the next extent that even the common things become sublime, or, as Paul puts it in 1 Corinthians 10:31, "Whether we eat or drink, we do it all to the glory of God." We become like Mary. Martha came to perform an act; Mary came to be acted upon. Martha came to prepare a meal; Mary came to be fed by the Bread of Life. Martha came to entertain; Mary came to have an encounter. Martha came to serve; Mary came to be served by the one who said, "I didn't come to be served, but to serve and to give my life, a ransom for many" (Mark 10:45). Brother Lawrence, the seventeenth-century monk from France, is well known for his conviction that it is practicing the presence of God so that even when you wash dishes, you are thinking about the goodness and glory of God.

Johann Sebastian Bach at times would sign the very bottom of his many original manuscripts, *INJ* (in the name of Jesus) or *SDG* (*Soli Deo Gloria*, to God alone be glory). When we bask in the sunshine of the Son of righteousness, we have a longing to see him more clearly, to love him more dearly, and to follow him more nearly. Of course, Jesus is the supreme exemplar, the supreme paragon, the ultimate model of one who did preaching as a contemplative theological task. In what was arguably Jesus' busiest day in ministry, after preaching, teaching, healing, and being with people all that day, "He got up a great while before day and went to a place to commune with his Father" (Mark 1:35). Surely Dr. Gardner C. Taylor must have been informed by this verse when he stated that he could have been a better and more effective preacher if he had prayed and read the Bible more.

Jesus communed with the Father because it was on his priority list. He was never called or paged during a Lord's Supper or prayer meeting, for he was always in communion with his Father. He practiced what he preached. According to Mark 3:13–15, he sometimes spent all night praying. The next morning after that time of prayer, Jesus called the Twelve to be with him and then to preach the gospel and cast out devils. They were called to be with him so that when they got ready to preach for him they would have anointing and power and authority to exorcise demons. They would have power because everything stemmed from being with him. Jesus would say the same thing about himself that he would say about us. In John 15:5, Jesus said, "Without me you can do nothing." If what we do for Christ is to have an eternal consequence, Christ must be involved in it; otherwise, it will never last. However, in John 5:19, Jesus said, "Whatever the Father does, the Son sees it and does it also." Jesus is saying, "I can't even do anything without my Father: He is the supreme example." We cannot do anything without the Son, and the Son cannot do anything without the Father.

To theologize, contemplatively speaking, is dangerous. When we come before the presence of God, God sees us as we are and knows that we are filled with the puss of sin. There are some things that have been entrenched in us for so long that we have to invite the Lord to take and abduct them so that he can lance them and let out what has been spiritually poisoning us. This is dangerous and penetratingly painful.

God cannot make us whole until we have been broken. God cannot fill us until we have been emptied. Clifton H. Johnson, in the book *God Struck Me Dead*, records the findings of two Fisk University professors who had interviewed several ex-slave exhorters and preachers in order to find out what characterized their call and defined their ministry. One thread that ran through the fabric of their call was death. When God called them, something within them died. They said they died to sin. They died to silence.[31]

James A. Sanders has stated that "Biblical characters do not primarily serve as models for morality, but rather as mirrors for

---

[31] Clifton H. Johnson, *God Struck Me Dead* (Cleveland OH: Pilgrim Press, 1993).

identity."[32] We must see ourselves in the person of Moses as those who murder others with slanderous tongues. We must see ourselves in Simon Peter, who asked the Lord to depart from him because he was a sinful man and who even at a later time departed from the Lord by denying him three times. We must see ourselves in David, who had been identified as the guilty one but then went on to write, "Search me, O God and know my heart. Try me and know my thoughts and see if there's any evil way in me and lead me in the way everlasting" (Psalm 139:23–24). The Greek word for confession is *homologeo*. It really means to agree with what God has said about us (see 1 John 1:9). Contemplative theologizing is both dangerous and penetratingly painful.

R. E. C. Browne believed that "ministers of the Word think about authority in solitude, they discuss it in the proper company, but for the greater part of their life they are not called to talk about authority but to speak and act with authority."[33] Are we still enough to let God speak to us? It is amazing what we hear God say when we sit down and are still. In fact, the greater emphasis in the Bible is not on the lips, but on the ear: "Be quick to hear and slow to speak" (James 1:9). The declaration of the Shema is Deuteronomy 6:4: "Hear O Israel, the LORD our God is One LORD." The young Samuel says, "Speak LORD, for your servant is listening" (1 Samuel 3:10). The prophet Elijah did not see the manifestation of God in an earthquake, the wind, or the fire, but rather discerned God's presence in the still small voice (1 Kings 19:12). Solomon prayed for wisdom. The Hebrew word for wisdom in this context means "a listening heart." He was praying, "Give me a listening heart that I might lead your people." Regarding preaching, this really places a demand on us because it means we have to deny ourselves in order to hear what God

---

[32] James A. Sanders, "Hermeneutics," *The Interpreter's Dictionary of the Bible* [supplementary volume] (Nashville: Abingdon Press, 1976) 406.

[33] R. E. C. Browne, *The Ministry of the Word* (London: SCM Press LTD, 1958) 29.

has to say. We can no longer *congregationalize* the text and say what the congregation wants to hear. We can no longer *denominationalize* the text and say what is going to please the denomination. We cannot *ethnicize* the text and say what is beneficial for the people of a racial hue. We cannot *fossilize* the text and *mute* the text so that it is frozen in time and no longer speaks to us today. We do not need to *adjust* the text. We need to *trust* the text. We do not need to *tame* the text or *sanitize* the text. Let the *text* be the *text.* There are some texts that stink so badly that they represent the sewage of scripture. Genesis 38 and Judges 19 are examples. In Genesis 38, Judah is both the father and grandfather of his offspring, Perez and Zerah, through his daughter-in-law, Tamar. In Judges 19, the Levite hears the cries of his concubine who is gang-raped throughout the night and proceeds to put her dead body on his beast, cutting her body into twelve parts and sending each portion to one of the twelve tribes of Israel.[34] Let the text speak. Do not tame the text. We must come to the place where we hear the text speak to us. We must be still and know that God is God and is sovereign in these texts of terror.

I believe that one of the greatest texts in all the Bible is Luke 1:57–79. Zechariah had gone to the temple to do his priestly course of duty. Because he didn't believe what God's messenger, the angel Gabriel, had said about him and Elizabeth having a child, God struck him dumb. Gabriel told Zechariah that he would be silenced for nine months, until after the baby had been born. The baby's name was to be John. I think that the greatest period in Zechariah's preaching ministry was that nine-month period when all he could do was listen to God. God put him on a divinely imposed sabbatical for nine long months. Finally, when the nine months were over and Zechariah and Elizabeth's son was born, he was asked to write his name down on a stylus. He wrote exactly what he had heard God say: "His name is John." I am convinced that had Zechariah written down Nehemiah,

---

[34] *The Holy Bible, King James Version.*

Joshua, Moses, or any other name, he would have remained silent. But when he wrote down what he heard God say, God loosed his tongue, and he wrote the great benediction song of scripture, the "Nunc Dimittis."

If we are going to have power in our preaching, we will have to say what God has said and speak exactly what God has spoken. Silence is not an option—it is a necessity. While on a cruise, I saw a young man wearing a tee shirt that read, "Save the hymnal." I approached him and asked, "Why are you wearing that shirt?" He responded, "Because I believe that the hymnal has sound theology."

God must be the center of Christian music. We are moving toward *anthropomusicology* (humanity as the center of Christian music) and away from *theomusicology* (God as the center of Christian music). The hymnal should be centered around *God*. The Bible is the written word of God, which exposes the incarnate word of God, Jesus Christ. In essence, the Bible is a *Him Book*. We worship in an audience of one: God, who is the reason we worship. Martin Luther believed that the devil should not have all the good tunes.

I believe that in the last fifty years, the greatest divorce that has taken place in the church is the divorce between the minister of Christian education and the minister of music. The minister of Christian education oftentimes has a great text but is victimized by insipid intellectualism. The minister of music may have a good tune but is often caught up in hyper-emotionalism. There needs to be a remarriage between a good tune and a great text. Both are needed. In Luke 2, the shepherds hear a great text from the angel, informing them that the Savior is born in Bethlehem. They are told not to fear, for the angelic pronouncement would bring them great joy, not only for them but for all people. This is a great text; however, they did not make their way to Bethlehem until they heard a great tune. Suddenly appearing with this angel was a multitude of the heavenly hosts, who were singing and praising God: "Glory be to God in the highest, and on earth peace, good will toward men." Their response to the great text, which was followed by the great tune, was to leave immediately and go to Bethlehem to observe what they had been told.

I recall hearing Dr. Haddon Robinson, of Gordon-Conwell Theological Seminary, share a story about a pastor of a Christian Reformed church in the Chicago area during WWII. He was close to his mother, who was a widow, and they had such a unique relationship that they shared their readings and meals together, and spoke often. When her son found a young woman that he was interested in marrying, he brought the young woman home to meet his mother. She gave her blessing to the marriage and said to him, "It's going to be difficult to find an affordable apartment in Chicago at this stage of your life. Why don't you move in this apartment, and I'll move upstairs?" The son agreed, but the mother said, "There's one stipulation to this agreement. You have got to continue to visit me once a week like you used to, and share your readings and a meal." The son said, "Oh, that's fine, Mama. That will be easy to do." For the first month, that is exactly what took place. But then the visits became phone calls, and the phone calls became less frequent. He began to feel guilty. On her birthday, he bought his mother a dress in her favorite color. Knocking on the door, he shouted, "Surprise! Happy birthday, Mama!" Looking rather forlorn, she took the dress. He sat down and said, "Mama, if you don't like the dress, the sales receipt is in the bottom of the bag." She said, "It is fine, son." He said, "Now look, Mama, we have been together for a long time. If you really don't like the dress you don't have to keep it." She said, "Son, I'll keep it." Sensing that he was troubled, she asked, "Son, what's wrong?" He said, "I can tell you don't like the dress." She took him by the hand and led him over to her closet. She opened the closet and said, "Son, do you see all those dresses that still have the tags on them? Son, I don't want those dresses, and neither do I want yours. What I want is you! I miss the time we used to spend together. You and I used to commune together. I don't want your dress. I just want you."

Preaching as a contemplative theological task must reunite paradise lost with paradise regained—God and humans walking together in the garden in the cool of the day. God not only wants us; God pursues us. In the eschaton, the task of preaching will be retired, but the privilege of contemplative theology will be continued.

Dr. Gardner C. Taylor, one of the greatest preachers in the history of the Christian church, must be regarded for more than his sagacious proclamation. As a preacher, he must always be reflected upon as one who grounded his proclamatory pronouncements in the matrix of contemplative theology, for he recognized that effective preaching requires more than intelligence—it demands intimacy with God. Like Dr. Taylor, praying and reading the Bible more will make all of us as preachers better and more effective in our calling and craft.

In Derrick Jackson's well-loved song "Just to Behold His Face," we sense the very essence of the purpose of heaven: "Not just to kneel with the angels and not to see loved ones who've gone; and it's not just to drink at the fountain that is under the great white throne; not for the crown that He'll give me that I'm trying to run this race; I know that all I want up in heaven is just to behold his face."[35]

---

[35] Derrick Jackson, "Just to Behold His Face," *African American Heritage Hymnal*. Arrangement by Charlene Moore Cooper, 584.

INCARNATIONAL PREACHING

Wallace Charles Smith

Rattling through televised religious programming, which features hour after hour of elegantly coiffed bejeweled preachers who look like poster children for Hollywood ad agencies, one cannot help but wonder if this proliferation of twenty-first century prelates presents an accurate picture of Corinthians: "We preach not ourselves, but Christ Jesus" (2 Corinthians 4:5, KJV). The dilemma of preaching is that the only way to preach Christ is to do so by preaching out of ourselves or, perhaps better said, out of who we authentically are. When we preach out of our authentic selves, we are practicing what I call incarnational preaching. *The incarnation is the Word becoming flesh.* To the church of the first century, this was critically important because the Word disconnected from the flesh was considered Gnostic and ahistorical.

The preaching tradition is not one of ghosts and phantoms. It is a tradition of real-life men and women who cried, laughed, suffered, and rejoiced, but who preached out of their own gifts and limitations to present an authentic depiction of the gospel message they presented. There is no better example of this tradition than Paul, who, thorn in the flesh notwithstanding, stood as the *parson*, the person charged with spiritual duties. Paul may be one of the most outstanding examples of the Word becoming flesh in his preaching, but he is surely not alone.

In examining the history of preaching, one observes that it is a history in which gallant men and women have suffered and have experienced great loss and pain for the sake of preaching. It is incumbent upon us to keep in mind as we preach that we stand not only in the shoes of Paul and John, but in those of such heroes as

Origen, St. John Chrysostom, Augustine, Luther, Calvin, and scores of unlettered Europeans, Latinos, peasants, Asians, Native Americans, and black slaves whose names will never appear among those of great preachers, but who suffered and gave profusely of themselves for the preaching of the gospel.

When the sense of holy awe is practiced, and as we realize the enormity of our task, the preacher is saved from the luxury of answering questions that no one is asking. In his sermon "Wide Visions from a Narrow Window," Dr. Taylor said that preaching is first and foremost the words that articulate "the deepest and truest longings of the human heart."[1] Whenever we humans attempt to speak of holy things, we cannot help but feel our complete inability to adequately handle the task. Those of us who make the attempt to preach face the impossible challenge of handling live, burning coals within the limits of unclean lips. We seek to brighten our vision even as we face the formidable task of looking through a glass darkly.

Preaching is the retelling of the greatest story ever told while attempting to preserve the excitement of hearing it for the first time, as did those disciples who went running from home to home, knocking on doors, and crying out to all who would listen, "The Lord has risen, indeed, and has appeared...."[2] It is a grown-up re-creation of life's inevitable sadness redefined in light of heaven's good news. Recalling the excitement of a child experiencing the tales of heroes and heroines while sitting around the licking flames of a campfire, the story must be told with this same freshness, excitement, and enthusiasm. The preacher must convey with joy and celebration in his or her voice the exciting reality that ultimately, by the power of God, the human spirit will triumph. Preaching re-creates a story in prose of the exile and faithlessness of a people chosen by God but

---

[1] Gardner C. Taylor, "Wide Visions from a Narrow Window," in *Quintessential Classics, 1980–Present*, vol. 3 of *The Words of Gardner Taylor*, comp. Edward L. Taylor (Valley Forge: Judson Press, 2000) 64-9.

[2] Luke 24:34 (KJV).

who too often denied God's power. However, it is also the poetic song of Daniel in the lion's den who emerged unscathed after a night surrounded by death, saying, "My God sent an angel and shut the lion's mouth."[3] The assumed tragedy of three Hebrew children unjustly placed in a fiery furnace is weighed against a song of celebration, for when the king came to look in the furnace it was not just the three but a fourth, and the fourth was likened unto the Son of God.[4]

I don't think anyone has defined preaching better than Phillips Brooks in the Yale Lyman Beecher Lecture Series when he described preaching as divine truth communicated through a personality. That may not seem like much on the surface, but when one begins to plumb the depths of this statement, one ends up in fairly deep waters. Are we, for instance, confident enough in who we are that we can stand before an audience competently, with all our warts and faults in full view, not attempting to hide ourselves behind some mask that we have carefully crafted over the years, so much so that we ourselves are not even sure where the mask ends and essential self begins? Is our preaching voice our own or some acquired sound from a beloved mentor? Are the ideas we preach our own, or do they parrot a tradition we feel we must uphold, be it evangelical, fundamentalist, or liberal? Are we truly called to do this work, or is this what our mothers, fathers, Sunday school teachers, or pastors always encouraged us to do?

Non-incarnational preaching is the de-fleshing of authentic personality from the preaching moment; it is skeletal preaching. It is laying bare the least amount of self-disclosure so that the resulting message has a third-person feel about it, almost like a term paper that is so heavily footnoted that the author has really said nothing genuine. When this happens, our preaching is not that which stands

---

[3] Daniel 6:22 (KJV).

[4] See Daniel 3:19–25 (KJV). The three victimized Hebrews were Shadrach, Meshach, and Abednego.

in the holy glow of the martyred, of those who suffered and died for the integrity of the Word. Inauthentic preaching is a tertiary quid, a third thing. In the words of William Shakespeare, it is "a tale told by an idiot, full of sound and fury, signifying nothing."[5] It bears the name but lacks legitimate power.

Legendary African-American preacher Nelson Smith, a former president of the Progressive National Baptist Convention, once told a story that captures this sentiment. He recalled that during the Depression era, he and his father, also a preacher, were traveling by train to a place where his father was to preach. When they arrived at the station, they exited the train and came upon a man on the platform who was selling pies. The man called out in a sonorous voice, "Cherry pies for sale; cherry pies for sale." The elder Smith bought each of them a pie, and they started eating as they walked along. When he took his first bite, there was a cherry *flavor*, and it was sweet and juicy, but no cherries. He took another bite and found the same thing: sweet cherry flavor but no cherries. He took a third bite, and it was the same as the first two. By now, he felt indignation at being duped by the salesperson. He took the pie back to the man and said to him, "You sold me this cherry pie. I have taken three bites of it, and there are no cherries." The man looked at Dr. Smith with impatient eyes and proclaimed, "Aw, Mister, I thought you knew when you bought it; that's just what they call the thing."

Preaching needs to be incarnational so that what we say and do is not just what we call the thing, but so that it comes out of a deep well of validity. For preaching to be incarnational, it must be the preacher himself or herself who shows up in the pulpit to preach. It can never be an imitation of another preacher. It can't be Charles Haddon Spurgeon or Gardner Calvin Taylor. (A preacher once said to me that Spurgeon has done more preaching since his death than he did when he was alive and that even in the twentieth century some of those

---

[5] Act 5, scene 5, line 26, *Macbeth*, in vol. 2 of *The Plays and Sonnets of William Shakespeare* (Chicago: Encyclopedia Britannica, Inc., 1952).

who purloin his sermons fail to delete the steamship illustrations.) *We* must be the one who both prepares and delivers the message. Otherwise, the sermon is nothing more than what one calls the thing.

Incarnational preaching links our stories with the biblical story. It is when we look at the book of Lamentations and Jeremiah's sorrow through our own loneliness, feeling of abandonment, and missed opportunities. Can we really preach the story of Abraham preparing to sacrifice Isaac without the voice of Isaac becoming the voice of some little one we love? How heart-wrenching that voice sounds when it is not from the rumblings of several thousand years ago but from several days ago, saying, "Daddy, where is the lamb?" (Genesis 22:7, KJV). What must it have been like for Peter, who in that misty morning thought he had successfully walled himself behind his lies only to hear the cock crow just as the master predicted? (Matthew 26:69–75). We make his story real to people by telling our own stories, disclosing our own failings and our own inabilities to be faithful to the things we say we love. We put flesh on the bones of preaching when we tear into our own skin and find the heart of a message beating not in past centuries, but in the hollows of our own chests, inside our own study place at the very moment of our meditation and preparation.

Preaching incarnationally requires the preacher to become free of the conventions, both external (proper form, word choice, etc.) and internal (fear of criticism, poor self-image, lack of authentic faith [values]), and to allow oneself the freedom to become a conduit for the Holy Spirit. The surest way for the preacher to free himself or herself is to realize that God is a liberator.

Throughout the biblical record the justice of God is the consistent theme that articulates God's liberating power. The story in Daniel 3 about the fiery furnace could be described not as God outside the furnace putting people in, but inside the furnace getting people out. God's liberating power is at its most awesome when we witness God's theater of redemption played out in three acts: Act

One, Good Friday, when, as the old preachers were fond of saying, "the moon hemorrhaged and dripped blood"; Act Two, a sorrowing Saturday, when, for a day, the Savior was relegated to a borrowed tomb; Act Three, a brand new day on which grieving whisper is turned into shouts of joy. On Easter Sunday morning, a tomb and the forces of death have been forced to relinquish their prisoner, and the Master is resurrected with all power in heaven and earth in his hands.

The greatest limitation to life was defeated. The preacher need not be confined by forces that might limit or restrain. Since death has been defeated, both internal and external forces that stand in the way of authentic preaching have been defeated as well.

Incarnational preaching in the first analysis is the retelling of the most powerful story ever known: the story of God working in history to restore creation unto God's self. When we practice incarnational preaching, which we define as being free to find our stories within the biblical story and to live those stories through the spoken word, certain common questions about preaching become inconsequential: Should a sermon have one point, two points, or more? Should the standard be three points and a poem? At a minister's conference I attended, someone once asked Dr. Taylor this very question, and he responded that every sermon ought to make at least one point!

In dealing with an incarnational approach to preaching, I do not argue for textual or topical preaching, manuscript preaching, use of notes, or memorization. These are stylistic decisions, and the best measuring stick is that which comes from scripture, namely that each of us should stir up the gift that is within (see 2 Timothy 1:6, KJV). The strong concern, though, is that, regardless of style, we come to see all effective preaching as being in one way or another authentically our own. Another way to put it is that in incarnational preaching, the message and the preacher become one; as such, style, through the preacher's ability to be free, determines itself. When we become free to present our sorrows and joys, our vocal inflections, facial expressions, and other rhetorical devices help the sermon come alive. But the only way a sermon is truly "enfleshed" is for the preacher to fully and totally embody the message.

As mentioned earlier, 2 Corinthians 4:5 states what one might perceive as a dilemma regarding this concept of incarnational preaching: "We preach not ourselves, but Christ Jesus the Lord." However, it is the intersection of two stories that makes incarnational preaching possible. First is God's story. God's story is the account of an all-good God who comes in the cool of the day, saying, "Adam, where art thou?" (Genesis 3:9). The tranquility of the God-human relationship has been rocked by the grievousness of sin and rebellion. As Dr. Taylor has stated in many of his sermons and lectures, most of the Old Testament is a recounting of the search for God's errant children. Because of sin, God is at a distance from creation. Again, according to Dr. Taylor, the voice of Job articulates humanity's search for God: "If I could but find him I would plead my case before his face" (Job 23:3). It is with the New Testament and the coming of Christ that these two searches reach their culmination. God finds humanity and humanity finds God in the birth of the Messiah, the incarnation. The word has become flesh and now dwells among us.

Christian preaching is finding that intersection where the word becomes flesh. The good news that we proclaim is that underneath our sorrowing circumstances, we maintain hope because nothing can separate us from the love of God in Christ Jesus. Our hope is not philosophical or ethereal. It is a reality that, in Jesus, the word became flesh. When we preach this message holistically, the word becomes flesh through us.

The methodology for establishing incarnational preaching is rooted in developing a homiletic lifestyle. This lifestyle is based on three forms of study and/or observation. The first, and most obvious, is the study of scripture. We must delve into texts so that they speak to us and to the conditions in which we find ourselves. This is more than just an academic exercise, although rigorous exegetical work is essential for effective preaching. The hard work of interpretation must be done squarely alongside careful reflection and meditation. As we do historical and linguistic analysis, we must raise not only the question of what the text says, but also what it means and, perhaps most importantly, "What does it mean to me?" How do the words of sacred scripture shape me, form me, and direct my pathways? If the Old Testament is a recounting of God's search for humanity, then as I study scripture and read about the escape route of the Hebrews from Egypt, along with the liberating presence that God established through Moses, I must also ask myself how God is searching for me and in what ways has God established a liberating presence in my life. The term *anamnesis*, "remember," is used to describe a historical reflection so profound that it not only exists in the past, but is also a present reality. Receiving the Lord's Supper is an example. When we break the bread and drink the wine, we are not only recalling the suffering, death, and resurrection of our Lord, but the experience is so powerful that the living Lord is present in that moment. Whether this is the actual presence or the symbolic presence is not the point; the point is that Christ being with us in that moment turns a memory into an actual living experience. At the moment of the breaking of the bread, through us the word has become flesh.

Those who are not from a sacramental tradition must not get bogged down at this point. In the so-called Free Church tradition, preaching is not considered a sacrament. However, when a sermon is prepared and delivered, there is that sacred moment when the searching God and the searching preacher meet. At that moment, not only does the word become flesh, but the preacher, through her or his flesh—that is, mind, body, and spirit—becomes the enfleshment of sacred truth. It is at that moment that preaching becomes incarnational and the preacher becomes authentically free. The study of scripture must be both academic and meditative if the incarnation of the Word is to be demonstrated in the sermon.

Our academic work provides the canvas on which the sermon is designed. When one learns to paint or draw, the first goal is learning to stay within the lines. That is where our exegesis comes in. Many who are parents recall fondly the point at which our grade-schoolers finally began to bring us their coloring books that demonstrated their ability to stay within the lines.

The process of exegesis can be practiced by a simple formula that, with diligence, becomes second nature. The first step is to read the text devotionally to assess what it says to us. How do we hear it? What do we feel it saying to us in our present condition? The next step is sorting through our preconceptions. What have we always believed the text is saying? What do we remember of it from Sunday school, conversations with friends, or sermons we have heard?

Thirdly, we compare translations. Is there something in the various translations that commands our attention? There is profound significance in the titles the New Testament writers used for Jesus. If one translation uses "Lord" and another "Master," it might trigger an insight we do not want to miss.

Fourthly, the preacher should look at the subjects in the text. If the author mentions a place like Sinai, Jordan, or Mt. Zion, it may mean there is a purpose in that stated locale.

Fifthly, one should examine concept and context of a text. Is there something in the way a pericope sits inside a chapter? The Gospel of Luke, for instance, features a number of critical theological interactions between Jesus and those he encounters after Luke declares that Jesus had set his face toward Jerusalem (Luke 9:51) in other words, that he was moving toward death and resurrection.

Within this context, a number of theological concepts emerge. During this travelogue, there are several types of persons encountered. There are those whom Jesus empowers by healing their predicament of powerlessness. There are the authorities, who form the increasingly calcified opposition. There are the disciples, who often fail to see the deeper implication of Jesus' ministry and teaching. Knowing the context contributes to a richer examination of the concepts. When the preacher enters fully into the process of exegesis, meaning begins to emerge. We begin to traverse the bridge between then and now. We become thoroughly in touch with the dynamics of the text and, in turn, begin to sense, see, and feel how those dynamics connect to our personal stories.

In preaching about the prodigal son (Luke 15:11–32), we are not just preaching about a lost boy who squandered his inheritance. We are preaching about all the blessings we have misappropriated, all the opportunities we have missed, and all the ways God has received us back, with warts and flaws, when we have simply come to our senses. The pain, degradation, and disruption of living in a pig pen comes alive when we exegete not just the text, but our own experiences.

The second form of study is personal, in-depth observation. This helps us to understand who we are in the light of biblical and theological realities. Every preacher who seeks to preach incarnationally must spend inordinate amounts of time getting to know himself or herself. Some of this can be done through prayer, meditation, and daily journaling.

Praying over a text should be given equal weight to consulting the finest commentaries. The mistake many of us make in praying is filling up the time with words. Prayer opportunities too often degenerate into our monologues before God. The psalmist put it best: "Be still and know that I am God" (Psalm 46:10). Nothing clears the mind of frantic thoughts and busyness more than prayer.

Prayer acts as a companion to exegesis because it provides the colors that will give life to the idea. Many of us also recall with our preschoolers that once they learned to stay within the lines, they next needed to grow to a place where they understood that cows were not green and grass was not red. Prayer offers us the right colors, nuances, and textures for what will go inside the lines of the canvas. When we are preparing to preach, we should be very intentional and unapologetic when it comes to asking God to direct us to the insights that will provide moral and spiritual help to our congregations. Once we have petitioned God for those directions, we must be patient and wait for God to open the windows and doors of heaven that the most helpful insights will come to us.

Meditation goes hand in hand with prayer. One way to understand meditation is to recognize that God gives us the gift of imagination. Meditation is one way to access that gift. Study provides the canvas on which we paint, and prayer offers the best and sharpest colors or insights with which to paint. However, meditation gives us the field of meaning that the painting ultimately is to contain. After we have prayed for the guidance that will give us insight, we need to use our imagination in order to walk through the passages with which we are working. In our moments of meditation, we should imagine ourselves with Jesus by the Sea of Galilee as those challenging and arresting words of the Sermon on the Mount were being uttered. What do we feel when we hear them? How do they impact us? What about them was neither affirming nor troubling? It is in moments of meditation that we become part of the text.

The third of the singular or private approaches to accessing our deepest selves is journaling. Journaling is a wonderful way to hear ourselves reflect on our relationships, encounters, and even casual interactions. Journaling means taking time every day, sometimes several times a day, to write in stream-of-consciousness fashion the things we have thought, the emotions we have felt, and the observations of the places and people we have encountered. Journaling helps us to avoid walking by unobservant when God attempts to get our attention. Exodus 3 relates the story of Moses and the burning bush. The text speaks metaphorically about Moses tending his flocks beyond the wilderness. What can be beyond the wilderness? The wilderness is already beyond civilization. What the text implies is that Moses was in a state of mind contrary to common daily thought. One could make the case that this was perhaps a non-rational, right-brain form of thinking. Obviously this is speculative, but it does indicate that authentic encounters with God take place when we find methods to enter the deepest places of our consciousness.

When we manage to quiet our business, inexplicable phenomena begin to show up. For Moses it was a bush burning, but not consumed. Daily journaling, along with prayer and meditation, is one way to still the spirit and become profoundly observant of what may seem inconsequential when we do not take the time to reflect. How many burning bushes, thought to be simple brushfires, are passed by in the course of a year by unobservant travelers? Moses received an awesome summons because he found a way to get deep enough into his soul to hear what others ignored.

In addition to study, prayer, meditation, and consistent journaling, there is another step to accessing the depths of one's soul. One should engage in some kind of counseling or therapy. This can be done either through the assistance of psychological professionals or through the help of venerable, wise guides. The fact is that most of us are blind to the dysfunctions and quirks that others can see clearly in us. For God's Spirit to show up in our preaching, we must come to grips with our fears and anxieties. All of the things that cause us to feel self-conscious direct the hearer's attention from God and onto us.

Much of the source of ineffective preaching is a simple woodenness that leads to a lack of spontaneity. The preacher needs to be free enough to laugh at thoughts and ideas that may not have come from careful scripting or rigorous preparation. A relaxed approach can be effective only if we have come to grips with, and are no longer intimidated by, the demons that hide inside our souls.

A large number of women and men who go into ministry do so because they have a tremendous need to be needed and/or liked. These factors present themselves in a number of pulpit sins that are all too common. A slavish adherence to a manuscript originates in the trepidation that to move away from the written document might accidentally cause one to split an infinitive, dangle a participle, or come across as too colloquial. The joy the congregation experiences in connecting with the preacher cannot develop if he or she is stiff, wooden, and un-spontaneous. The fear that causes the preacher to disconnect from the hearer is not normally due to some heinous crime, perhaps one of the seven deadly sins of which he or she is bitterly ashamed. Usually it is just the preacher being uncomfortable with himself or herself.

The soil out of which this anxiety emerges is the fear that we are not good enough for the task. After the murder of Abel, Cain feared that if he were found in exile, he would be killed. Preachers who bring self-conscious fears to the preaching moment are unaware that God's calling on our lives is the mark God places upon us to protect us from the anxieties that lurk deep in our souls. Some soul growth work can be done privately through prayer, meditation, and journaling. Other such work needs the feedback of trusted guides, counselors, or prayer warriors. Those who come out of dysfunctional families need to hear impartial voices affirm them as individuals of self-worth. When we were children, the voices of parents were like the voices of gods. We were too young and undiscerning to dismiss out of hand the putdowns and slights of our childhood. We were not mature enough to understand that verbal assaults on our being had nothing to do with us and everything to do with our parents' sicknesses and unresolved issues. When we trust God to send us righteous, godly people who will affirm us and validate our personal value and worth, our preaching will slowly but surely be freed from the self-consciousness that makes the preaching moment more about us than about God. One way to understand 2 Corinthians 5 is that we really must not preach ourselves because if hearers see more of us than God, the message will always be obscured by their focus on our unresolved issues rather than on the illumination they should receive from the goodness and grace of God.

Another insight that helps explain the soul work needed to preach incarnationally comes from systems theory. In a systems theory of organizational behavior, the case is made that people in groups, when confronted by challenge, move into flight or fight mode and thus become anxious and reactive. The way to keep a system from anxious reactivity is for the leader to maintain a non-anxious presence.

A preaching moment is, by definition, an anxious reactive time. The realities of human disobedience, faithfulness, and sinfulness are the constellation in which worship orbits. The degree to which the preacher remains calm, assured, and relaxed determines the extent to which the audience will be the same. Incarnational preaching is rooted in the way the preacher connects with his or her authentic self. The exegesis of scripture, prayer, meditation, and journaling all contribute to a confidence by the preacher that makes him or her much more in tune with the inner life of the spirit. When that spiritual confidence exudes, the hearers experience no disconnection between what the presenter is saying, how it is being communicated, and the person doing the speaking. The sermon then takes on the air of authenticity. A preacher who is more comfortable with self models confidence in God's story of redemption and evidences faith through that confidence. The preacher then stands in the pulpit as a non-anxious presence, and the congregation in turn moves toward being a non-reactive system.

In sum, incarnational preaching is not a technique, an approach to exegesis, or a style of delivery. It is a way to live in a sermon that the sermon becomes who we are, not just what we say. Method acting draws on some of these same principles, although acting and preaching diverge at one critical juncture. Method actors work assiduously on their imaginative understanding of the role being performed. The incarnational preacher is not pretending to wrap self in the flesh of the part. He or she lives the presentation because it is our story and God's story about us. We are the parents, who, like

Abraham, face responses to dictates from God that simply do not make sense. We are the people facing fiery furnaces, whose fears are so extraordinary that the faith to face these challenges needs to be even more extraordinary. We are the disciples who sit around hushed and astonished because, although Jesus is alive, we have acted as if his power was not what he had promised us. Incarnational preaching is where our story and God's story intersect. And by telling our story, we have, in faith, represented the story God has given to us all.

PULPITS WITHOUT PURPOSE

Cleophus J. LaRue

One morning, in a small village at the southernmost tip of India, I sat across the breakfast table from an Indian scholar who had just completed a book on preaching in the Indian context. Upon learning that I taught preaching in an American seminary, he leaned across the table and told me that during his research on preaching throughout the world, he had come to the conclusion that white American mainline preaching was in trouble because it focused too much on process and not enough on purpose.[1] He said he thought that American homileticians tended to focus too much on the how-tos of preaching and not enough on the whys and wherefores. Moreover, he thought Americans were bogged down in form and structure but seriously lacking in biblical depth and substance. While he was much more positive about the preaching of black Americans—especially the preaching of the civil rights era—owing to their proximity to white mainline preaching, he thought blacks were also in danger of adopting the practice of preaching from what he called "pulpits without purpose," a result of preachers who neglect their primary mission—to preach the unsearchable riches of Jesus Christ.

While I cannot speak for Indian preaching, or to the decline of white American mainline preaching, I do believe that if African Americans are not careful, we will indeed be guilty of mounting pulpits without purpose. I believe that the world is changing about us

---

[1] The "mainline" refers to those Protestant ecclesiastical institutions that, for decades, have enjoyed an unofficial "establishment status" in American culture. Related terms for the mainline are "old-line" and "sideline." See Thomas C. Oden, *Turning around the Mainline: How Renewal Movements Are Changing the Church* (Grand Rapids: Baker Books, 2006) 37–9.

so quickly, that we are so caught up in the new and the now, and that we are so faddish to a fault, that it is all too easy to forget our primary reason for standing behind that sacred desk every Sunday morning. I understand that everything changes and nothing stays the same. I understand that there is no single way to preach Jesus. And I know there is nothing wrong with new ways of preaching Jesus, as long as it is Jesus who is being preached.

Anyone who is at all attentive to the present church scene must be aware that in every denominational tradition, new forms of congregational life and new challenges to many long-established church practices are emerging. The signs of change are visible in all areas of church life. Our traditional churches now stand alongside seeker churches, cell churches, mall churches, seven-day-a-week churches, next churches, nondenominational churches, and even parachurches. Whatever we choose to call these new and different— and, in some cases, large and fast-growing—nontraditional congregations, they probably are the most visible and talked about new church forms of the past thirty years.[2] Some say the fact that they are relatively new allows them to be more creative, more cutting-edge, and more open to change than traditional churches. Many a young pastor has run into difficulty trying to move a traditional church along too hurriedly. Some pastors resign in disgust, and some are voted out in disgust. Others stand and fight and take the spoils of victory or the remnants of defeat. Still others simply step down and organize a new work in what they call "a different part of Zion." Suffice it to say, our churches are changing.

Not only are there changes in our churches, but there are also changes in our worship practices, including liturgy, music, and preaching. Although some congregations seek to retain their longstanding traditional liturgical practices, most are in great flux.

---

[2] Jackson W. Carroll, *Mainline to the Future: Congregations for the 21st Century* (Louisville: Westminster John Knox Press, 2000) x; and Alister E. McGrath, *The Future of Christianity* (Malden MA: Blackwell Publishing, 2002) 40–71.

Many congregations, especially those influenced by the "seeker church" movement, have thrown out their traditional liturgical practices in an effort to reach the Baby Boomers and Generation Xers who have left the church in significant numbers in recent years.[3] Still other congregations have kept traditional services intact but have introduced alternative worship as a way to satisfy different constituencies within the congregation. Many are characterizing these services as either *traditional* or *contemporary*.

All around us, churches are experimenting with worship, trying to discover what works and what does not, what will draw people and what will drive people, what will make them come in the first place and come back in the second place. Such experiments with worship frequently lead to conflicts, or so-called "worship wars." In other churches there also have been disputes about traditional language about God. Some say they are uncomfortable with traditional Trinitarian language about God the Father, God the Son, and God the Holy Ghost, preferring instead Creator, Redeemer, and Sustainer. Some even go a bit further, preferring as their Trinity the language of Mother, Lover, and Friend.

Some churches have rewritten many of their old hymns, and some have discontinued certain well-loved hymns that they say are offensive to some because of their language and imagery. Some have rewritten "Amazing Grace" because it has the word "wretch" in it, and they say some people in this day and time may take offense at being referred to as a "wretch."[4] Some churches have discontinued singing "Onward Christian Soldiers" because they say it encourages military aggression.[5] On the other hand, some hold fast to the old hymns, refusing to change one iota. A Presbyterian pastor in

---

[3] Seeker churches are defined as those churches that design their services and programs to attract those who are unchurched.

[4] A wretch is defined as a miserable, unhappy, unfortunate person. Some have replaced it in their hymnals with the word "soul."

[5] Carroll, *Mainline to the Future*, x.

Philadelphia, who refused even to consider a genre of music other than traditional hymns, said he simply could not bring himself to sing what he called "that 7–11 music—the same seven words eleven times."[6]

Pentecostal practices are having a significant impact on African-American congregations in storefronts and traditional churches across the denominational spectrum. As Jackson W. Carroll points out, this neo-Pentecostal movement—especially as manifested in some of the African Methodist Episcopal churches—combines a deep Pentecostal piety with involvement in progressive politics and political activism, including a particularly strong concern for the plight of African-American men.[7]

In recent years there has been an explosion of African-American worship on television.[8] Although being on television in and of itself is not a bad thing, the desire to copy what is seen on television without any kind of theological filter to separate the wheat from the chaff can have a debilitating effect on unsuspecting congregations. Television is, by its very nature, an entertainment medium, and owing to its widespread influence in our lives, we are in danger of amusing ourselves to death.[9]

One night, as I watched a sermon on television, I noticed people walking up to the pulpit area and throwing money at the preacher's feet while he was preaching. I wondered about the theological significance behind that act. Just because you see something on television is no guarantee that there is a theological justification for

---

[6] From an unpublished paper presented at a Homiletical Feast Conference in Tampa, Florida, 10 January 2004.

[7] Carroll, *Mainline to the Future*, x–xi.

[8] Jonathan L. Walton, "A Cultural Analysis of the Black Electronic Church Phenomenon" (Ph.D. diss., Princeton Theological Seminary, 2006). Walton has written a very telling dissertation on the black church and television.

[9] Neil Postman, *Amusing Ourselves to Death: Public Discourse in the Age of Show Business* (New York: Penguin Books, 1985) 4.

the act itself. Without a doubt, television is here to stay, but we must think theologically, critically, and reflectively about its use in our religious experience. It is a medium that has transformed our culture and set us on an uncertain course, and if we are not careful, "TV religion" could become just one of any number of ways that we seek to entertain ourselves.[10]

All of our worship practices are caught up in change. Many church leaders desire to stay relevant by keeping up with the times and trying to stay at the forefront of new ways of worship, while other churches resist change completely. But change is nothing new in black churches. It has been with us in every age, although it has always been difficult to implement change in established, traditional, institutional churches. For example, historians point out that in the nineteenth century, some in the African Methodist Episcopal Church did not approve of organs and choirs, considering them to be the work of the devil. Some clergymen, such as Bishop Henry McNeal Turner, thought the clergy should wear robes to give greater dignity to the worship service. But although AME bishop Daniel Alexander Payne believed that the AME Church should have educated ministers and dignified services, he opposed robes for AME clergy, preferring instead the plain dress of Richard Allen.[11] Moreover, Bishop Payne favored a strict adherence to the worship service outlined in the AME discipline and was, therefore, opposed to dance, song, and spirit possession.

Payne especially disliked the ring shout practiced by some black Methodists, where the participants clapped their hands and stamped their feet until they were overcome by the Holy Spirit, and he also opposed the singing of cornfield ditties such as, "Ashes to ashes, dust

---

[10] Ibid., 114–24.

[11] Stephen W. Angell, *Bishop Henry McNeal Turner and African-American Religion in the South* (Knoxville: The University of Tennessee Press, 1992) 148–49.

to dust, if God won't have us the devil must."[12] Payne thought such rites were "ridiculous and heathenish," and did more harm than good, for in his eyes such carrying on disgraced and corrupted black Christianity. Another controversy was raised during the period after the Civil War when some northern AMEs wanted to drop the word "African" from the AME name.[13] The point I'm trying to make is this: There have always been disagreements about the best way to be the church and to have church in the black church.

Black Baptists have also had their difficulties with change.[14] Gospel music and gospel choirs, for example, cramped the style of many black Baptist churches in the first half of the twentieth century. So offensive was gospel music to some in mainline American black Protestantism that some churches were known to throw out the gospel singers. Michael Harris, in *The Rise of Gospel Blues*, reports that one of the gospel singers who got thrown out of church in the early part of the twentieth century was a woman named Mahalia Jackson. Shortly after moving to Chicago from New Orleans, Jackson joined a group named the Johnson Singers, which sang gospel music throughout the city. But when a Chicago pastor heard this new type of music called *gospel music*, he was so offended that he threw Jackson and her group out of his sanctuary, saying, "Get that twisting and jazz out of this church."[15] On her way out the door, Jackson looked back at the pastor, no doubt in a tone of defiance, and said, "This is the way we sing down south."[16] Still, she was forced to leave the church.

---

[12] Clarence E. Walker, *A Rock in a Weary Land: The African Methodist Episcopal Church during the Civil War and Reconstruction* (Baton Rouge: Louisiana State Press, 1982) 22–4.

[13] Angell, *Bishop Henry McNeal Turner*, 149–50.

[14] See James M. Washington, *Frustrated Fellowship: The Black Baptist Quest for Social Power* (Macon GA: Mercer University Press, 1986).

[15] Michael W. Harris, *The Rise of Gospel Blues: The Music of Thomas Andrew Dorsey in the Urban Church* (New York: Oxford University Press, 1992) 258.

[16] Ibid.

In every age, as new ways of having and being church emerge, there will always be some resistance. In our rich black religious history, a group of congregants who decided to wear pulpit gowns on Sunday met with some resistance. And when another group decided to put a pipe organ in the church, they met with resistance too. There will always be people who try to hang on to the old and others who try to break forth into the new, and both groups mean well. All sides must remember that many find it difficult to keep up with or to become comfortable with rapid and relentless change. Traditional church is an institution, and the nature of institutions is that they move slowly.

What are we to make of all the changes that are upon us now, and how are we to deal with them? First, we need to understand that change will always incite resistance from some congregation members. Anything new or different will rub some people the wrong way, and they will try to resist the change, usually by saying, "But we have never done it that way before around here." Or they will say, "This is a Bible-believing church, and we have a certain way of doing things around here," suggesting that their church traditions strictly follow the scriptures. But neo-Orthodox theologian Karl Barth has reminded us that "there has never been…an intrinsically sacred sociology of the church."[17] No full-blown, biblically mandated way of having church is outlined in the scriptures.

Congregational patterns and practices in Christian churches have not only varied considerably over time, but they have also differed substantially within each given time period. Church practices run the gamut, and they are less and less dictated by denominational beliefs and more and more influenced by the customs we see in churches in our local area or models we pick up at conferences or on television.[18] Sometimes we initiate a change in our churches simply because we don't want the pastor down the street to get too big a jump on us in

---

[17] Carroll, *Mainline to the Future*, 1.
[18] Ibid., 7.

implementing something new that might prove to be effective. But although change will frequently trigger some kind of resistance, we must remember that just because a tradition is long standing does not make it biblical, and just because something is new does not make it unbiblical.

Second, we must also understand that even though some in our congregations will always resist change, some changes are unavoidable in our current, rapidly changing era. We are living in a posttraditional age. The term "posttraditional" does not suggest that we have moved beyond tradition, but that we have moved to a place where inherited traditions are likely to play increasingly less decisive roles in the way we understand and order our lives. Time-honored ways of doing things change, and we have to adjust to that.[19] There was a time when women did not wear slacks to Sunday worship and might be asked to leave the church for attending "the moving picture show." There was a time when black Baptists did not applaud in church; instead, they said "Amen," because applause was considered appropriate for an audience being entertained, not for a congregation engaged in the worship of God. There was a time when some churches held fast to the closed Communion rule, and if you were not a Baptist in good and regular standing in that congregation, you could not participate in the Lord's Supper. There was a time when some churches would serve the Lord's Supper only on Sunday evening, because they said "supper" was an evening meal and was not supposed to be eaten at midday. But things change, and we must learn to separate custom and tradition from the non-negotiables of the faith.

Many people now feel that a variety of traditions no longer carry the weight they once did. People are guided and directed more by an inward authority. No longer do we rely without question on traditional formulae for doing things or on long-established

---

[19] Ibid., 9.

institutions and their representatives to give us directives for living or for how to have and be the church. Today, people rely on themselves and their own experiences to find appropriate ways to respond to the changes and challenges that arise in their lives and in their church experiences, and this approach is likely to continue in the future as well. Change is upon us, and we can no longer exert the kinds of controls over our congregants that we used to use when we could simply tell them, "The church says...."

Third, as we try to deal with the changes and challenges that are upon us, we must never forget whose church it is in the first place. If we forget to whom the church ultimately belongs, we run the risk of preaching from pulpits without purpose. Jesus said, "Upon this rock I will build my church and the gates of hell shall not prevail against it" (Matthew 16:18 KJV). Before we get all hung up about who's up and who's down, who's packing them in and who's barely hanging on, who has correctly perceived which way the winds of change are blowing and who is being left on the steps of yesterday's Holy Ghost headquarters—before we get caught up in all of that, we need to remember whose church it is. I know some people who have been at their posts for so long that they begin to refer to it as "my church." But it really does not belong to us. Throughout Christian history there has been a rhythm to church life and church growth. Church existence and continuation are not solely in our hands; churches come and go, they start up and die out, they rise and fall, sometimes because of what we do and sometimes in spite of what we do.

The missionaries from centuries past, who sailed the seas and traveled through *terra incognita* (unrecognizable territory) to carry the good news of Jesus Christ, did not have near the anxiety we have about what it takes to evangelize the world and to nurture, grow, and develop a church in the midst of changes and challenges. They knew better than so many of us today that they did not have the final say over the church's ongoing vitality and strength, because they knew it did not belong to them. As European missiologist Andrew Walls points out, those missionaries, when seeking to determine the efficacy and effectiveness of their work in Christ, were guided by three tests. I commend those tests to you today.[20] The first was the *church test.* The first sign of the legitimate expansion of the influence of Christ is the presence of a community of people who willingly bear his name.

The second test the old missionaries used to determine the efficacy and effectiveness of their work in Christ was the *kingdom test.*[21] The kingdom test stands for signs of the kingdom of God within your midst. Some church folks do not like signs of the kingdom because they are more interested in attending glorified social clubs than they are in attending to the inbreaking activity of God. But kingdom movements call the church to repentance and to alertness to the presence of Christ within.

Finally, there is a third test the old missionaries used—the *gospel test.*[22] The gospel test asks, "Is Jesus Christ being preached within our midst?" You cannot build a church on announcements and extracurricular activities. No church can be stronger than the gospel it proclaims. The church lives in her preaching—always has and always will.[23] Luke said Jesus came preaching and teaching. Paul said it pleased God through the foolishness of preaching to save those who believe. P. T. Forsyth said that with its preaching, Christianity stands or falls.[24] Paul Scherer said Jesus always knew what came first, so with confidence he turned to those around him and said, "As ye go…preach."[25]

---

[20] Andrew F. Walls, *The Cross-Cultural Process in Christian History* (Maryknoll NY: Orbis Books, 2002) 8–26.

[21] Ibid., 13–18.

[22] Ibid., 18–25.

[23] John Bright, *The Authority of the Old Testament* (Grand Rapids: Baker Books, 1989) 162.

[24] P. T. Forsyth, *Positive Preaching and the Modern Mind* (London: Independent Press, 1907) 1.

[25] Paul E. Scherer, *For We Have This Treasure* (Grand Rapids: Baker Books, 1943) 21.

In our ever-changing world, if we forget to preach Jesus Christ and Him crucified (1 Cor. 2:2 ESV), we run the risk of preaching from pulpits without purpose even though our churches may be on the cutting-edge of change and bubbling over with worldly success. To preach Jesus in this post-Christian world is our most compelling challenge and charge, for there is still power in the heart of that old story: For us—he took a birthday in time and was born of suspect parentage, in a third-rate country, in a forgotten corner of the world. He gave up his rightful seat in that celestial city that was older than Eden and taller than Rome. He traded in the praises of angels for the sin-stricken curses of lost humanity. He traded in a crown for a cross and a throne for a tomb. For us—Jesus the judge was judged in our place. And for us—God raised him from the dead on the third day. Amen![26]

---

[26] Karl Barth, *Church Dogmatics*, vol. 4 of *The Doctrine of Reconciliation* (Edinburgh: T. & T. Clark, 1956) 211–82; and Edward R. Hardy, ed., *Christology of the Later Fathers* (Philadelphia: Westminster Press, 1954) 359–70.

GARDNER TAYLOR AS
INTERPRETER OF SCRIPTURE:
HERMENEUTICS FOR HOMILETICS

William H. Willimon

In *Life Together*, Dietrich Bonhoeffer addresses the matter of reading scripture in light of the preacher's primary calling to serve the Word. Bonhoeffer warns us preachers that interpretation of the Bible for preaching is a perilous task full of possibilities for sin:

> It may be taken as a rule for the right reading of the Scriptures that the reader should never identify himself with the person who is speaking in the Bible…. It will make all the difference between right and wrong reading of the Scriptures if I do not identify myself with God but quite simply serve Him. Otherwise I will become rhetorical, emotional, sentimental, or coercive and imperative, that is, I will be directing the listeners' attention to myself instead of to the Word. But this is to commit the worst of sins in presenting the Scriptures.[1]

After reading and listening to a couple hundred of Dr. Gardner Taylor's sermons, I can say with confidence that Dr. Taylor never commits Bonhoeffer's "worst of sins." He is a right reader of scripture par excellence, a mark of Dr. Taylor's obedient service to the Word. In all of his sermons, Dr. Taylor manages to be ever so much more interested in the Word than in himself or even his listeners.

I heard Dr. Taylor preach "In His Own Clothes" at the Hampton Institute some years ago.[2] It was electrifying. I present this analysis of that sermon not only because "In His Own Clothes" is a

---

[1] Dietrich Bonhoeffer, *Life Together*, trans. John W. Doberstein (San Francisco: Harper & Row, 1954) 55–6.

[2] Gardner C. Taylor, *Quintessential Classics 1980–Present*, vol. 3 of *The Words of Gardner Taylor*, comp. Edward L. Taylor (Valley Forge: Judson, 2000) 116–21.

fairly typical example of a Gardner Taylor sermon, but it also reveals his methods of hermeneutics for preaching.[3] His text was Mark 15:20 (KJV): "And when they had mocked him, they took off the purple from him, and put his own clothes on him, and led him out to crucify him."

The first thing we note is that, contrary to the way most of us were taught to interpret scripture, Taylor's sermon focuses upon one single sentence within a very dramatic biblical story. Actually, the sermon focuses upon one phrase in that sentence. Taylor begins his sermon with the astounding statement that "short of the cross itself and the betrayal by Judas, what the soldiers did to Jesus may well have been the most humiliating part of our Lord's suffering and death for you and me." Bypassing the soldiers' mocking and even their leading Jesus away to crucifixion in the one-sentence text, Taylor instead focuses upon the way Jesus was dressed for crucifixion.

He begins in a measured, thoughtful tone of voice: "We may be greatly wronged and deeply hurt, but we want to be able to hold on to our human dignity, the feeling that we are a part of the family of humankind." In spite of great humiliation, some people nobly "hold their heads high and bear bravely whatever it is they must go through." Very quickly, the preacher hones in on his major connection with the text:

> There is something uniquely cruel in being laughed at and mocked, set apart from one's fellows and made the target of ugly jibes, cruel comment, and cutting laughter. One of the most painful and sinister weapons used historically against black people in this country was mockery and ridicule. Physical features were caricatured and exaggerated, and so the large white-lipped, wide-eyed, blackened faces in minstrel shows became the notion of the way black people looked and acted. I am not far enough from the experience of that

---

[3] I was also helped by the sermon and commentary by Dr. Taylor in Don M. Wardlaw, ed., *Preaching Biblically: Creating Sermons in the Shape of Scripture* (Philadelphia: Westminster Press, 1983).

mockery to be able to see the art in this kind of thing, no matter what the occasion may be. The purpose of the foot-shuffling, head-scratching, wide-grinning, ghost-frightened darky was to ridicule, scorn, and humiliate.[4]

Note that Taylor uses Jesus, in his humiliation, as a kind of figure, a type that connects with us in our humiliation, particularly the humiliation heaped upon African Americans. After having linked the ancient text with our modern humiliation, he turns directly to the humiliation of Jesus: "Far crueler than our own experience was the kind of scorn and ridicule that the soldiers heaped upon our Lord on the night leading to his crucifixion.... They blindfolded our Lord and then struck him a stinging slap in the face taunting, 'Prophesy. Who is it that smote thee?' Then they did spit in his face to add to the outrage. Each new assault seemed designed to outdo the last.... They scourged the Lord."[5] The preacher then goes into some detail about the horrors of the Passion: "The victim was stripped down to the waist and was stretched against a pillar with hands tied. The instrument of torture was a long leather strip, studded with pieces of lead and bits of bone. The whip left lashes, and the lead and bone tore out chunks of flesh. Some died under the lash.... After the Lord was scourged with the lash, sentence was pronounced, and it was the sentence of death by crucifixion, the most awful and painful of the Roman methods of execution. Lifted on a cross."[6]

The preacher's voice rises and energy increases, almost hammering the gory details into the hearts of his listeners:

> The condemned slowly died, and the vultures and carrion crows might dispose of the body.... These men were hard-bitten professional soldiers who chafed at their unpleasant assignment in such a hot, fly-ridden place as Palestine and among all of those

---

[4] From Taylor's sermon "His Own Clothes," in *Quintessential Classics 1980–Present*, 116.

[5] Ibid., 116–17.

[6] Ibid., 117.

strange and offensive people. They took their pastime and sport when and where they could find them. One of their pleasures was to taunt and torture convicted criminals who cringed before them like cornered and helpless animals. The Son of God was turned over to them, and they went to work with their cruel jibes.[7]

Note how, in this first third of the sermon, the preacher has coaxed his congregation into the sermon by connecting the text with their context and also by providing rich details. And yet the preacher wisely refuses to say too much about the historical background of Roman crucifixion, for to do so would be to risk presenting this event as an historical episode. The preacher clearly wants to claim that this excruciating experience is a prefiguring of a type of experience that some of his listeners have actually had themselves. Thus, his brief historical details amplify the story in a way that makes it vivid.

Now, Taylor settles upon that which fascinates him most about the text, slowing down, stressing each word to be sure that his congregation shares in his exegetical discovery, making sure that they know this is the key to the sermon:

> The whole detachment gathered in their barracks with the Savior of the world before them.... They stripped him of his clothes. Having picked up some thread of the charge that Jesus claimed to be a king, they jammed a reed in his hand to mock a scepter, plaited a crown made out of thorn bush for his brow, and flung around the Lord's shoulder an old, faded red tunic, the scarlet cloak that was a part of the parade uniform of the Roman soldier. All this was done to mock him.... "We will be your devotees and subjects, King Jesus. Look at us kneeling before you," and then their loud, uncouth laughter rang and echoed through the barracks.[8]

Deftly, the preacher moves from the mock robe that was put on Jesus to the mock honor that many pay to Jesus today. One can hear

---

[7] Ibid., 117–18.
[8] Ibid., 118.

the touch of irony in his voice: "There are still many who put cloaks of imitation honor and false respect on the Lord Jesus as surely as those soldiers put their old scarlet robe on the Savior.... One says, 'I respect and honor Jesus. His golden rule is enough religion for anybody.... I admire his life and believe it to be a thing of beauty. His ethics are splendid principles.'"[9] The preacher thus turns the tables on the mockers, doing some mocking of his own: "It is all right for those who need it, but I do not go to church. I do not feel and need of it, really. And so saying, they feel they have delivered themselves of something very profound...chic and fashionable. Well, I had a dog, a blooded Doberman pinscher, who never went to church either.... He was a dog. Now, what is your reason?" Taylor turns his derision upon some in the church who "put garments of mock royalty on the Lord and who call his name but who feel no deep loyalty to him, no crowning and controlling love for the Lord, who has done so much for us. You may see them now and again in church, now and then among the people of Christ. They throw their leftovers at the Lord who made us all, as one would toss scraps to a pet dog. They are neither hot nor cold, and to such the word of the Revelation applies, 'I will spew thee out of my mouth'" (Revelation 3:16 KJV).

The preacher ventures even further, out beyond the bounds of the congregation to a consideration of the moral failings of the na-tion: "'What is wrong with us as a nation?' One word is the answer: godlessness.... In the wager of a gun lobby and money that stops congressman from passing a gun law. In greed and bigotry and the attitude 'anything goes.' In lies and deceit.... Listen to any national telecast. See how all of our national interest is built around what some self-serving people in Washington do: crime, scams, confusion.... Godlessness! And until we turn to the Lord, it will not get better; it will get worse."[10]

---

[9] Ibid.
[10] Ibid., 119.

And now the preacher turns the text on himself, slipping deftly from the third to the first person: "Have I put fake garments on the Lord Jesus? Have I cloaked the Savior of the world in scarlet robes of pretense, claiming that I honor him as Lord while my heart is far from him?" Then the preacher takes a metaphorical turn that uncovers the richness of the text:

> When the soldiers had tired of their ugly game of ridicule and making sport of the Son of God, they took off the old scarlet tunic and put his own clothes back on him…the final preparation for crucifixion. They put on our Lord his own clothes. And "his own clothes" says worlds to us. We need to see him as he is, "in his own clothes," not mocked and ridiculed by false respect and pious hypocrisy.… Looking at Jesus as he is, we see ourselves as we are.… When we see him in his own clothes as he is, we want to do better.… Jesus in his own clothes going to Calvary did his best.… In his own clothes he went to Calvary and made everything all right, not temporarily all right but for always.… The crooked way has been made straight; we may arise and shine for light is come. It is all right now.[11]

The sermon ends in grand crescendo, as Taylor shouts, overflowing with emotion, and the excited congregation rises to its feet and begins to clap thunderously and to shout in celebration with him:

> We shall see him yet in other clothes.… Christ shall appear no longer with an old, faded red cloak around his shoulders, no longer mocked by soldiers, no longer wearing simple garments of this earth. Every eye shall see him. We will see him as heaven's King, victor over death, hell, and the grave, the admired of angels. Every eye shall see him. Ten thousand times ten thousand and thousands and thousands of angels and the triumphant sons and daughters of God will escort him. His raiment will outshine the sun. And on his vesture, his clothes, a name will be written, "King of kings and Lord of lords."

---

[11] Ibid., 120–21.

Shall we not shout his name who has lifted us to heights sublime and made us his own people forever?[12]

The congregation goes wild with shared jubilation. In all the concluding shouting and clapping, it is clear that the preacher wanted to achieve more, in his biblical interpretation for the congregation, than mere understanding. He wanted nothing less than ecstasy, and he got it.[13]

While the preacher has clearly made it his business to learn about some of the historical details of the text, and to freely share those in his sermon, there is no sense that the preacher feels in any way compelled to answer historical-critical questions about the text. Nothing is allowed to come between the text and the immediate claim of the text upon the contemporary congregation. If anything, the preacher appears to be more concerned with the world "in front of the text," the world of the community of faith today, than (as in historical-criticism) the historical world behind the text. Our challenge in understanding Mark's Gospel, the preacher thus implies, is not one of history (how and when and if these things "really happened"), but rather one of faith (are we willing to follow the same crucified Jesus Christ as Lord now?). Taylor quite comfortably assumes that the biblical story is our story, moving quite easily from the text to our context and then back again, from today's headlines and TV shows to an explosive eschatological vision of the last things and the ultimate triumph of the crucified Jesus Christ as the reigning Lord.

I agree with Warren Stewart's assertion that "the genius of black preaching is grounded in its almost 'intuitive' ability to fulfill effectively and accurately the primary purpose of hermeneutics in biblical interpretation, which is 'rightly handling the word of truth'

---

[12] Ibid., 121.

[13] Henry H. Mitchell shows how this concluding celebration is a hallmark of African-American preaching in *The Recovery of Preaching* (New York: Harper & Row, 1977) 54–73.

(2 Timothy 2:15 KJV)."[14] As Henry Mitchell puts it, "The Black preaching tradition has for generations, even centuries, reached these depths intuitively, almost always without the preacher being aware of how or why."[15] I agree as long as this almost "intuitive" ability is in no way considered to be less than a complex, valid, intellectual hermeneutic.

In his masterful study of the preaching of Martin Luther King, Richard Lischer noted that King's study of scripture at Crozer Seminary, during which King was first introduced to historical criticism of scripture, could not have been "more at odds with his own tradition," attempting to teach King to distance himself from "the alien world of the Bible."[16] King joined other Crozer students in imbibing the notion of "progressive revelation" that had been popularized by Harry Emerson Fosdick. Lischer praises King in particular, for having the good sense to ignore "the method's reduction conclusions," and the African-American church in general, for shunning the historical questions that obsessed historical criticism because "its disinterested objectivity was as useless in [King's] crusade to the nation as it was in the ministry of the African-American church."[17]

This sounds a bit like what Dr. Taylor said in an interview:

> One of the sad parts of the lives of seminary students, and in my own time too, is that they study so much about the Bible and not enough of the Scriptures. I am not sure that you can simply study the Bible and get what I am talking about. I think you can get the raw material out of the Bible, but I think one's own being has to be stamped on, and even more than that, stamped into the Scriptures,

---

[14] Warren H. Stewart, Sr., *Interpreting God's Word in Black Preaching* (Valley Forge: Judson Press, 1984) 6.

[15] Mitchell, *The Recovery of Preaching*, 30.

[16] Richard Lischer, *The Preacher King: Martin Luther King Jr. and the Word That Moved America* (New York: Oxford University Press, 1995) 199–200.

[17] Ibid., 200.

and the Scriptures have to be stamped into your personality so that one lives in the then and the now, in the Scriptures and then in what's going on now. And I don't think you can ever separate them.[18]

In opposition to the Enlightenment stress on objectivity and stepping back from the biblical text, Lischer says, "The African-American tradition of interpretation, however, did not pass through the Enlightenment, never enjoyed the leisure of disinterested analysis, and therefore did not distance itself from the Bible or settle for moral applications. The cruelties of slavery made it imperative that African Americans not step *back* but step *into* the Book and its storied world of God's personal relations with those in trouble."[19] African Americans, stripped of their history, were "*enrolled* in the world of the Bible."[20] "In His Own Clothes" demonstrates the propensity of African-American preaching to do "eyewitness" hermeneutics in which the preacher becomes an eyewitness, reporting to the congregation, thus enrolling them in the story. George Lindbeck notes that faithful biblical interpreters think that "no world is more real" than the world that is created by the biblical text. The world of the scripture has the capacity to "absorb the universe."[21] Gardner Taylor demonstrates this world-absorbing dynamic in his sermon.

Gardner Taylor takes a seemingly small detail in a grand narrative—Jesus was dressed in the dress of a fake king, then clothed in his "own clothes"—and works this up into a lively word that sets a

---

[18] Cleophus J. LaRue, ed., *Power in the Pulpit: How America's Most Effective Black Preachers Prepare Their Sermons* (Louisville: Westminster John Knox Press, 2002) 149.

[19] Lischer, *The Preacher King*, 200.

[20] Henry Mitchell says that "Greatness in the Black pulpit almost invariably involves the ability to get into parts, especially biblical parts, with as much ease and impressiveness as one gets into one's own." Mitchell, *The Recovery of Preaching*, 38.

[21] George A. Lindbeck, *The Nature of Doctrine: Religion and Theology in a Postliberal Age* (Louisville: Westminster John Knox Press, 1984) 117.

congregation aflame. Is this making too much of a rather small scriptural detail? Harvard's James L. Kugel has shown that early biblical interpreters saw the entire Bible as a "divinely given text," a rich, though mysterious literature that provoked constant discovery of hidden meanings.[22] Modernity attempted to reduce scripture. Modern biblical study, says Kugel, a Jew, is indebted to Spinoza, who stressed that scripture mainly means what it literally means. The simple, literal reading is to be preferred over the symbolic, metaphorical meaning. Scripture, said Spinoza, is not eternally true but rather is historically true, true for some people living at a certain time but without much relevance for our time. Spinoza thus paved the way for historical criticism's treatment of scripture as a source of information about ancient cultures. Modernity rendered us into scripture's examiners rather than scripture's hearers. Scripture as the medium for a living, speaking theological agent is lost in favor of scripture as a kind of archeological dig.[23] Kugel makes the somber verdict that "modern biblical scholarship and traditional Judaism are and must remain completely irreconcilable."[24] Could the same be said of modern biblical scholarship and Christianity?

Taylor once confided, "I find myself in the same situation as P.T. Forsyth who said, in his 1907 Lyman Beecher Lectures that although as a scholar he agreed with the historical critics who did not believe in 'verbal inspiration' of Scripture," and yet as a practicing preacher Taylor, along with Forsyth, had so often witnessed the

---

[22] James L. Kugel and Rowan A. Greer, *Early Biblical Interpretation* (Philadelphia: Westminster Press, 1986).

[23] My stress on divine agency is, of course, indebted to Karl Barth, whose *The Word of God and the Word of Man*, trans. Douglas Horton (Glouser MA: P. Smith, 1978) recovered for modern theology a sense of the Word of God as active and alive.

[24] James L. Kugel, *How to Read the Bible: A Guide to Scripture, Then and Now* (New York: Free Press, 2007) 681.

fecundity and activity of scripture that it was a constant struggle for him not to believe in the verbal inspiration of scripture!²⁵

Thus, Taylor's interpretation is metaphorically rich and imaginative, encouraging the congregation imaginatively to place themselves within the biblical story because of what Taylor believes about the nature of scripture. Far from treating the Bible as a repository of allegedly "biblical principles," or as a collection of ancient precepts that are sometimes helpful today (the bane of much preaching today), the preacher subsumes the congregation into the biblical story. Taylor obviously assumes that, in dealing with biblical literature, he is dealing with a symbolically charged, readily available, and revelatory text. Even seemingly insignificant details of the text—Jesus' clothes—are assumed by the preacher to have sweeping revelatory significance. There is no attempt to pare the text down to the one "right" reading, the primary message, the essential thing—all dearly beloved methods of biblical interpretation in the modern age. Rather, there is sheer enjoyment in the story, great wonder and delight in seeing the text fulfill the expectations of the community—this ancient story is our story.

As Taylor puts it, "I think the first thing a person ought to do is just go back and start reading the scriptures imaginatively. One ought to walk up and down the street on which the scripture lives. Catch the atmosphere, cloudy or sunny. What are the neighbors like? Get into it that way."²⁶ Or as Bonhoeffer put it,

> The church's encounters with Scripture, force everyone who wants to hear to put himself, or to allow himself to be found, where God has acted once and for all for the salvation of men. We become a part of what once took place for our salvation. Forgetting and losing ourselves, we, too, pass through the Red Sea, through the desert, across the Jordan into the promised land. With Israel we fall

²⁵ Gardner Taylor, "Shaping Sermons by the Shape of Text and Preacher," in Wardlaw, *Preaching Biblically* (Philadelphia: Westminster Press, 1983) 137–52.

²⁶ LaRue, *Power in the Pulpit*, 148.

into doubt and unbelief and through punishment and repentance experience again God's help and faithfulness. All this is not mere reverie but holy, godly reality. We are torn out of our own existence and set down in the midst of the holy history of God on earth. There God deals with us, and there he still deals with us, our needs and our sins, in judgment and grace. It is not that God is the spectator and sharer of our present life, howsoever important that is; but rather that we are the reverent listeners and participants in God's action in the sacred story, the history of the Christ on earth. And only in so far as we are *there,* is God with us today also.[27]

It is for this reason, scripture's ability to be vividly contemporaneous, that Lischer says that African-American biblical interpretation tended to be "figural" in decoding contemporary events through the figures of the Bible. These preachers avoided biblical literalism, remembering when such biblical interpretation was born (does not the Bible acknowledge slavery? Therefore, who are we to challenge slavery?), remembering how literalism was used against them to justify and defend their oppression in slavery. On the other hand, when white interpreters went "spiritual" in their interpretation, blurring the plain sense of the biblical word, black interpreters went literal—taking scripture's liberating imperatives with absolute seriousness.

Dr. Taylor's biblical interpretation "In His Own Clothes," and indeed in most of his sermons, tends to make heavy use of typology. Typological interpretation claims continuity between figures who appear in scripture and who reappear in history. After noting the use of typology in the preaching of Martin Luther King, Jr., Lischer says that "typology is the most important form of figural interpretation for it allows for the fullest participation of one reality in another. Allegory, which is the assignment of external values to textual figures, plays a less significant role in the same tradition."[28]

---

[27] Bonhoeffer, *Life Together*, 44.
[28] Lischer, *The Preacher King*, 202.

In Taylor's sermon, Jesus' clothes become a typology for who Jesus was and for that mission from which the world could not dissuade him. The world tried to dress up Jesus in a way that was not who he was, and the world attempts the same with us. Taylor weaves contemporary struggle into the biblical narrative and marvels with wonderment about how the biblical narrative illuminates contemporary sin and evil. Thus, his typological interpretation enables Taylor to probe the lives of his listeners.

As Lischer says, for the black preacher "there is nothing in the Bible that one does not meet here in the world. And there is nothing in this world—no cruelty, stupidity, struggle, or marvel—that one cannot find in the pages of Scripture."[29] Laid over our contemporary culture and the present-day church, through figural and typological interpretation, the biblical text becomes a lens, a way of bringing certain things into focus. African-American experience of humiliation and ridicule is claimed as a creative means whereby the text is unlocked and allowed to speak. The preacher's notation, early in the sermon, of the congregation's experience of such oppression serves as a way of inviting them into the interpretive process by implying that some within the congregation may indeed know more about the message within the text than the preacher himself knows. This is a delightful homiletic device.

In his sermonic encounters with scripture, Gardner Taylor never questions whether or not scripture wants to be contemporaneous. I wonder if some of our biblical interpretation is, even if unconsciously, an attempt by us preachers to disarm scripture, to rob the Bible of some of its contemporaneous clout. Walter Brueggemann says that the question before us preachers is not the vague, metaphysical speculation, "Is God's word powerful?" Rather, in regard to God's word, the question is this: Dare we embrace the word's contemporaneity, God's "present-tense struggle among us"?

---

[29] Ibid., 201.

Brueggemann then asks, "Can the synagogue and the church, the communities committed to this prophetic claim, do the hard, demanding intellectual, rhetorical work that will construe the world according to this memory and this discourse?"[30] In "In His Own Clothes" Gardner Taylor deftly, adeptly led a congregation to construe the world according to this ancient text, thus making God's story their own, without modifying the story to suit the confines of the limited modern worldview.

To be sure, Taylor explicitly relates the sermon to the needs and the culture of his predominately African-American congregation. But what happens when one is not speaking to a congregation full of people who have actually known the racial injustice of which Taylor speaks? And what happens to the sermon when it is in the hands of a preacher who is less attentive to, and adoring of, the biblical text than Gardner Taylor? When does "relating the text to the congregation" become an abuse of the biblical text because few in the congregation have experienced such injustice? I wonder if much of today's preaching, mostly in the therapeutic mode—consumed with the trivialities of middle-class North American culture, obsessed with narcissistic preoccupations in which scripture has no interest, unbearably positive, practical, and accessible—is a commentary on the audience we have unwittingly created for the sermon.

Too much allegedly "culturally sensitive" preaching appears merely to pander to the concerns that everyone brought to church with them, despite Jesus, concerns that are of no concern for scripture. The sermon is reduced to helpful hints for happier lives; the gospel is pared down to what already consumes us rather than prophetically judging those concerns. The gospel is commended as the solution to problems that do not appear to trouble the gospel (a meaningful life, happiness, a sense of deeper purpose for us as individuals, and so forth).

---

[30] Walter Brueggemann, *Texts That Linger, Words That Explode: Listening to Prophetic Voices*, ed. Patrick D. Miller (Minneapolis: Fortress Press, 2000) 41.

In the first part of Taylor's sermon, when he speaks of the humiliation that people sometimes suffer at the hands of their fellow humans, we expect him to launch into a sermon on our humiliation and how we are to overcome it—the therapeutic gospel. But Taylor is too enamored with the text itself, too Christologically grounded, to indulge the sermon in merely human, therapeutic, self-help matters. He quickly returns to The Story, to the Christ who stands before us, clothed in mock clothing of empire. Taylor's sermon thus becomes a critique of much contemporary preaching that too quickly leaps from the text to our narcissistic context and becomes distracted from scripture's essentially theological concerns as theology is jettisoned for interests that are mostly anthropological.

As I expected, when I listened to the tape of "In His Own Clothes," I was jolted by the remarkable difference between Taylor's sermon as actually recorded and as the sermon appears on the printed page. His sermon in its oral presentation considerably raised the bar on good biblical interpretation. The text was not simply interpreted, but allowed to live, permitted to do its work among the congregation, performed, enacted. It was good to be reminded that Mark's Gospel is a sermon before it is abstract theological exposition. It is safe to assume that the dynamic of a preacher adopting a congregation into the narrative of the Passion is closer to Mark's originating intent than most that passes for biblical interpretation today. As Paul says, "Faith comes through hearing" (Romans 10:17). It is the sound of proclamation on human lips that saves, not its appearance on the printed page.[31] Scripture wants more than mere intellectual assent; it demands performance, embodiment, incarnation.

---

[31] James Simpson, *Burning to Read: English Fundamentalism and Its Reformation Opponents* (Cambridge: Harvard University Press, 2007) shows well that evangelical Christians made a mistake in privileging the written over the oral word, in allowing print to dominate their encounters with scripture. Print, by its nature, excludes, circumscribes, and limits what is communicated to itself. The embrace of the "literal sense" of scripture led to modern Fundamentalism and its problems, a sort

Cleophus J. LaRue recalls, as a first-year seminary student, being invited by Gardner C. Taylor to preach at Concord Baptist Church of Christ in Brooklyn.[32] On the way to the sanctuary for the service, Taylor turned to LaRue and asked how many years he had served his church in Texas before heading to Princeton Seminary. He told him ten years. Taylor shook his head in disapproval, saying, "I don't think I would have stepped down after so many years." LaRue said that Taylor's comments crushed him because Dr. Taylor had been influential in his desire to further his theological education.

Taylor thought about what he said for a moment and then turned to LaRue once again and said, "I take that back. You've done a noble thing and God will not allow himself to remain in your debt. God will honor your sacrifice."

In a way, Gardner Taylor's life illustrates the truth that God pays God's debts. Any sacrifices we make, or risks we take, when we step into the ministry of the pulpit, when we dare to put ourselves in service to God's word, are paid back generously by God. God gives response. Despite all the reasons why people may not hear, people *do* hear, step forward, and respond. The biblical text speaks, summons,

---

of a-theistic reading of scripture. Fundamentalism implied that scripture could speak because it was true whereas the church has always taught that scripture speaks only through the power of a God who enables it to speak. As Simpson says, "Only oral or unwritten context made sense of written texts"(233). In other words, scripture, printed and static, must have preaching to make it make *theological* sense.

[32] As recounted in *From Midterms to Ministry, Practical Theologians on Pastoral Beginnings*, ed. Allan Hugh Cole, Jr. (Grand Rapids: Eerdmans, 2008) 152.

and lives now. Christ walks among his people. The satisfaction that we preachers receive in that is a sign of God's generosity in paying back God's debts to us.

PART THREE

VOICING TRUTH WITH GRACE

WHEN PREACHERS PREACH,
DOES GOD SPEAK?

David G. Buttrick

The title of the chapter asks a seemingly odd question, but a controversy that blew up in the 2008 presidential primary prompts the question. I refer to the flap that ensued when someone swiped about thirty seconds from a Jeremiah Wright sermon and put the video clip on Internet display. The full sermon rambled a bit but was basically biblical. Wright argued that human governments, including our own government, can never be an ultimate trust. He listed things that might make us sing "God bless America," but also listed injustices done that could prompt a different lyric, "God damn America." The sermon concluded by calling for us to put our trust in Jesus alone. The video clip, however, featured only the brief but passionately delivered contrast, "God bless" and/or "God damn" America. Public disapprobation flared, demanding that candidates denounce such language. One candidate was obviously hesitant; the other was outraged, saying in effect, "If I heard a preacher so speak, I would leave the church." The reaction was extreme, for leaving a church is never easy; over time, churches become family. Yet behind campaign rhetoric, there was a deeper issue. Could God have been speaking through Jeremiah Wright's sermon, though the words offended America's proud patriotism? In black churches, congregations appear to believe that preachers speak God's word. In white congregations, such conviction seems to have faded, but still may be residually present. The stir over Dr. Wright's sermon raises the issue. So, again, when preachers preach, can God be speaking to us?

To be honest, most twenty-first century thinkers would reject the claim. They would label the statement blatant anthropomorphism. How could God, a mysterious, unseen, transcendent Consciousness, speak, particularly in something as antiquarian as a robed preacher declaiming from a pulpit? In our modern age, such a notion boggles most minds. Yet Reformation theologians such as Martin Luther so argued; and before the Reformation, early Christians so believed. To push back further into the historical past, obviously the Hebrew Bible tells of God putting a message on the lips of awed Isaiah, and before him Jeremiah, and before him Elijah, all the way back to Moses. So, clearly, the Bible backs the proposition: God can and does speak through chosen human voices. These days, the scientific community would surely be skeptical, and, to be truthful, most of us find the whole idea somewhat odd. To begin with, the notion of a transcendent God (with vocal chords?) speaking our languages strains credulity. Then, to add complexity, the idea of God speaking words through chosen human voices is simply too much for us here-and-now practical people. The notion brings to mind Edgar Bergen, a ventriloquist, with a cheeky, wooden Charlie McCarthy on his lap, pulling strings to make the lips move while he himself gives speech to the dummy. To us semi-rational people, the whole idea does seem preposterous.

Of course, lest we forget, were we *not* taught in Theology 101 that God's power is unlimited? Surely our great God—who created the universe, who flung stars into space and shaped continents in the midst of primal seas, who dreamed up such wonders as the bounding kangaroo and the astonishing duck-billed platypus—knows no limits. Almighty God's unlimited freedom prohibits the word "can't." Presumably, if God wanted to speak, God could speak in any language. The possibility may seem anthropomorphic, attributing human speech to a God who is, by definition, transcendently "Other;" nonetheless, in some manner God must be able to transmit meaning to human creatures. From the first chapter of Genesis where, with a mighty "word," God calls the cosmos into being, to the last chapter of Malachi, which concludes with God promising us a future, Hebrew scriptures venture the notion of a talking God. Nowhere is the claim more blatant than in the prophetic tradition. In the prophetic calls, God promises to be with prophets, supplying words for them to speak. No wonder Isaiah celebrates God's wondrous word: "For as the rain and the snow come down from heaven, and do not return there until they have watered the earth, making it bring forth and sprout, giving seed to the sower and bread to the eater, so shall my word be that goes out from my mouth; it shall not return to me empty, but it shall accomplish that which I purpose, and succeed in the thing for which I sent it" (Isaiah 55:10–11). Did you catch the phrase, "My word that goes out from my mouth?" The Hebrew Bible seems to believe in a conversing God.

What about the Christian scriptures? After Pentecost, obviously the situation has changed. The gathered community has received the Spirit, *a Spirit of prophecy*, promised by the prophet Joel: "In the last days, it will happen, God says, that I will pour out my Spirit upon all flesh, and your sons and your daughters shall prophesy, your young men shall see visions, and your old timers dream dreams. Even on my men slaves and my women slaves, in those days I will pour out my Spirit; and they shall prophesy" (Acts 2:17–19).[1] Though the whole Christian community possessed a prophetic Spirit, some special roles were soon defined in the life of the community, roles determined by a distribution of the Spirit's gifts (1 Corinthians 12:6–11). Paul picks out a pattern: "God set up the community, so first apostles, second prophets, third teachers; then all with gifts of leadership, with gifts of healing, helpers, officials; all who speak with tongues" (1 Corinthians 12:28). Notice that when it came to speaking, there were apostles, the chief first-century preachers, but additionally there were prophets and

---

[1] Citations from Christian scriptures are my own translations.

teachers. Were the apostles preachers who delivered and defined the faith, while prophets discerned the way in which faith addressed particular situations that communities might encounter? Did teachers then explore the faith, often drawing on traditions of Israel?

The Christian prophets are intriguing.[2] In 1 Corinthians 14:4, Paul draws a line boldly between prophecy and tongues: "Those who speak in tongues build themselves up; those who prophesy build up the community." Subsequently, Paul advises, "Let two or three prophets speak and others discern" (14:29). After all, in the Spirit the community can discern, weighing words of prophecy, assessing their insights and validity. In Paul's discussion, prophets appear to be congregational members. Other sources seem to suggest that, later, some prophets became itinerant, gaining wider influence as they visited other congregations. But what is most important to our discussion is that prophetic oracles were thought to be the continuing voice of an ascended Jesus. As a result, messages from the prophets have been woven into our Gospel records as words of Christ. Notice again that we are dealing with people who, in the Spirit, believed they were speaking with the voice of the risen Jesus Christ.

As Christian communities gradually became churches with a usual patterned life, did prophecy die down? When the apostles died off, did prophecy pass away as well? No. Early Christian preachers seem to have incorporated Paul's list of speakers into one office. They were apostolic as they passed on the church's faith, but insofar as they spoke to changing situations with insight, they incorporated the prophetic calling as well. Of course, in the Spirit congregations were still to weigh the spoken words they heard in light of the gospel message.

---

[2] Two scholars have studied the prophets in early Christianity; see David Aune, *Prophecy in Early Christianity and the Ancient Mediterranean World* (Grand Rapids: Eerdmans, 1983) and M. Eugene Boring, *The Continuing Voice of Jesus: Christian Prophecy and the Gospel Tradition* (Louisville: Westminster John Knox Press, 1991).

Since the beginning of the twentieth century, we have witnessed the rise of redaction criticism. Scholars are able to delineate early texts from later texts, early records of Jesus' words from subsequent additions. It is likely that many of the additions derive from unnamed Christian prophets. Their words, weighed by the communities of faith, were understood to represent the continuing voice of Christ and thus were incorporated in early collections of Jesus' words—parables, teachings, and controversial sayings.[3]

If we turn to the Reformers, we find the tradition continuing. To Luther as to Calvin, when a faithful preacher speaks, the preacher is the voice of God! Luther insisted that the church was a "mouth house" and not a "pen house."[4] Listen to Luther announce God's speech: "Hear, brother: God, the creator of heaven and earth, speaks with you through his preachers.... God himself, is speaking."[5] Dennis Nygren sums up Luther's theology of the pulpit: "Luther's God is not an impassive deity of the Greeks, but an ever-present deity who hides in human speech, who is active in preaching through human voice. Accordingly, the faithful hearers will respond: 'Pay attention, we are hearing God's speech.'"[6] For Luther, preachers were called to announce the *gospel* message. Yes, insofar as the Bible contains good news of the gospel, scripture may be labeled the word of God as well. But, for Luther, God's primary mode of communication is a spoken word.

---

[3] Boring, "Part Three: Prophetic Sayings of the Risen Jesus in the Gospels," *The Continuing Voice of Jesus*, 189–272.

[4] *Luther's Works*: American Edition, 55 volumes. Edited by Jaroslav Pelikan and Helmut T. Lehman (St. Louis: Concordia Publishing House and Philadelphia: Fortress Press, 1955-1986). See companion volume p. 63 for Church Postil 1522.

[5] WA TR 4, 531, no. 4812. D. Martin Luther Werke: Kritische Gesamtausgabe, Tischreden. 6 vols. (Weimar: Hermann Böhlaus Nachfolger, 912-1921).

[6] Dennis Nygren, "Theology of Preaching in Martin Luther," *Themelios* 28/2 (Spring 2003): 48.

John Calvin differs from Luther because he begins with scripture as the word of God, and then turns to address the subject of preaching. But he is as insistent as Luther in asserting that preachers are "the very mouth of God."[7] In his *Institutes*, Calvin writes that "[God] deigns to consecrate to himself the mouths and tongues of men [sic] in order that his voice may resound in them."[8] God's choice of human vocal chords is a sweet concession to our human frailty: "[God] prefers to address us in human fashion through interpreters in order to draw us to himself rather than to thunder at us and drive us away."[9] For both Reformers, a talking God addresses us by setting his message on the lips of chosen preachers.

Nicholas Wolterstorff, in discussing the whole idea of a talking God, has established a series of useful analogies.[10] At the outset, he is careful to limit his discussion to *illucutionary* statements, phrases that are speech-acts, commanding, ordering, or prompting actions.[11] For example, there is the case of a presidential proclamation that some staff member drafts and a president signs. The drafted words go down in history as the president's own declaration.[12] There are more everyday examples: When a boss dictates a letter, a secretary types his spoken words, word for word. But often the boss will say to send off a letter to so and so and say such and such. In this case, the secretary writes words that, presumably, the boss will peruse and approve with a signature. But if boss and secretary have worked together for some

---

[7] "John Calvin," in *Homilies on I Samuel XLI* (Copus Reformatorium XXXIX) 705.

[8] "John Calvin," in vol. 2 of *Institutes of the Christian Religion*, ed. John T. McNeill, trans. Ford Lewis Battles (Philadelphia: Westminster Press, 1960, 1977): 1018.

[9] Ibid., 1018.

[10] Nicholas Wolterstorff, *Divine Discourse: Philosophical Reflections on the Claim That God Speaks* (Cambridge New York: Cambridge University Press, 1995).

[11] Ibid., 37.

[12] Ibid., 38.

time, when she opens the mail, the secretary may simply answer obvious letters and then submit them for authorization. She writes what she thinks the boss would say, and does so as much as possible in his style. To push the process further, a boss leaving town may ask a secretary to write to several people and to sign the letters for him. We might move matters further and suggest that someone who knows the boss by reputation could compose a statement saying what he supposes the boss would say in a given situation, and do so without any actual authorization. Subsequently, the boss might hear about the statement and, without an authorizing signature, let it speak for him.[13]

Wolterstorff sees all these structural analogies happening in scripture and early Christian literature. But with the rather developed skills of an analytic philosopher, he defends the basic notion of God's communication through chosen human voices. He insists that though there is a distinction between dictated words and words spoken but not formally authorized, one way or another, God's messages are delivered.

Wolterstorff then turns to chase down examples of authorization.[14] For example, an ambassador is permitted to speak for a president in certain limited ways. In day-to-day affairs, the ambassador speaks for the president unless a situation arises that pushes the limits; the ambassador must then get in touch with the president for further advice and authorization. Wolterstorff finds that the analogy explains odd prophetic passages in which a prophet speaks for God but includes some "I" language from God as well. Wolterstorff worries his analogies in many different ways, finding repeated insight into biblical and early Christian tradition.

Obviously, we can apply his logic to preaching. Some years ago, the splendid homiletician Fred Craddock wrote a little book titled *As*

---

[13] Ibid., 38–42.
[14] Ibid., 42–57.

One without Authority.[15] His concern: We are offended by high-pulpit declamations, robed in an aura of divinity. Preachers are human beings. We are bound to agree that preachers have no intrinsic authority. Nevertheless, we must not forget that they are in a way authorized by God. As Paul puts it, "We are ambassadors for Christ" (2 Corinthians 5:20). So though we have no personal authority, and need not pose as angelic messengers singing high-flown prose, still we are under authorization—and not by ecclesial agency alone. Further, insofar as inevitably we speak to situations with prophetic urgency, we sometimes do so with a sense of direct commissioning. We may not burn inwardly as Jeremiah did, but perhaps we do feel impelled by the Spirit. At other times, all we have is a general sense of responsibility, knowing that we do speak in God's name. Though Craddock is quite right in insisting that we have no intrinsic authority, is there not a theological possibility to keep in mind? *God might be speaking in our speaking!*

Now let us switch focus and talk about listeners, beginning with the following example: Some years ago, a young woman I know was faced with a decision. Would she, a southern girl, pack up and go to graduate school in New York? She was frightened at the prospect, but in church on Easter Sunday, she heard a preacher preach on the fearful women at the tomb, who were told to go and tell the news of the resurrection. The preacher's sermon echoed a phrase: "Don't be afraid; just go!" The words did seem to speak directly to her need. She packed up and went off to graduate education in New York. Her story is not as singular as it may seem. Again and again, Christians do seem to feel that they have received divine messages designed for them personally, messages from God delivered via human voices.

---

[15] Fred B. Craddock, *As One without Authority: Essays on Inductive Preaching* (Enid OK: Phillips University Press, 1971). Subsequent editions have been published by Abingdon Press (Nashville) and Chalice Press (Saint Louis).

Recall St. Augustine, who, in a period of some personal distress, overheard school children running down the road beside his residence sing-songing a teacher's phrase: "Tolle lege, tolle lege" ("Take and read, take and read"). Immediately, Augustine picked up the scriptures and read what seemed to him a message from God: "Not in reveling and drunkenness, not in lust and wantonness, not in quarrels and rivalries. Rather, arm yourselves with the Lord Jesus Christ, spend no more thought on nature and nature's appetites." Augustine, reciting words of scripture, added, "I had no wish to read more and no need to do so. For in an instant, as I came to the end of the sentence, it was as though the light of confidence flooded into my heart and all the darkness of doubt was dispelled."[16]

In these cases, what are we dealing with? Both people were in crisis, confronted with a decisive moment in their lives. Both had some basic knowledge of Christian faith; even if uncertain, they did believe in God. Still more, both had some respect for the words they heard as possible words of God. The woman's father had been a preacher, and she had come to regard sermons, at minimum, as something important having to do with God. But Augustine was definitely predisposed, for he had heard the story of St. Antony:

> I had heard the story of Antony, and I remembered how he had happened to go into a church while the Gospel was being read and had taken it as a counsel addressed to himself when he heard the words, *'Go home sell all that belongs to you. Give it to the poor, so that the treasure you have shall be in heaven; then come back and follow me.'* By this divine pronouncement he had at once been converted to you."[17]

---

[16] *Confessions*, VIII, 12. Also, see *The Works of St. Augustine: The Confessions*, John E. Rotelle, O.S.A. ed. (New York: New City Press, 1997) 193.

[17] Ibid., VIII, 12.

So both people heard the spoken words with some predisposition to receive them as significant. In each case, the words seemed to address their inner turmoil with a command that resolved doubt and opened a path into the future: "Don't be afraid; go!" and "Tolle lege." How can we understand such stories? What can we say? Were these moments simply subjective happenings, accidents of speech colliding with particular needs within persons of faith? Most likely, we could classify them as personal and, possibly, as psychologically interesting. But just to be quirky, let's mention a theological question that can never be answered with certainty: In view of the need and the outcomes, was that great improviser God involved? Did God, in effect, authorize the commanding words?

Let's drift back to the Jeremiah Wright video clip used during the 2008 primary presidential campaign. The clip was, of course, a nasty campaign ploy. Wright was slandered, his thirty-five years of ministry impugned, his denominational affiliation called into question. In a personal press conference, his anger was obvious. But the episode did underscore a profound difference between the African-American church-going community and much of the Caucasian church-going community. Most black pastors believe that God has called them to preach, much as were prophets in the Hebrew Bible. They have been picked out and sent to speak God's message. What's more, their congregations share the same understanding. The phrase that Martin Luther King, Jr. used, "I've been to the mountain top," was instantly grasped by African-American listeners as a preacher's metaphor. King meant that, like Moses, God had given him a message to speak; in effect, God set words on his lips. The notion that when faithful preachers preach, congregations may hear the voice of God is still resident in the black church.

So what has happened to the same tradition in white churches? Yes, most ministers do have a sense of calling, and they do believe that they are to speak on *behalf* of God. But do they understand their call within the prophetic model? Do they see themselves as an Amos or a Jeremiah? Would they identify with Moses coming down from the mountain? Probably not. We mainline types have been ordained and installed in pulpits by denominational judicatories; and though acting for God, as we all know, denominational judicatories seldom look much like God. These days, most mainline clergy are apt to embrace a therapeutic model for ministry. They do not define ministry within a prophetic model; more significant, neither do their congregations. Are ministers merely institutional servants? Perhaps to most mainline congregations, that's exactly what they are. No wonder the prophetic voice has largely disappeared from mainline pulpits! And no wonder that Jeremiah Wright's words could seem utterly alien!

The Christian gospel is good news. Essentially, it is a message of God's undeserved free love for us wayward human beings. Of course, the gospel message includes an emphatic announcement of forgiveness. Still more, the context of the message is a table set for us with wine to share and bread to break. Christianity puts a table in the midst of every congregation where we can feast as God's new humanity, citizens of God's social order, what Jesus named the "kingdom of God." And there's the rub! There is still a big difference between Jesus' images of kingdom and contemporary life in the United States. Thus, the good news of the gospel has a prophetic edge. Maybe church-goers demand a feel-good gospel, but without the call to citizenship in God's new social order. No wonder we mainline types were offended by a clipped-out phrase from a prophetic sermon. Lately, the prophetic voice of Jesus has been silenced in most white congregations.[18] And few of us who preach suppose a God who wants to speak through our words.

---

[18] A few years ago, I contributed an essay to a volume titled *What's the Matter with Preaching Today?*, ed. Mike Graves (Louisville: Westminster John Knox Press, 2004). I came to the conclusion that "the matter with preaching today" was a

Here's a little personal postscript: Some years ago, I was teaching a seminar for doctoral students in homiletics. One student tossed in a surprise question: "Who do you think is the best preacher in America today?" I answered, "Gardner Taylor." Looking around at a seminar room largely filled with white faces, I was not surprised that the class looked baffled—we are so racially isolated one from another. But an African-American student, after laughing a little, told the class all about Gardner Taylor.

A week later, I showed up at the seminar armed with no more than a few paragraphs from a Gardner Taylor sermon. I went to work and did a complete rhetorical analysis, parsing every sentence, every word. I noted the sounds of words, charting how the sounds were distributed in relation to subject matter. I pointed out internal vowel rhymes, some matters of syntax. I noted how speeding up or slowing down language established rhythms. I spent nearly two full hours on the analysis of Taylor's stunning language. When we were done, the class was convinced that Gardner Taylor was a brilliant preacher whose range of gifts was truly astonishing. Then the African-American student added, "But you've got to hear him. He's like the voice of God!" Having gone to hear Dr. Taylor whenever I could, I nodded in agreement, "Like the voice of God."

---

general silence of the pulpit when the United States launched a wicked, preemptive war in Iraq. Preachers had lost prophetic courage.

ANOINTED WITH FIRE
THE STRUCTURE OF PROPHECY IN THE
SERMONS OF MARTIN LUTHER KING, JR.

Richard Lischer

One intuitively associates Gardner C. Taylor, whose lifetime of ministry is recognized with thanksgiving in this volume, with the preaching of Martin Luther King, Jr., for two reasons. The first is biographical. Taylor was a longtime friend to the King, Sr., family. Young Martin grew up amidst the company of preachers in a rhetorically charged atmosphere of homiletical connoisseurship. Some of the greatest twentieth-century representatives of the African-American tradition in preaching passed through the doors of Ebenezer Baptist Church during "young Mike's" childhood. Later, when Martin, Jr., had become the leader of the American civil rights movement, Taylor was deeply involved in the effort to raise money and offer support in any way possible. Together, King and Taylor worked to link a Baptist coalition to the civil rights movement and in 1961 helped found the Progressive National Baptist Convention.

The second connection between the two men is homiletical. Taylor is widely acknowledged as one of King's most important mentors and pulpit role models. I have written elsewhere about Taylor's stylistic and theological influences on King, as well as their differences. Rhetorically, "the Taylor style relies on a voice like a pipe organ; its stunning vocal range produces an equally impressive emotional range but one that never degenerates into posturing or histrionics. Taylor is able to achieve profound emotional contact through his natural timbre;…in comparison with the most acclaimed preachers, Taylor's high baritone is purer, his low more richly resonant, and the mastery of his vocal instrument more complete."[1]

Theologically, Taylor's decades of full-time parish responsibility have evoked from him a broadly evangelical approach both to the word of God and the human condition. Unlike King, whose sermons are informed by a generous dose of theological liberalism, Taylor's sermons are marked by a balance between political liberalism and theological evangelicalism, the latter expressed by his greater attention to doctrine and biblical interpretation. Everything, he says, is conditioned by the plight and the hope of the black experience in America. And, indeed, when he takes on the subject of race, Taylor's sermons often flash a sense of the ironic that is absent from King's preaching. Yet, in Taylor, one also hears greater reverence, if that is the word, for the biblical text and particular attention to Christian character, which are the marks of pastorally inflected prophetic sermons.

Both are widely considered "prophetic" preachers—Taylor in ways that are oriented to a pastor's duties in a congregation, King more aggressively and politically so. In what follows I want to sketch the structure of prophecy in King and by doing so illumine the same tradition in Gardner C. Taylor. The first difficulty we face is the absence of an accepted definition of prophetic preaching. The word "prophetic" frequently acts as a cover for the preacher's anger or current political commitments. It often focuses exclusively on social critique, which is but one important dimension of the prophet's manifold vocation. Prophecy is too often confused with the word of one righteous preacher deposited upon the heads of an unsuspecting congregation. It was for these reasons and others that at the height of the Vietnam War a theologian at Yale called for a "moratorium on prophetic preaching." His frustration is easy to understand, but ours

---

[1] Richard Lischer, "Gardner C. Taylor," in *Concise Encyclopedia of Preaching*, ed. William H. Willimon and Richard Lischer (Louisville: Westminster John Knox Press, 1995) 466.

is a generation that has been schooled in the prosperity gospel and other forms of cheap grace. We cannot afford a moratorium on prophecy these days.

Prophetic preaching consists in speech and symbolic actions that follow the implications of God's holiness and revealed acts to their most concrete, vivid, and public conclusions. What is whispered in closeted places of fear and suffering, the prophet proclaims from the housetops. Prophecy begins in dissatisfaction with the present state of things—King's refrain was, "Let us be dissatisfied"—and ends in the imagination of an alternative future.

The prophet is the consummate outsider. Whether a court prophet like Isaiah or a bomb-thrower like Jeremiah, all prophecy eventually entails conflict with the most powerful regimes and myths of its day. One cannot draw a straight line from Martin Luther King, Jr., to Barack Obama, as if the latter stands in succession to the former, for they held/hold different offices. One spoke truth *to* power; the other embodies that power with all its possibilities for good or evil. The president is a potential audience to the prophetic word. Prophecy, therefore, may have dangerous consequences for the one who utters it. In *Stride toward Freedom*, King identifies suffering as the most important characteristic of the prophet: "Any discussion of the role of the Christian ministry today must ultimately emphasize the need for prophecy. Not every minister can be a prophet, but some must be prepared for the ordeals of this high calling and be willing to suffer courageously for righteousness."[2]

No prophet is self-appointed, but the question is, "Who is the boss?" Early in his ministry King made it clear to his congregation at Dexter Avenue Baptist Church in Montgomery, Alabama, that he did not work for them. In many of his sermons he minimized the congregation's role as a mediator of the divine call. He defiantly insisted, "I got my guidelines and my anointment from God

---

[2] Martin Luther King, Jr., *Stride toward Freedom* (New York: Harper, 1958) 210.

Almighty. And *anything* I want to say, I'm going to say it from this pulpit."[3] And yet the church did offer pervasive definition to his prophetic self-understanding. The prophetic function is assumed in the African-American church because the church is locked in tension with white institutions. Its suffering and hope are experienced six days a week and duly registered every Sunday. The prophetic vocation, therefore, is the expected vocation for any leader in the African-American church. Thus, before he became a civil rights leader King had already taken his place in the tradition of black church protest that included Richard Allen, Henry Highland Garnet, Henry McNeal Turner, Reverdy Ransom, and many others.

The wise rabbi Abraham Heschel said it is a mistake to identify prophecy with a moral idea or to misidentify the prophets as guardians of morality. In his classic *The Prophets,* he insists that the prophets do not care that the people have broken the moral law, the law of decency, or even the Ten Commandments. Their sin is that they have violated the majesty of God, whose holiness alone can evoke worship and acts of mercy that are worthy of God.[4] Heschel would have seconded the comments of Amos Wilder, who dismisses sanctions that are ultimately based on self-interest, such as rewards and punishments, as unworthy of prophetic obedience. The true sanction for behavior—the "essential sanction"—is nothing less than the essence of God: "I am the Lord your God." "Be ye perfect as your Father in heaven is perfect."[5]

Martin Luther King, Jr., did not explicitly ground his prophetic demands in the holiness of God, but in what amounts to the same thing, the righteousness of God. In his sermonic narration of his own

---

[3] Martin Luther King Jr., "Guidelines for a Constructive Church," *A Knock at Midnight* ed. Peter Holloran and Clayborne Carson (New York: Warner Books, 1998) 111.

[4] Abraham J. Heschel, vol. 1 of *The Prophets* (New York: Harper, 1962) 217.

[5] Amos N. Wilder, *Eschatology and Ethics in the Teaching of Jesus* (New York: Harper, 1939) 47, 57ff.

call, which occurred more than a year into his first pastorate—his so-called "Vision in the Kitchen"—he remembers hearing a voice tell him, "Preach the gospel, stand up for the truth, stand up for righteousness."[6]

In King's mind, holiness was closely associated with God's righteousness, and that righteousness expresses itself in acts of liberation. Thus, God's history with Israel is an essential sanction for King's prophetic message. King's proto-liberationist message is grounded in the exodus from Egypt. Although he did not preach frequently on the exodus account, its message of the liberating God underlay much of what he had to say. In more than one of his sermons, King cries, "Whenever God speaks, he says, 'Go forward!'" Deliverance is the figure in the historical carpet; he reprises it in his accounts of colonialism in Africa and the struggle for civil rights in the American South.[7] Rhetorically, no matter what their text, King's sermons reflect the weariness with captivity (evidenced in the fatigue and discouragement of the preacher), the people's growing dissatisfaction (the pace quickens), expressions of outrage or pure rage, a sense of passage, the breakthrough to hope, and the final celebration of this hope as a form of encouragement for the congregation. In this formal sense, virtually all of King's sermons are "exodus-speak"—prophetic messages of deliverance and hope.

A third and final warrant for prophetic speech was the ministry, death, and resurrection of Jesus, and especially his ministry. King typically encouraged clergy to perform a ministry like that of Jesus, who began in the temple or synagogue but then went out into the streets where he engaged in acts of mercy and justice. Eventually, King merged his message of suffering with the model of Christ's ministry and spoke increasingly of his own ministry as the

---

[6] Clayborne Carson, ed., *Symbol of the Movement, The Papers of Martin Luther King Jr.,* (Berkeley: University of California Press, 1992) 114.

[7] See Richard Lischer, *The Preacher King: Martin Luther King Jr. and the Word That Moved America* (New York: Oxford University Press, 1995) 210–17.

embodiment of the Lord's. While there was much to imitate in Jesus' outreach to others, even more was to be gained by conforming one's life to the divine pattern of death and resurrection.

What is the anatomy of a prophetic sermon? Despite its direct derivation from God, prophetic speech (humanly speaking) originates in the prophet's profound awareness of and sensitivity to suffering caused by injustice. Thus, it originates in discernment. It entails re-cognition of terrible discrepancies that many religious people take for granted. Heschel writes, "The world is a proud place, full of beauty, but the prophets are scandalized, and rave as if the whole world were a slum."[8]

The divine compassion places God in the midst of the human predicament. The prophet, as God's representative, mirrors God's own pathos of which Heschel speaks so eloquently: "[God] is also moved and affected by what happens in the world, and reacts accordingly. Events and human actions arouse in Him joy or sorrow, pleasure or wrath. He is not conceived as judging the world in detachment. He reacts in an intimate and subjective manner, and thus determines the value of events."[9]

Given God's involvement with the world, it is not surprising that the emotion most characteristic of the prophet is not rage, but grief. Jeremiah gives full expression to his grief: "My anguish, my anguish! I writhe in pain! Oh, the walls of my heart! My heart is beating wildly; I cannot keep silent" (Jeremiah 4:19). In his last Sunday morning sermon, preached at the Washington National Cathedral, King recounted his recent visit to Marks, Mississippi, located in Whitman County, the poorest county in America, where he saw "hundreds" of black children with no shoes to wear, who were subsisting on berries and wild game: "I must confess that in some situations I have literally

---

[8] Heschel, vol. 1 of *The Prophets*, 3.
[9] Abraham J. Heschel, in vol. 2 of *The Prophets* (New York: Harper, 1962) 4.

found myself crying."[10] The prophet's grief reflects the tragically needless separation of God's people from the gifts of their creator. Such a separation can have no good outcome; it will produce nothing but suffering.

The prophets also rage against the willfulness and obstinacy of those who contribute to suffering in the world. In King, the rage came late. After years of building bridges toward those who opposed him, he began to react angrily toward deepening poverty, white liberal backlash, and Vietnam. Something in him turned. Most of the denunciations the media has unearthed in Jeremiah Wright had an earlier life in King's sermons, though in King they are almost always delivered with a note of prophetic sadness. In 1967 he sorrowfully indicted America as a racist country founded on a racist compromise. He accused it of genocide against Native Americans. In comments on Vietnam, he said his own country was the greatest purveyor of violence in the world. He wondered out loud whether African Americans should celebrate the approaching bicentennial since the promise of America had never been fulfilled in their lives. The title of his last sermon, which because of his death he never preached, was "Why America May Go to Hell."[11]

The prophet is a compulsive truth-teller. He translates the pathos of sorrow or anger into the logos of hard, factual analysis. As Walter Brueggemann has shown in *The Prophetic Imagination*, the prophet begins by naming the evil. What King's opponents called southern folkways in housing, education, and entertainment, the prophet names "segregation." What white Christians labeled freedom of assembly in matters of religion, King names "hypocrisy." Military superiority and today's fixation on security the prophet would have surely named "idolatry." What the Klan called the maintenance of civil order, the prophet names "terrorism."

---

[10] "Remaining Awake through a Great Revolution," *A Testament of Hope*, ed. James M. Washington (San Francisco: Harper & Row, 1986) 272.

[11] See Lischer, *The Preacher King*, 157–62, 300–302.

Following Brueggemann's analysis, we can appreciate how prophetic speech destabilizes the myths of a dominant regime or culture.[12] What are these myths? That "we" are God's chosen people; that God expects us to defeat our enemies; that with God's help we can dominate the world benevolently; that freedom has no limits; that anyone can make it in America; that people are poor because they don't want to work; that those who suffer did something to deserve it; that all people are equal; that justice is blind; that this country is a melting pot; that you can have it all; that America is great (as Tocqueville said) because America is good.

The prophet can only say no to these sentiments by contrasting them to something better, purer, or more eternal. Telling the truth may involve many types of rhetorical proofs, ranging from history to sociological analysis, but for the prophet and the Christian preacher the truth is always grounded in the essential sanction of God's nature and revealed will. In his final sermon King said, "We're going to win our freedom because...the eternal will of the almighty God [is] embodied in our echoing demands."[13] Thus, the prophet has very few texts. He or she focuses on God's revealed will and the church's duty in light of that will: righteousness, deliverance, covenantal love, grace, community, reconciliation, the hope of peace, the family of humankind. King preached prophetically on these and other themes. He dwelt on two in particular: God's perennial act of deliverance based in the exodus and the divine imperative to love one another. One of his most creative innovations was to inject Christian love into the discourse of social resistance. In his controversy with the black nationalists, he insisted that God wants all people to be free, but not "by any means necessary."

The prophet is a public theologian. It is the unparalleled extent to which King was able to transfer the sacred themes of synagogue

---

[12] Walter Brueggemann, *The Prophetic Imagination*, 2d ed. (Minneapolis: Fortress Press, 2001) 21–58 and *passim*.

[13] "Remaining Awake," 277.

and church into the public arena that entitles him to the prophetic mantle. Religion has always taken part in public discourse in America. The question has never been, "Do religion and politics mix in American culture?" Rather, it is, "What kind of religion will it be?" Some religious leaders have made their mark by trimming and restricting the key categories of prophetic religion; others, like King, have spent their lives expanding the same themes, such as the image of God, justice, and reconciliation, in order to give them wider political application.

The prophet speaks in a timely fashion. He or she is forever answering the question, "What time is it?" Historical exegesis is the easy part of preaching; what comes more wrenchingly is the contemporary meaning of the text. The preacher asks and answers her own question: What is God doing *now*? Bonhoeffer's famous question contains the seeds of prophecy for any sermon: "Who is Jesus Christ for us today?" That is, who is the Christ? What does he mean *pro nobis*, for us? What would he have us do today? One Sunday, King addressed the perennial eschatological question, "When is the day of the Lord?" His eschatological answer: "When Mississippians quit killing civil rights workers."

In his "I Have a Dream" speech, King spoke of "the fierce urgency of now." Forty-five years later, Barack Obama used the same phrase with which to address a new era and a different set of moral and political problems. Both uses of the phrase illustrate what Aristotle called *phronesis*, the aptitude for discerning not the eternal verities but what is true and best for *this* particular time and place. Such wisdom characterizes the pastor, prophet, or anyone who proclaims the word of God in a timely fashion.

That discernment applies to the style and language of the message as well. Prophetic speech employs a mixed rhetoric—down to earth in terms of its human audience yet sublime in its reflection of God's holiness. Ezekiel poses the dilemma of the American prophet: "For you are not sent to a people of foreign speech and a hard language…whose words you cannot understand" (Ezekiel 3:5–6). Although the revolutionary Frantz Fanon insisted that any liberator must adopt a different language than the oppressor's, American religious reformers have generally pursued justice by means of their inherited religious vocabulary. King not only employed the great and well-known themes of the Bible, but he peppered his sermons and speeches with the clichés of civil religion as well. His early rhetorical strategy was to achieve the identification of black aspirations with mainline religious and political sentiment. And it worked—to a point.

But as he did it, King was quietly training the resources of the prophetic tradition against the complacency of those who assumed they were its custodians. It was a magnificent rhetorical strategy: by focusing on the great themes of biblical religion, he united an army of supporters among believers of all races and traditions, and at the same time he skillfully isolated the opponents of these broadly held values. Only when his opposition hardened and the isolated opponents began acting like a majority did he revert to the more primal method of confrontation. He was no longer the seer speaking from the heights of the Lincoln Memorial. In Memphis he said, "God sent us here to say to you that you're not treating his children [the sanitation workers] right." In another sermon he said that America's "hands are full of blood."[14]

Given the magnitude of the problems the prophet faces and the majesty of his revealed message, any hint of introspection, self-absorption, or emotional purgation has no place in prophetic discourse. When King spoke of himself in a sermon, it was always to make a larger point. For all his rhetorical talents, he himself remained hidden behind and subservient to the speaker's mask. By today's standards he told relatively few anecdotes, but even his narratives were grounded in the larger story of God's deliverance of a people.

---

[14] See Lischer, *The Preacher King*, 157–62, 177, 181–82.

He was never diverted from the main plot. What Heschel says of the biblical prophets is a perfect description of King's technique: "The prophet seldom tells a story, but casts events."[15]

King cast events by deploying large, public metaphors and figures of speech. He created pictures big enough that everyone could find a place in them. The sheriff's deputies became "the iron feet of oppression." Those who deserted the cause of freedom dwelt in "the dark chambers of pessimism." The ups and downs of the movement were transformed into "the sunlit paths of inner peace" or "the dark and desolate valleys of despair." King also used sharp language from which qualifications and second thoughts were cleanly removed. He did not say, "It seems to me" or "In my opinion." He avoided the passive voice and the subjunctive mood. He was rarely conversational. Instead, he crafted proverbial antitheses, such as "We've allowed our technology to outrun our theology" or "If a man hasn't found a cause worth dying for, he's not fit to live"—expressions that sharpened his message and enhanced its authority.

The prophetic function for which King is most famous is the envisioning of an alternative reality. The prophet is a *seer*, one who sees things others cannot quite make out. Moreover, the prophet sees in priestly fashion *on behalf* of others who wouldn't mind seeing but whose eyes are dimmed by the cataracts of hopelessness or hate. When the people of Israel despaired of their freedom, it was Isaiah who saw on their behalf a desert with a great freeway running through it. With the people of God languishing in terminal exile, it was Ezekiel who saw a cemetery come to life. In a segregated nation, King was given to see a reality that was still hidden from our eyes: black children and white children playing together, and their parents sitting at a table and treating one another as kin. In spring 1963, with the city of Birmingham in chaos and its jails bursting with black teenagers, King came to the Sixteenth Street Baptist Church and gave

---

[15] Heschel, vol. 1 of *The Prophets*, 7.

a speech on love, which he ended with a vision of hope and reconciliation in "a New Birmingham." Isaiah would have been proud.

King's prophetic witness was burned into the soul of the nation before it flamed out and was extinguished. Gardner C. Taylor's exercise of the prophetic was of a more ecclesial nature. It was rooted in one Brooklyn congregation and took the form of one sustained ministry of pastoral care and preaching. His calls for justice in America were necessarily balanced by the pastor's duty to provide moral guidance to his flock. In a 1969 sermon, Taylor spoke as a prophetic pastor when he said, "Nothing is more tragic about the long season of injustice in this country than what it has done to so many young people and to their hopes and aspirations. At the same time, no disadvantaged young person ought to let the delinquencies of society make a delinquent of him. I know the problems such young people face, but I know the answer also: 'In all thy ways acknowledge him, and he shall direct thy path.'"[16]

Eleven years older than King, Taylor's witness continues to instruct and inspire forty years after his young friend's voice was silenced. Together, they endure.

---

[16] Gardner C. Taylor, *The NBC Radio Sermons, 1959–1970*, vol. 1 of *The Words of Gardner C. Taylor*, comp. Edward L. Taylor (Valley Forge: Judson Press, 1999) 73.

A GOOD MAN SPEAKING WELL:
THE HOLY RHETORIC OF GARDNER C.
TAYLOR

O. C. Edwards, Jr.

A festschrift is supposed to honor the person to whom it is presented, but I must confess that it is a far greater honor for me to be asked to contribute to this one than any that Dr. Taylor will receive from having my essay included, even though I intend to praise him highly.

I cannot claim to be well acquainted personally with the honoree, although I have met him and have had the privilege of hearing him preach once or twice. We have even written a small book together, one of the volumes in an early series of Fortress Press's *Proclamation* homiletical aids.[1] I had the responsibility for the exegesis and Dr. Taylor that for the homiletical interpretation, but I am afraid that he had little opportunity to make use of my exegesis because I was late getting it in and he had to go ahead without me, which was probably just as well.[2]

---

[1] O. C. Edwards, Jr., and Gardner C. Taylor, *Pentecost 3*, from series *Proclamation 2, Aids for Interpreting the Lessons of the Church Year,* ed. Elizabeth Achtemeier, Gerhard Krodel, Charlie, P. Price (Philadelphia: Fortress Press, 1980).

[2] When reading his sermons, I looked out for any that may have been written near the time of our *Proclamation* volume on a passage that we had commented on to see if he had followed his own suggestions, but found only one overlap between what he said in a sermon and what he had written in our little book, a quotation from Alexander Maclaren, *Pentecost 3*, 64, and *Sermons from the Middle Years, 1970–1980*, vol. 2 of *The Words of Gardner Taylor*, comp. Edward L. Taylor (Valley Forge: Judson Press, 2000) 155. I am indebted to Dr. James Dunkly, theological librarian at the University of the South, Sewanee, Tennessee, for

The title of this article is an allusion to the way the great Roman teacher of rhetoric, Quintilian, defined the perfect orator: "The first essential of such an one is that he should be a good man, and consequently we demand of him not merely the possession of exceptional gifts of speech, but of all the excellencies of character as well."[3] If moral qualities are required of the generic orator, then *a fortiori* they should be expected of the preacher, however often individual members of both the general and specific categories have fallen short. Happily, in our subject, moral and rhetorical excellence coexist in perfect harmony, and I think it not too much to say that it shows in his face. He glows with the sort of light that illuminates the face of John Wesley in Nathaniel Hone's portrait hanging in the National Portrait Gallery in London, the sort of expression I think earlier painters tried to indicate by halos.

The purpose of this essay is to analyze what, from a human point of view, makes Taylor's sermons so effective. While no one can know how the Holy Spirit works in the minds of preachers and in the hearts of their congregations, one can observe the techniques by which oral communication achieves its goal. The way I will go about doing that will be first to examine in detail one sermon and then to discuss an aspect of Taylor's preaching that does not appear in that sermon but does appear in many others he wrote. In doing so, I will confine my observations to his words on the printed page. I will say nothing about his delivery, because I have observed too little of it, which is a great deprivation. The little I have seen makes me willing to believe Richard Lischer's claim that Taylor used his voice even better than Martin Luther King, Jr., a high compliment indeed. In comparing the two, Lischer said, "Taylor's high is purer, his low more

---

making available to me the books I needed to write this essay, something he has done for me on many other occasions as well.

   [3] Quintilian, *Institutio oratoria*, Books I-III, trans. H. E. Butler, Loeb Classical Library (Cambridge MA: Harvard University Press, and London: William Heinemann Ltd., 1980) 1:9.

richly resonant, and the mastery of his vocal instrument is more complete than King's."[4]

By the same token, I will not be able to set his sermons in the context of the services of worship at which they were delivered, showing how all the other elements of the event reinforced what was done in the pulpit, for the simple reason that I have never had the privilege of praying at Concord Baptist Church in Brooklyn. I imagine its liturgy has much in common with that of many other large black congregations, but I have not seen so much as a bulletin for one of the services. This means that what I discuss will be much less than the total worship experience, but what I will discuss is worthy of study in its own right.

In order to prepare for this task I read all of Taylor's sermons found in the set of volumes compiled by Edward L. Taylor.[5] To indicate the range of these it will be helpful to list the titles, along with their publication dates.

Volume 1, *NBC Radio Sermons, 1959–1970* [1999]

Volume 2, *Sermons from the Middle Years, 1970–1980* [2000]

Volume 3, *Quintessential Classics, 1980–Present* [2000]

Volume 4, *Special Occasion and Expository Sermons* [2001]

Volume 5, *Lectures, Essays, and Interviews* [2001][6]

Volume 6, *50 Years of Timeless Treasures* [2002]

My problem was how to choose one sermon to analyze from such a rich trove. Edward Taylor favored sermons from volume 4, *Special Occasion and Expository Sermons* (2001), saying that they "demonstrate Dr. Taylor's literary genius to an extent that cannot be offered to a Sunday morning congregation populated by people of

---

[4] Richard Lischer, *The Preacher King: Martin Luther King Jr. and the Word That Moved America* (New York: Oxford University Press, 1995) 50–51.

[5] Although both Taylors grew up in South Louisiana, I have seen no indication that they are related to one another.

[6] I did not read this volume since the works in it are not sermons.

various backgrounds and ages."[7] It seemed to me, however, that my purpose would be best served by choosing an example of his ordinary Sunday preaching, the sort of thing responsible for his reputation. It also seemed best to choose a sermon from his most mature period, one from volume 3 or volume 6, representing the same era, Taylor's last years at Concord before retirement.

The sermon I eventually settled on was "Three Days That Changed the World."[8] I was, however, a little embarrassed to discover from an internal reference that the published version of that particular sermon had been delivered in Dallas rather than at Concord.[9] Recognizing, however, that Dr. Taylor often preached on the road sermons that he had originally developed for his home congregation, I decided that this one that shares so many qualities with the sermons known to have been preached in his regular pulpit that I could stick with my choice.

The text for "Three Days That Changed the World" is taken from 1 Corinthians 15:3–4: "For I delivered unto you first of all that which I also received, how that Christ died for our sins according to the scriptures; And that he was buried, and that he rose again on the third day according to the scriptures." The first thing to be noticed is that Taylor quoted from the King James Version (hereafter KJV). In a way, that is not surprising, because virtually all his texts and other biblical citations are from the KJV, but this is a little surprising today when there are many newer translations. Some of the newer translations can claim to be more accurate translations of the biblical writings, drawing as they do from texts in the original languages,

---

[7] Gardner C. Taylor, *Special Occasion and Expository Sermons*, vol. 4 of *The Words of Gardner Taylor*, comp. Edward L. Taylor (Valley Forge: Judson Press, 2001) xiii.

[8] Gardner C. Taylor, *Quintessential Classics, 1980–Present*, vol. 3 of *The Words of Gardner Taylor*, comp. Edward L. Taylor (Valley Forge: Judson Press, 2000) 188–94.

[9] Ibid., 193.

fuller knowledge of those languages and the contexts in which the documents were written, and employing English in a contemporary idiom rather than a form of the language spoken 400 years ago. Whatever the explanation is, it cannot be charged that Dr. Taylor was unaware of the modern alternatives because he cites them from time to time. I noted references to the Revised Standard and New Revised Standard Versions and the translations of Edgar Goodspeed, James Moffatt, Ronald Knox, and J. B. Phillips. My guess is that Taylor felt the KJV would be more familiar to his parishioners; even more importantly, he might consider its language more elevated and evocative than current English, an opinion in which he would be joined by countless others. It appears to me to be a conscious choice of rhetorical strategy.

To begin our study of what Dr. Taylor was inspired to say on this text, it will be helpful to have not so much an outline of his sermon as something close to what David Buttrick would call his series of move statements, enabling us to follow the logic of the way Taylor developed his sermon. As I understand it, it goes something like this: (1) Spurgeon said that apostolic preaching "set the world on fire" because New Testament preachers always preached the resurrection.[10] (2) One of the chief achievements of Satan is that we preach it only on Easter. (3) R. W. Dale arranged for an Easter anthem to be sung in his church every Sunday. (4) So Taylor wanted to preach on "Three Days That Changed the World." (5) Many days are world changing, such as those of great battles for nations, and of graduations, and marriages for individuals, but Christians have the greatest three days. (6) First, the day of the crucifixion: all theories of the atonement put together are not enough to tell its significance. (7) Scripture has little to say about the second day except for 1 Peter 3:19, which says that Jesus preached to "the spirits in prison."

---

[10] These move statements are numbered for easy reference later. For more reading about "move statements" see David G. Buttrick, *Homiletic Moves and Structure* (Philadelphia: Fortress Press, 1987) 72-73.

(8) Taylor has no warrant to preach a second probation, but could Jesus have preached in vain? (9) The third day should always be in our preaching: the grave held Moses, Abraham, Isaiah, and David, but could not hold Jesus. (10) In every circumstance of life, it needs to be said that Christ lives. (11) That will be the burden of all Taylor's preaching. This is an example of what Edward Taylor meant when he said, "[Gardner Taylor's] message moves toward its purpose as a staircase headed to the top floor of a mansion."[11]

The difference between "moves" and "points" can be noted here. "Move" is a more dynamic concept than "point." If this sermon were outlined in the traditional way, it would be a classical three-point sermon with each of the days being a point and the three points being preceded by an introduction and followed by a conclusion. Thus, the first five moves listed above would be the introduction, the sixth would be the first point, the seventh and eighth would be the second, the ninth would be the third point, and the tenth and eleventh would be a segue of the third point into the conclusion.

Taylor's sermons take their hearers through a process in which each move is developed in a precise way that brings it to life. Many homileticians claim a preacher is ready to preach only when the entire sermon can be summarized in one sentence. But if one sentence says it all, why are those other sentences necessary? The answer is that the truth of the one sentence must be experienced. It is not enough merely to recognize what is being said, much less simply to hear it. That truth must come alive for the hearer. A good sermon leads the congregation through the progressive stages in which it is developed so that at the end its members do not merely understand what is being said, but experience its truth as well. As Taylor himself expressed it, "Jesus kept telling us that the only way we can somewhat grasp the wonderful and unspeakable relation God bears to us and we

---

[11] In his introduction that appears in each volume of *Words*. The words quoted appear on p. 6 of every volume, except vol. 5, where they appear on p. 7.

to him is by illustration, example, by comparison, by 'like.'"[12] He has far more tools to accomplish this, though, than what are usually understood to be "illustrations."

Taylor begins this sermon with a reference to a classic preacher from the past, Charles Haddon Spurgeon. Edward Taylor says that in Gardner Taylor's preaching "can be found a mix that includes a sort of grand nineteenth-century Victorian style, the richness of the African American folk tradition, and a unique interpretation of modern homiletical theory."[13] Taylor himself testifies to the importance of the second of these influences when he says, "Most of the things I talk about are things that have come to me, filtered through my own mind and imagination, from those preachers I heard in my earliest years."[14] The first and third influences are acknowledged in his many references to the great preachers of the past and present. An incomplete list of those cited includes Spurgeon, R. W. Dale, Frederick Robertson, Joseph Parker, John Hutton, Alexander Maclaren (apparently his favorite), John Henry Jowett, G. Campbell Morgan, Arthur Gossip, George Truett, Donald Barnhouse, Harry Emerson Fosdick, Clovis Chappell, George Buttrick, Paul Scherer, James Stewart, Carlyle Marney, and Joseph Sittler. To these could be added Taylor's friends whose preaching he admires, such as Sandy Ray and Vernon Jordan.

The use that he makes of his study of other preachers he indicated in his Beecher lectures when he said, "Any preacher greatly deprives himself or herself who does not study the recognized masters of pulpit discourse, not to copy them but rather to see what has been the way in which they approached the scriptures, their craftsmanship,

---

[12] Gardner C. Taylor, *50 Years of Timeless Treasures*, vol. 6 of *The Words of Gardner Taylor*, comp. Edward L. Taylor (Valley Forge: Judson Press, 2002) 196.

[13] Ibid., p. 6 in most volumes.

[14] Ibid., 225.

their feel for men's hearts."[15] On the rare occasion when he has drawn more fully on the work of someone else, he indicates that dependence by a note saying that he is indebted to the particular preacher for the germ, kernel, or structure of a sermon.[16] This reminds us that Shakespeare borrowed some of his plots, but his use of them was greater than that of those who originated them.

Taylor uses the reference to Spurgeon at the beginning of "Three Days That Changed the World" to get his congregation thinking about what he wants them to consider. Cicero said that the introduction to a speech should make the audience well disposed to the speaker, attentive, and receptive.[17] In the case of Taylor, the favorable disposition of hearers could usually be taken for granted. So for all practical purposes, he needs to use the introduction to get them starting to listen carefully and to being open to applying what the preacher says to their lives. He needs to get them interested and focused.

A study of his sermons shows that he has no one standard way of doing this. Sometimes he will tell a story; sometimes he will start right in interpreting the text; sometimes he will raise a question he wants the congregation to think about; sometimes he will do something else entirely. In this sermon he begins by citing the authority of Spurgeon. He establishes authority by saying that Spurgeon had "a preaching ministry as far as hearers were concerned unrivaled by any pastor in the English-speaking world."[18] The relevance of Spurgeon is made evident by his charge that many churches of Spurgeon's time, unlike those in the New Testament, were "so staid and so chilled." The implication is that the condition still continues. This becomes the problem for which a solution is

---

[15] Gardner C. Taylor, *How Shall They Preach* (Elgin IL: Progressive Baptist Publishing House, 1977) 63–64.

[16] Taylor, *50 Years of Timeless Treasures*, 11, 57, 131.

[17] *Benevolus, attentus, docilis* in Cicero, *De Inventione* I.xv.20.

[18] Taylor, *50 Years of Timeless Treasures*, 188.

sought, a condition that his hearers' church needs to avoid and presumably can avoid by applying the remedy that Spurgeon recommends. That remedy was a homiletical one, but it was not a matter of either rhetorical method or the correct sermon form of taking a biblical text. Rather, Spurgeon said, it had to do with the subject matter of *preaching:* "the reason why the apostolic preaching set the world on fire was that the New Testament preachers always preached on the Resurrection."[19] Taylor then applies the diagnosis and remedy proposed in Spurgeon's sermon to the congregation he is preaching to that day by saying, "I am convinced that it is one of the chief achievements of Satan that we preach the Resurrection only on Easter Sunday, for here is the central truth of the Christian faith. Here is what supremely sets it apart."[20] He adduces further justification for preaching the resurrection by citing R. W. Dale's practice of having an Easter anthem sung in his church every Sunday.

On the basis of the foregoing argument for such proclamation, Taylor announces that he will proceed to preach on "Three Days That Changed the World" and reads as his text the verses from 1 Corinthians (15:3–4) quoted above. This calls for two observations. The first is that his introduction leads us to anticipate a sermon on the resurrection alone, not on the crucifixion, Jesus' preaching to the spirits in prison, *and* the resurrection. The second observation is that his text speaks of our Lord's dying for our sins and being buried and his rising again, but makes no reference to the way that Holy Saturday intervened between Good Friday and Easter. This is to say that to some extent the text is a pretext in that it does not warrant all that is discussed in the sermon. My saying this is not intended as a criticism but rather as a way of pointing to the variety of legitimate uses of scripture in preaching. (It is probably saying also that Taylor decided the subject for his sermon before he chose the text, but he is not by any means the first to do so.)

---

[19] Ibid.
[20] Ibid., 189.

This calls us to consider what he hoped to accomplish in this sermon. One of the things I admire most about Taylor's preaching is that he is not Little Johnny One-note. There are many different purposes that one discovers for his sermons. Some of them seem evangelistic and call for members of the congregation to accept the Lord Jesus Christ as their Savior. Others have a pastoral purpose; it appeared to me that most of the NBC radio sermons preached in volume 1 were aimed to assist those who heard them to go back into a cold world and make it through another week. Another purpose of many entire sermons and of parts of even more is Christian witness against social evils.

There were a number of other purposes in addition to these that Taylor preached to fulfill, but it seems to me that in this sermon his aim is to celebrate the reality of the saving work of Christ as the church understands it, the entire Paschal event. It is kerygmatic preaching, but it is also Taylor's triumphant witness to his own experience of the truth of the gospel, a witness that he expects either to call forth recognition and concurrence in his joy on the part of the congregation or a yearning to share that experience on the part of those who have not yet done so. It is essentially an ecstatic celebration. This is related to Gerald Davis's statement that "closure is rarely found at the end of an African-American sermon. The sermon is open-ended."[21] I cannot say that this is usually the case with Taylor's sermons, but it does seem to apply to this one. That being so, the way he makes each of his three points is essentially climactic, as we shall see below.

Before looking at the three points of the sermon, it is important to note that while three-point sermons were a staple of twentieth-century preaching, they occur infrequently among those found in the volumes of Taylor's *Words*. For instance, in volume 6 we find "God's

---

[21] Gerald L. Davis, *I Got the Word in Me and I Can Sing It, You Know: A Study of the Performed African American Sermon* (Philadelphia: University of Pennsylvania Press, 1985) 80.

Three Great Sabbaths"[22] and "Three Testing Times,"[23] a mere two in a volume of forty-one. It is more common for Taylor to make one point clearly and effectively.

Taylor begins his first point by saying, "The First Day—Friday. A hill shaped like a skull, a corpse, a tomb," summarizing the entire event by a stark listing of three of its elements.[24] Then he raises the question of the meaning of those elements, stating that "some of the noblest minds of these two millennia have wrestled with the meaning of that first day,"[25] and lists some of them: Irenaeus, Origen, Augustine, Anselm, Aquinas, Barth, Tillich, and Luther. He quickly sketches in some of the theories of the atonement: the legal, the moral, and the revelatory. Then he moves on to tell his personal reaction: "As a boy I could not read the account of our Lord's death without tears coming into my eyes, and I still cannot."[26] The rest of the paragraph is vintage Taylor:

> For I know in some way I have never been able to explain that he took a lick that was meant for me. I know that where our slates were all blotched and marred, he made them clean. And I know that he got under a load that I was meant to carry and that where the charges stood against me, he cleared them. If in Eden I see a tree forbidden, at Calvary I see a tree forgiving. If in Eden I see a tree prohibited, at Calvary I see a tree provided. But in some way deeper than I can ever say, he made it all right with my soul. He manumitted the slave's bondage, brought the exile back to his native land, put the orphan at the father's table and called him a child, an heir. I know that at

---

[22] Taylor, *50 Years of Timeless Treasures*, 131–36.

[23] Ibid., 137–42.

[24] The rhetorical figure of *synecdoche*, where a part is substituted for the whole.

[25] Taylor, *50 Years of Timeless Treasures*, 190.

[26] Ibid., 191. In between is a short paragraph about Caiaphas and his vestments and apparently pseudo-nurses in uniforms that I cannot make heads or tails of. I assume this is a topical reference to something anyone not at the service where the sermon was preached would not know about. If so, it would have been humor to draw in the audience.

Calvary that first day, my condition was forever altered and changed, and I am now a child of the royal house. Was it for crimes that I have done He groaned upon the tree? Amazing pity! Grace unknown! And love beyond degree! Well might the sun in darkness hide And shut his glories in, When Christ the might[y] Maker died For man, the creature's sin.[27]

Albert J. Raboteau tells of how the traditional black preacher starts off slowly in his delivery but picks up that pace and begins to chant at the emotional peak of the sermon.[28] He could have gone on to say that even those in the learned tradition who do not chant have climaxes[29] in their sermons. This is remarkably true of Gardner Taylor, of whom Richard Lischer said, "He was one of the few who could generate passion while retaining his composure."[30] One of the characteristics of Taylor's climaxes is a compressed listing of elements. Indeed, the presence of such a list can be an indication that a climax is occurring. An example of such a list occurs in the next to last paragraph of a sermon he preached to the Baptist World Alliance: "We are the community of the responsible, for we are under imperious orders to commit ourselves to his purposes until 'the kingdoms of this world are become'—every bastion of bigotry, every installation of pride, every pocket of rebellion, every rebel frontier, every castle of pretension, every region of false servility must

---

[27] Ibid., 191.

[28] Albert J. Raboteau, *Slave Religion: The "Invisible Institution" in the Antebellum South* (Oxford: Oxford University Press, 1978) 143–44.

[29] I am not using "climax" in the technical rhetorical sense in which the last word in one clause or sentence becomes the first word in the next, but merely to describe the crescendos that occur with such surging power in African-American sermons.

[30] Lischer, *The Preacher King*, 51. In the same paragraph he says, "His was the grand style to which King and many preachers of his generation aspired but never quite attained."

become—'the kingdoms of our Lord and of his Christ; and he shall reign for ever and ever.'"[31]

Another element is his use of the same word or phrase at the beginning or at the end of every clause or sentence in a sequence.[32] This sort of listing occurs at the beginning of Taylor's treatment of Good Friday with the names of the great theologians who have tried to state an adequate theory of the atonement, and occurs in a different way in the short summaries of several of those theories that come next, while the paragraph in which Taylor states his personal sense of the inadequacies of all the theories has examples of succeeding clauses beginning with the same words. And what he says about his inability to cope with this great mystery is the figure of *adynaton*, claiming that it is impossible for one to state the reality adequately. Thus, what Taylor has to say about the crucifixion and what it means for us is the sort of emotional peak that I am calling a climax.

Something else that is characteristic of many of Taylor's climaxes—and those of African-American preaching in general—is the quotation of a hymn such as occurs at the end of his first point in the sermon on "Three Days That Changed the World." The hymns may be spirituals or come from classical Protestant hymnody. And they may be quoted at length or only be alluded to in the way Taylor uses a phrase as a part of his own sentence. I suspect that these allusions are intended to prompt his hearers to remember the whole passage and put its force behind what he is saying.

This may also be a good point at which to observe Taylor's effective use of language. A case in point is his summary of one of the interpretations of the atonement:

> And there is the revelatory doctrine that God revealed the heartbeat of his love at Calvary and at the same time unmasked the

---

[31] Taylor, *Special Occasion and Expository Sermons*, 79.

[32] The repetition at the beginning of clauses is called *anaphora* and that at the end is called *epistrophe* in the technical vocabulary of rhetoric.

powers of evil, pulled off their cloak of honor, and showed them to be a wicked government in alliance with a blasphemous religion turned against the fairest the world has ever seen. For the cross forever reveals the wickedness of men, and we see over and over again conniving political operators joining hands with prostituted religionists to crucify the best the world has ever seen.[33]

This language is part of what Lischer had in mind when he spoke of the "grand" tradition of preaching to which Taylor belongs. In his Beecher lectures, Taylor attributes his skill in this area to parental influence: "I am thankful that I was born to parents who, though not highly educated by today's standards, had a natural feel for the essential music of the English language wedded to an intimate and emotional affection for the great transactions of scriptures. Somehow, in the way they thought and spoke, what is African found a cordial meeting with what is Anglo-Saxon."[34] Please note that I have called his use of language "effective" rather than "impressive." While it certainly does impress as well, there is no indication that he was trying to call attention to his extensive vocabulary. Indeed, I have the impression that as he has matured in his preaching style, his language has become less grand, that he has forsaken any ambition he may ever have had for a reputation for art in order to be unmistakably clear in his proclamation of the gospel.

The second day that changed the world was Holy Saturday. In speaking of it, Taylor uses something like the rhetorical device of *paralipsis*, pretending to pass over something in a way that calls attention to it. While repeatedly insisting that he has no warrant to preach a second probation, he powerfully reveals his hope for one. I find this passage so moving that I wish to quote it in its entirety, making no change beyond italicizing his repetitions of his lack of warrant, his use of "until," and a few other key passages:

---

[33] Taylor, *50 Years of Timeless Treasures*, 190–91.
[34] Taylor, *How Shall They Preach*, 13.

Concerning the second day, the scriptures do not speak much. The third chapter of 1 Peter at verse 19 says "He was freed in the spirit and went and preached to the spirits in prison."[35] Now, *I am not under any warrant to preach any second probation,* the doctrine that gave rise to the whole Roman Catholic doctrine of purgatory.[36] Those of us who have lost kin who did not accept Christ feel sometimes a strange sadness, for *I am among those.* And I do not know the meaning of this cryptic passage that he went and preached to the spirits in prison, *nor do I have warrant to preach a second probation.*

But I do read again the word our Lord spoke about a shepherd. Was he talking about himself? Is he the one who left the ninety and nine and went searching for one lost sheep who had strayed, beguiled by some tempting tuft of grass or led by some inviting waterfall? *Until...I do not know* how long *until* is, and *I have no warrant to preach a second probation,* and I shall not. But *until...*not *until* the darkness falls. But *until...*not *until* the chill of evening comes. But *until...*not *until* briers cut the Shepherd's hands. But *until...*not *until* thorns cut and lacerate the feet. But *until... Until... I do not know* how long *until* is. *I do not know* what he preached. Did he take that text from the old book, "Arise, shine for thy light has come"? *I do not know.* Or did he utter again the words he spoke when he addressed himself to the deepest places of Lazarus' death and said, "I am the resurrection and life"? *I do not know.* But he preached to the

---

[35] Taylor's rendition, 1 Peter 3:19 (KJV).

[36] The doctrine of purgatory, as I understand it, does not teach a second probation. Rather, purgatory is "the place or state of temporal punishment, where those who have died in a state of grace expiate their venial sins and undergo such punishment as is still due to forgiven sins, before being admitted to the Beatific Vision" ("Purgatory," *Oxford Dictionary of the Christian Church,* 2d ed. [New York: Oxford University Press, 1974]). In other words, the soul's final destination has already been decided before death, but some saved souls need preparation to be ready to stand in the presence of God. This misunderstanding of detail, however, does not undercut the essential point Taylor is making.

spirits chained in darkness. *In vain, I do not know.* I leave the second day.[37]

In a short paragraph Taylor makes the transition to his third point, the resurrection, and does so in such a way that, if the first and second points were left out of the sermon, the transition would join seamlessly with the introduction and we would have a short, powerful, and perfectly integrated sermon: "The third day should be in all our preaching all of the time—all of the time. Ah, my brother, you have no better word to preach than that third day. It belongs to no one Sunday of the year; it belongs to the kerygma of the Christian proclaimer always—the third day."[38] But I for one am grateful that he did not omit those two points because it is far more important to preach such good news than it is to have an outline that flows smoothly.

His report of the resurrection is an *ecphrasis,* the sort of vivid description that creates a sense of virtual presence, a sense of being there. The temptation once again is to quote it all, but space is running out.

The final words in this *ecphrasis* are, "Christ lives!" In the remaining part of the sermon, about a page long, these words become a constant refrain, repeated twenty times. This section consists of the final two moves in the list of move statements above: "In every circumstance of life it needs to be said that Christ lives" and "That will be the burden of all Taylor's preaching." The first move is a short paragraph, exhorting members of the congregation in Dallas, and the second takes up the last three paragraphs. Taylor says that he had recently undergone surgery and while doing so he came to an even deeper awareness of the living Christ with the result that for the rest of his life he will make that the main theme of his preaching. He wants all corrupt rulers and politicians to know this truth that he will

---

[37] Taylor, *50 Years of Timeless Treasures,* 191–92.
[38] Ibid., 192.

proclaim whether he is preaching before huge crowds or to tiny congregations.

In his final paragraph he bursts forth in even more joyful celebration:

> When time hoarsens this voice and whatever ring there may be in it, I shall whisper, however throatily, Christ lives! When I come down to the slippery shores of Jordan, I have but one crossing password, Christ lives! I shall pass through its swelling current with those words upon my heart, Christ lives! When I stand on the shores of everlasting deliverance, I shall repeat those words, Christ lives! When the gates of new life open to me, I will shout again, Christ lives! As I go stately stepping up the broad avenues of the glory land, I shall salute angels and archangels, prophets, priests, and kings, with the glorious words, Christ lives! When I kneel down at the lily-white throne and look at his nail-pierced feet, surrender my commission and thank him that he made me a preacher—a preacher down here—I shall cry out once more, Christ lives![39]

How I would have loved to hear him say those words! What Taylor said of his friend Sandy Ray could easily be applied to himself: "When the glad thunders of that voice reached his climactic theme, the heavens seemed to open and we could see the Lord God on his throne."[40]

While that completes what I have to say about "Three Days That Changed the World," I must say one more thing, or this treatment of Taylor's preaching will be even less adequate than it is. I have said that he did not have just one message, but I have not discussed so far any of his topics that did not come up in this one sermon. Something must be said, however, about the way that he dealt with social issues in general and race relations in particular. A lot of his attitude toward the matter can be seen in the way he began his sermon on the Sunday after Mrs. Martin Luther King, Sr., was shot: "I do not relish

---

[39] Ibid., 192.

[40] Taylor, *Special Occasion and Expository Sermons*, 141.

preaching which is joined too closely to current events, since it can become merely the preacher's comment on the passing scene. On the other hand, I shudder at the thought of preaching which never comes within sight of human affairs and happenings."[41]

While Taylor can and does preach prophetic sermons, most often he will work a statement in as part of his development of another theme. Not that there is anything hesitant or compromising about what he says, but he makes the point in passing and lets it go at that. I believe that practice must be related to something he said in relation to Martin Luther King, Jr. He talked about the lineage of King's (and his own) people, "who by the power of God were told one thing and heard another." The people who "had sat in the slave galleries of churches…heard the preachers say to them one thing, but they heard something else."[42] It was said to them, "'You are ordained of God to be slaves,' but they heard, 'Before I'd be a slave, I'd be buried in my grave and go home to my Lord and be free.'"[43]

Later he calls this a "slave glossalalia" whereby "a translation would occur somewhere between the preacher's utterance and the slaves' hearing."[44] Gerald Davis said that one of the main purposes of traditional black sermons has been to enable their hearers "to live a fully experiencing daily, secular existence" in a world dominated by whites.[45] I said above that it appeared to me that most of the NBC radio sermons had the pastoral purpose of assisting those who heard them to go back into a cold world and make it through another week. Although Taylor's radio audience almost certainly consisted of far more whites than blacks, they could appreciate what was said as commentary on the difficulties of their own lives and probably remain unconscious of the special meaning the message had for the

---

[41] Taylor, *50 Years of Timeless Treasures*, 90.

[42] Taylor, *Special Occasion and Expository Sermons*, 107.

[43] Ibid.

[44] Ibid., 124.

[45] Davis, *I Got the Word in Me*, 64.

rest of his audience. (This coded quality may account for the way that no more explicit preaching on race relations occurs than the good amount that does.) Certainly, there is no hesitation in his prophetic spirit. Some speaking in code is characteristic of many of Taylor's other sermons as well, and that makes him not only a preacher for all seasons, but a preacher for all peoples as well.

While we have by no means exhausted the subject of the secret of the power of Taylor's preaching, a bit more of it can be seen in the introduction to a sermon he preached in 1975: "This morning will not be the first time I have tried to hold up this text before your hearts and minds—mark those last words, 'hearts and minds,' for this preacher has no desire to speak to either of these worthies without the other. You will be, I hope, in the wrong church this morning if you want the preacher to get at your feelings while your mind is excused; likewise, I pray, if you want to think without feeling."[46]

In his preaching deep thought is combined with powerful emotion. That by itself, however, does not make him the consummmate artist he is, for "the successful artist is constantly studied with the hope that the *how* may be found out. Let a preacher attain any eminence in pulpit work, and such a one will be bombarded in conferences and seminars times without number as to how it is done. The best human answer is that technique can be taught; art cannot.... A master cook can give accurate recipes, though I am not sure they often do, but getting the feel to make the food come out right is a different matter."[47]

For Gardner C. Taylor's rare combination of strong faith, deep thought, powerful emotion, and high art, we can only say, "Thanks be to God for raising him up."

---

[46] Taylor, *50 Years of Timeless Treasures*, 108.
[47] Taylor, *Quintessential Classics*, 169.

POETIC PERSUASION:
A MASTER CLASS ON SPEAKING
TRUTH TO POWER

Teresa L. Fry Brown

The first day of class, students enrolled in the introduction to preaching classes are challenged with the task of such critically engaging questions as the following: Why do we preach? When do we preach? What do we preach? What do we do when we are preaching? With whom do we preach? What is the role of the preacher in the life of the church and community? What are the expectations of the preacher and listener during this holy communicative engagement? These seemingly simplistic questions at times leave students with confused looks on their faces regardless of the amount of their preaching experience. In the discussion of the preaching task, one has only to listen briefly to some contemporary popular preaching models to ascertain that the possibility of any consideration of these inquiries of the preaching task is grossly deficient. Preaching at times seems to have evolved into a monologue, eisogeted, clichéd, self-indulgent harangues focused on individual gratification from a monogrammed God who is only concerned with wealthy, able-bodied, gender-specific, paid spokespersons. In other instances the preaching task is dialogical, exegeted with integrity, relevant to the needs and concerns of the listener, and encapsulating a liberating God of promise and hope to all of God's people. While my introduction to preaching students intentionally pursue the questions of preaching's purpose for fourteen weeks, Gardner C. Taylor poetically persuades us to wrestle with the preaching task as a vehicle to speak truth to power in an unending master class about why, when, and how we preach.

In his classic *How Shall They Preach*, Dr. Taylor outlines the necessity of critical engagement and purpose for the "presumptuousness of preaching."

> To seek and find God's movement in human affairs and to cry out, passionately pointing to where that stirring is discernable though scarcely ever indisputable, is the preacher's task. To hear and to suffer deeply with "the still sad music of humanity" and then to offer to it the wonderful gospel of healing and wholeness is the preacher's privilege. We are called to listen and to identify the tread of the eternal God's sovereign purpose, marching in private and public affairs of men.[1]

Preaching is an intimate personal identification with the existential situation of the listener. During the act of preaching there is a genuine identity of preacher with people's lives, personal involvement, and gut-level emoting. Preaching is communication in the concrete, filled with language and images from day-to-day details, dynamics, sights, sounds, smells, tastes, texture, and life scenes. Preaching revisits the familiar through recognition of the frame of reference of listener and identity with the hearer's environment. One delivers the sermon in a manner in which the hearer is able to see and hear self within sermon.[2] Gardner Taylor describes the preaching task as active. The preacher "seeks," "finds," "cries out," "hears," "suffers," "offers," "listens," and "identifies." The preacher is never passive, waiting for a sermon to fall from the sky. It is a privilege, not an entitlement, for the persons called to share God's word with God's people. This essay will discuss the purpose of the preached word, the effective use of persuasive language, and the necessity of speaking truth to power, using the words of Gardner C. Taylor.

---

[1] Gardner C. Taylor, *How Shall They Preach* (Elgin IL: Progressive Baptist Publishing House, 1977) 38.

[2] Henry Mitchell, *Celebration and Experience in Preaching* (Nashville: Abingdon Press, 1990) 79–84.

Poetic Persuasion

The prophetic nature of preaching is meant to address what was deemed not of God and point persons toward life-changing decisions that meet God's standards of behavior as recorded in the biblical text and as revealed to the preacher. The preacher must realize that we often see only the surface issues. The preacher must *mine the deep*. Knowledge of the congregation is enhanced when preachers spend time listening to the levels of conversation. Foundational to prophetic preaching or speaking truth to power is proficiency with sermonic language.

Theologian Paul Tillich once wrote that "words that are used most in religion are those whose genuine meaning is also completely lost…. Such words must be reborn, if possible; and thrown away if this is not possible."[3] Language has power. It is not simply referential; it is creative. Language determines the reality of those who share it. Preachers who apologize after every sentence for fear of hurting feelings diminish the authenticity and power of the message. At the other end of the spectrum are preachers whose language reflects a hierarchical view. They enter the pulpit to teach their listeners a lesson, assuming they are holier than everyone else in the church. A cognitive dissonance sets up, for example, when a preacher addresses the topic of equality in the reign of God while using derogatory or oppressive language or imagery.

Sermons need a fresh flow of language to avoid being disconnected from the listener's vocabulary, culture, mindset, standard and non-standard language usage. Language helps us to construct meaning. For example, metaphors, verbal images, analogies, and paradigms provide new ways of poetically talking about God and instill new linguistic possibilities for speaker and listener to image an "awareness of the unseen and the seen." In his sermon "Laodicea, Part III: The Door of the Soul," Taylor employs phrases such as the

---

[3] Paul Tillich, *The Eternal Now* (New York: Scribner's, 1963) 94.

salvation of Dismas on the cross by describing him as "on the very edge of hell, hanging over that bottomless abyss of endless nothingness," judgment as "sweeping and withering," God as the "tender, pleading, kindly inviting," knocker, or the beautiful image, "My shadow is already behind me, the sign that the sun is far, far along," to describe the maturing of life.[4] The richness of the poetic imagery gives new meaning to an often avoided text. Homiletically, Taylor possesses an incomparable command of sermonic imagery and captivating language that educates those in a technological, sound-byte, visual-image-laden society that words do still matter.

The preacher's use of musicality is the linguistic intonation, ebb and flow, call and response, inflection, and physicality inherent in the many forms of black and charismatic preaching. It often evokes and expresses the emotional content of the sermon.[5] Taylor said, "Life is rarely one thing or the other. It is almost always a mixture of joy and sorrow, of gladness and grief, of sunshine and shadows, of sickness and health, of life and death. This is life, and preaching ought never be far away from tears and laughter. Any preaching that is going to search hearts of people must search them at the depths of their gladness and at the most profound moment of their grief."[6] Taylor's language does not manipulate, demean, brutalize, or obscure the word of God or the listener. Rather, his word choice allows space for the listener to visualize, imagine, construct, or sense other possibilities on their own creative terms. His use of multiple levels of language engages each listener. Using vivid, attractive, and engaging language,

---

[4] Gardner C. Taylor, "Laodecia, Part III: The Door of the Soul," in *Special Occasion and Expository Sermons*, vol. 4 of *The Words of Gardner Taylor*, comp. Edward L. Taylor (Valley Forge: Judson Press, 2001) 253–58.

[5] William Turner, "The Musicality of Black Preaching: A Phenomenology," *Journal of Black Sacred Music* 2/1 (Spring 1988): 21-34.

[6] Gardner C. Taylor, "Three Women and God," in *Quintessential Classics, 1980–Present*, vol. 3 of *The Words of Gardner Taylor*, comp. Edward L. Taylor (Valley Forge: Judson Press, 2000) 196.

the intellect and emotion are enjoined as persons reconsider their faith.[7] The preaching moment brings us face to face with God. The efficacy of the sermon must be a reinforcement of the convictions the listeners already have as the speaker and the listener are invited to think again about beliefs: "And let me say to you quite honestly, the strongest preaching that you will ever do will be in what you are. If you have principles and decency and purpose and a determination not to exploit your people, there will be people who will look to you and glorify God in heaven. The God of heaven will honor your ministry far beyond what you will able to scramble and scrounge and plot and scheme to receive. God will do it."[8]

In his sermon about "Three Women and God," Taylor begins the sermon by reminding the preacher of the necessity of inclusivity in preaching ("We almost always preach about men"). By inclusivity he means not only gender, class, ethnicity, age, and race, but he states that good preaching must "search the hearts of people" and mine the "depths of their gladness and of those profound moments of grief."[9] Preachers encounter life issues with a depth of spirituality and pathos that few others have the opportunity to do. Preachers are called on to rekindle the vitality of life, to call the people to live as Christ, and to refocus on the distinctiveness of faith. Preachers must develop a multisensory and multilingual approach to articulation of the faith. In a sermon on homelessness, Taylor broadens the concept from physical to spiritual homelessness that is devoid of cultural exclusion: "Now it is the preacher's responsibility and privilege to remind homeless people of some 'abidingness'; of some permanence for

---

[7] Mark Gallie and Craig Brian Larson, *Preaching That Connects: Using the Techniques of Journalists to Add Impact to Your Sermons* (Grand Rapids: Zondervan, 1994) 16–21.

[8] Taylor, *Quintessential Classics*, 196.

[9] Ibid.

which all of our hearts deeply and passionately yearn, because we have to keep moving on and on and on."[10]

Taylor compellingly engages the listener through not only his metaphoric sermonic discourse, but also through linguistic "earthing" of his memories by weaving quotations from philosophers, teachers, scholars, congregants, family members, friends, and the depths of a panorama of literary citations. This allows space for the listener to mine his or her own life to attach relevance to the purpose of the preached word. It universalizes human experience, and the word becomes communal rather than a monologue of selected "personal testimonies" on a subject.

Speaking Truth to Power

On any given Sunday, one may hear religious discourse that is intentionally marginalizing and denigrating to humanity. One may become aware of the absence of silence about contemporary social issues due to apathy or apprehension of termination. One may also hear liberating, life-affirming rhetoric that recognizes the promise of God that all are welcomed into the kingdom.

The concept of speaking truth to power originated with the Quakers, a religious group that, in the 1600s, stated that "everyone contains a spark that can be reached with prophetic voices." The American Friends Service Committee's (AFSC) most influential pamphlet, *Speak Truth to Power*, was published in 1955 as an antiwar pamphlet written by Milton Mayer.[11] Even those in positions of power who are not willing to listen, or who are brutal and insensitive, can be convicted to change or correct behavior, to formulate new paradigms if one is bold enough to "speak truth to power," to say a

---

[10] Gardner C. Taylor, "Healing Our Homelessness," *The African American Pulpit* 10/2 (Spring 2007) 86-9.

[11] "Speak Truth to Power," n.d., archives of the American Friends Service Committee, General Administration, Information Services, Publications-Speak Truth to Power, Correspondence, Philadelphia, PA, 1954.

word, to tell the truth, to utter a defense of freedom, to look a wrongdoer in the face and say enough is enough. The ability to speak truth to power should never be taken for granted regardless of who seeks to silence the masses.

The late Salvadoran archbishop Oscar Romero reminded us of this not long before his assassination in 1980: "A church that doesn't provoke any crisis, a gospel that doesn't unsettle, a word of God that doesn't get under anyone's skin, a word of God that doesn't touch the real sin of the society in which it is being proclaimed, what gospel is that?... Those preachers who avoid every thorny matter so as not to be harassed, so as not to have conflicts and difficulties, do not light up the world they live in."[12] Homiletics scholar Charles Campbell, in his book *The Word before the Powers*, reminds us that to speak truth to power means to speak up and to eliminate isolation, demoralization, diversions from the issues, language and image that delude and capture minds, trivialize the Christian message, and failure to speak out on difficulties publicly. To speak truth to power means to evaluate the particularities of the web of oppressions that slowly strangle the life out of our individual and collective lives. To speak truth to power is redemptive preaching that provides space for individual and communal change in the lives of listeners.[13]

Taylor's sermons, essays, and speeches are replete with instances of addressing the power disparities of this life. In a sermon called "The Key to It All," Taylor preaches about God's care of people's needs by retelling Jesus' seaside final-examination discourse with Peter. He speaks of God's longings for restoration and reconciliation and the sense that no one cares for them. With the breath of a

---

[12] Oscar Romero, *The Violence of Love: The Pastoral Wisdom of Archbishop Oscar Romero*, trans. and comp. James R. Brockmen (New York: Harper & Row, 1988) 64.

[13] Charles Campbell, *The Word before the Powers: An Ethic of Preaching* (Louisville: Westminster John Knox Press, 2002) 33–39, 90.

comma, like a pop test to see if preachers are paying attention, he begins a homiletical praxis critique:

> Ah, the question is to all preachers, all Christians, do you have anything to say to anybody that will make heaven seem a little nearer to earth? Have you anything to say that will take the bitterness of despair and make them feel that they are not orphans underneath an uncaring sky but they are sons and daughters of the Father's house? Have you anything to say to lift up heads that are bowed down and dry eyes that are set with tears? You've got it if you love the Lord. He'll give you what to say, and he'll teach you how to say it. And he'll tell you when to say it, and he'll tell you where to say it.[14]

Taylor is clear that speaking truth to power is undeniably related to the biblical text, not the preacher's agenda. Preachers must understand the difference between prophetic preaching and political moralizing: "Prophetic preaching rises out of the Scriptures; moralizing is self-generated and arises from social mores and personal predilections."[15]

Preachers are to rely on God's guidance for what and when to preach. Preachers are to present the acknowledged Word of God, regardless of translation, verbally and nonverbally with such presence, power, passion, and purpose that the listener or observer senses the impulse of change or conversion in his or her own life. We each are called to speak truth to power in our own way. It is under divine intercession that one is able to address social injustice as persons who work to alleviate the social invisibility, silencing, or moral denigration of any person or group. Social justice begins when each person evaluates his or her own complicity in social denial of another's humanity. Social justice begins when each person takes responsibility for creating a beloved community where all persons are free. There

---

[14] Taylor, "The Key to It All," in *Special Occasion and Expository Sermons*, 139.

[15] Samuel D. Proctor and Gardner C. Taylor, with Gary V. Simpson, *We Have This Ministry: The Heart of the Pastor's Vocation* (Valley Forge: Judson Press, 1996) 128.

are many more who hear God's call for justice and can visualize and imagine a time and a place when, as the prophet says, justice covers the earth like the waters in the beginning when God called chaos to order. Howard Thurman, in his book *The Luminous Darkness*, asks us to imagine a time and place when we reject stereotypes, report prejudice, and do justice.[16] This is also Taylor's instruction to each preacher.

The preaching moment is not a place for cheap grace or a quick fix, but of patient endurance, anticipation, and confidence that the end of the matter at hand is the not-yet but soon. The sermon is more than a theoretical exercise in biblical scholarship; it is a practical, day-in and day-out application of faith to a particular situation.[17] The purpose of preaching entails being a relevant preacher. Relevant preachers must speak to the hungers of all people who sit in the pews—not just economic hungers, but the hunger to be socially free. All people need a sense of place, roots, and history. Sermons are to effect behavioral change through conversion, discipleship, forgiveness, honesty, generosity, and humility.

Preachers are called to do more than console and answer questions. Preachers who speak truth to power avoid pop psychology-based sermons and group counseling from the pulpit that leaves more persons in pain after the "living word" than before the sermon. The "just have faith," "tell all of your story now," "get over it," "it wasn't that bad," "it's all your fault" mantras of many contemporary preachers will not do. Taylor distances himself from such a trend in the middle of his sermon about societal influences and engagement of enemies by stating, "I am against a disembodied faith which does not take into account that we have to live amidst physical sights and

---

[16] Howard Thurman, *The Luminous Darkness* (Richmond IN: Friends United Press, 1989) 100.

[17] Teresa Fry Brown, "An African American Woman's Perspective," in *Preaching Justice: Ethnic and Cultural Perspective*, ed. Christine M. Smith (Cleveland OH: United Church Press, 1998) 49.

sound. A ghost Christianity cut loose from the earth—misty, vaporous, suspended, so to speak, in midair—does not honor our Lord Jesus."[18] One can envision faith floating away as clichés overshadow God's salvific plan and careful critical engagement of the "web of systemic oppressions"[19] that people face daily.

Relevant preachers are called to address the lived experiences of all the people and those people, places, and things that comprise exploitation, marginalization, powerlessness, and imperialism and the hopeful expectation of their eradication. One who speaks truth to power works to end practices that establish, maintain, and perpetuate subordination, exploitation, marginalization, powerlessness, cultural imperialism, "othering," systematic violence, and subjugated knowledge. It is pointing to the fire on the outside of the cave, the light of truth, God's call on the people of faith.

In *How Shall They Preach*, Taylor poetically directs preachers to their ultimate purpose and the purpose of preaching:

> But there is a Gospel and you have been privileged to be summoned to declare it. It can stand people on their feet for the living of their days. And also—what a privilege, almost too precious to be mentioned—it may be that the Gospel which you preach will then steady some poor pilgrims as they come to where the bridgeless river is and some of them, feeling the spray of Jordan misting in the face, just might thank God as they cross the river that He made you a preacher.[20]

It is Taylor's proclamation pedagogy that unequivocally seeks to model a homiletical theory and praxis based in the lived moments of humanity's quest to know God. His syllabus is a captivating representation of preaching excellence. His delivery dances with word

---

[18] Taylor, "Chariots Aflame," in *Special Occasion and Expository Sermons*, vol. 3 of *The Words of Gardner Taylor*, 70-4.

[19] Christine Smith, *Risking the Terror-Resurrection in This Life* (Cleveland: Pilgrim Press, 2001) 20–21.

[20] Taylor, *How Shall They Preach*, 94.

choice, historical references, sharing personal experiences and utter love of the biblical text, and is worthy of imitation but cannot be truly duplicated. Taylor could have chosen to stop there and be touted as one of the greatest preachers known to humanity, but he is also a master teacher at heart. His passion for the lives of all persons seemingly leads him to an unsuspecting and at times disarming pause to converse directly with preachers.

In the midst of telling "that old, old story," Taylor pauses, looks directly at us, raises his voice in a commanding yet instructive cadence, and reminds us that our duty, our purpose, our intention as preachers is to speak life in the midst of death-dealing situations, to release captives in oppressive conditions, and to confront anyone who is in opposition to the liberative activity of God. His teaching urges all preachers to linguistically proclaim, with what I call *metamorphic boldness*, the possibilities for transformation. Taylor charges all preachers to step out of the status quo to seek language and content that shakes dungeons and makes chains fall off. In order to pass his comprehensive final, we must strive to address whole persons in the congregation, not just those who can pay attention or pay admission. If we follow his instructions, our preaching will be a holistic communicative act. It will engage the spiritual, intellectual, social, psychological, and economical yearnings, needs, questions, and issues of all of God's family.

The spring 2000 [millennial] issue of *The African American Pulpit* contains the sermon "A City with Other Walls," in which Taylor preaches about the positive and negative aspects of physical, spiritual, and psychic walls, weapons, and will. Again, he pauses in the sermonic content and testifies, "I would rather my hand be cut off than that it raise itself against the Lord's purposes. I would rather the tongue was plucked out of the mouth than that it be employed to try to block the purposes of the everlasting God."[21] That master

---

[21] Gardner C. Taylor, "A City with Other Walls," *The African American Pulpit* 2/2 (Spring [Millennium Issue] 2000): 22.

teacher, in stylized prose, hints that we have an obligation to proclaim God's Word within God's purpose, not our agenda. What is our purpose in preaching? Why do we preach? With whom do we preach? What do we preach? These questions seem to be a part of every lecture by this master teacher in an unending semester of introduction to preaching as he poetically persuades us to speak truth to power.

WHAT HAPPENED TO SACRED ELOQUENCE? (CELEBRATING THE MINISTRY OF GARDNER C. TAYLOR)

Martha Simmons and Brad R. Braxton

What Makes Gardner Taylor Unique?

So much has been said about Gardner Taylor in countless books and essays and as countless preachers introduced him prior to a sermon. In preparation for this essay, we asked ourselves this question: What is the one thing about Dr. Taylor that everyone would agree makes him uniquely Gardner Calvin Taylor? Yes, he is a preacher of almost indescribable skill. We can all agree on that. Yes, he belongs on any list of great pulpiteers. We can all agree on that. But what is the one characteristic that places Dr. Taylor in a class by himself?

Is it Dr. Taylor's voice? Speaking of a select group of preachers (that surely would have included Dr. Taylor had he been alive in the nineteenth century), Thomas Potter said in 1866:

> And what a voice! A voice which is never hoarse, broken, soured, irritated, or troubled by worldly and passionate struggles of interest peculiar to the time; a voice which, like that of the thunder in the clouds, or the organ in the cathedral, has never been anything but the medium of power and Divine persuasion to the soul; a voice which only speaks to kneeling auditors; a voice which is listened to in profound silence, to which none reply save by an inclination of the head or by falling ears—those mute applauses of the soul!—a voice which is never refuted or contradicted, even when it astonishes or wounds; a voice, in fine, which does not speak in the name of opinion, which is variable; nor in the name of philosophy, which is

open to discussion; nor in the name of country, which is local; nor in the name of regal supremacy, which is temporal; nor in the name of the speaker himself, which is an agent transformed for the occasion; but which speaks in the name of God, an authority of language unequaled upon earth, and against which the lowest murmur is impious and the smallest opposition a blasphemy.[1]

As important as voice is to any preacher, is it voice that places Dr. Taylor in a class by himself? Dr. Taylor has long been a member of that fraternity of preachers—many of whom now reside in eternity—known for their superb voices. There was Sandy F. Ray, of whom Dr. Taylor once said, "He was President of Preachers, ambassador plenipotentiary from the court of King Emmanuel.... Our history has not produced his equal.... At the height of his pulpit oratory, it was hard to tell whether one heard music half spoken or speech half sung."[2] Then there was William Augustus Jones, Jr., with whom Dr. Taylor also had a longtime friendship. In addition to eulogizing his friend Sandy Ray, Taylor also eulogized his friend William Jones. Taylor said Jones's voice "was a unique instrument that filled a room; it was without blemish or hint of quiver."[3] Dr. Taylor clearly understands the centrality of a preacher's voice in the homiletic task. As he appreciated the voices of his peers, we have appreciated the lyrical, poetic tonality in Dr. Taylor's voice. Taylor's voice is measured, melodic, and possesses the clarity of a prophet and the compassion of a pastor. While his voice is marvelous and should be compared with the voices of other great preachers, we do not believe that it is his voice that places Gardner Taylor in a class without peer.

---

[1] Thomas J. Potter, *Sacred Eloquence: The Theory and Practice of Preaching* (Dublin: James Duffy, 1866) 19.

[2] Eulogy of Sandy F. Ray: A President of Preaching," as delivered by Gardner C. Taylor, *The African American Pulpit* 4/1 (Winter 2000–2001): 58.

[3] A conversation between Martha Simmons and Gardner C. Taylor, September 2008.

Is it his ability to persuade, or argue a point, or in the parlance of black preachers, "press his claim"? Undoubtedly, Dr. Taylor's powers of persuasion are legendary. He shows a keen understanding of texts, culture, philosophy, poetry, homiletics, science, and other areas of knowledge. He carefully wields information as if he has obtained doctoral degrees in multiple academic disciplines. In his ability to argue a homiletic case, Taylor was joined by other great contemporaries. For example, one calls to mind the late J. H. Jackson, who was known as a barrister in the pulpit. Jackson was so persuasive that he homiletically argued his way into remaining the president of the National Baptist Convention, USA, Inc., longer than any other person—even against the opposition of Dr. Taylor and Dr. Martin Luther King, Jr.!

When recalling persuasive preachers, we also must mention Samuel DeWitt Proctor, another of Taylor's longtime friends. Proctor nimbly practiced what preaching professors tell students: "Argue yes. But all the while, persuade, persuade, persuade!" Also on the list of persuasive contemporary black preachers is Charles Gilchrist Adams. In multiple crescendos, Adams presses home a point until even the angels pause to hear the evidence presented.

Then there was Dr. Martin Luther King, Jr., the American Moses and successor to the Reverend Vernon Johns. Dr. King's ability to construct a rhetorical case for peace and justice, among his other grand achievements, made him a man for the ages. Countless books and articles on King attest to his persuasive prowess. Dr. King also was a close friend of Dr. Taylor, and they often vacationed together. Taylor was King's favorite preacher. Taylor would not personally rank his persuasive powers among the likes of Jackson, Proctor, Adams, and King, even though Taylor need not take a backseat to any of the aforementioned greats as it relates to rhetorical persuasion. While Taylor's powers of persuasion are considerable, the uniqueness of his homiletic gift is ultimately not found in his persuasive ability.

What is it, then, that makes Taylor unique? What is it that all agree has made him the heralded preacher he is? Without fear of contradiction, we believe that the one thing that has gained Gardner Calvin Taylor a definitive place on every preaching list or ranking of the last half century is his *eloquence!* While his eloquence is but one characteristic of his impressive preaching arsenal, it is the signal characteristic for which we salute him.

Our reflection on Dr. Taylor's eloquence led us to an important and connected issue. It occurred to us that the gift for which we so revere Dr. Taylor—eloquence in the pulpit—is now, sadly, a very rare occurrence. As a part of Martha Simmons's varied roles with *The African American Pulpit* across a decade, she has read at least 1,500 sermons, mainly from preachers of the last twenty-five years. Then, as one of two editors of a forthcoming anthology on black preaching, she read an additional 400 sermons and biographies of preachers from 1750–2005. As a professor of preaching for nearly a decade, Brad Braxton has listened regularly to numerous sermons as student preachers have proclaimed the gospel. After reading, studying, and listening to so much preaching, we were led to title this essay, "What Happened to Sacred Eloquence?"

Yes, some good preaching has occurred in the last twenty-five years, but not much of it would be considered eloquent. Some of it was quite doctrinal, some colorful, and some entertaining, but rarely eloquent. Occasionally at revered black religious conferences (such as the Hampton Minister's Conference) or denominational conventions, we may hear a prophetic voice here and there, but rarely eloquence. When we turn on televisions, we might witness local preachers doing commendable ministry as they preach to the faithful. We also might see preachers who broadcast nationally and internationally. However, as we change the channel or turn off the broadcast, we do not walk away saying, "My, what a Spirit-filled, eloquent word." What happened to sacred eloquence?

The Role of Rhetoric in the Making of Gardner Taylor

Rhetoric constitutes a large part of the skill-set or underpinning for eloquence in the pulpit. Aristotle said rhetoric is "the faculty of discovering in any particular case all of the available means of persuasion."[4] Cicero said, "Rhetoric is one great art comprised of five lesser arts: *inventio, dispositio, elocutio, memoria,* and *pronunciation* [or invention, arrangement, elocution (style), memory, and delivery]. Rhetoric is speech designed to persuade."[5]

Augustine, the esteemed African bishop, was once a teacher of Latin rhetoric. After his conversion to Christianity, he became interested in using the "pagan" arts of rhetoric for spreading Christianity. His new use of rhetoric is explored in the fourth book of his *De Doctrina Christiana* and laid the foundation for what would become the discipline of homiletics, the rhetoric of sermons. According to Fred Craddock, "it was Augustine who officiated at the wedding joining the rhetorical principles of Cicero to the growing and changing ministry of preaching.... Augustine's adaptation of rhetoric for preaching came to America and dominated the study and practice of homiletics well into the twentieth century."[6]

Later, in *On the Preparation and Delivery of Sermons,* John Broadus modernized the Augustinian rhetorical understanding of preaching and captured the homiletical attention of several

---

[4] Aristotle, *Art of Rhetoric,* English trans. J. H. Freese (London: Heinemann, 1926, 1959) 1.1. This edition, first published in 1926, had Greek and English parallel text.

[5] Marcus Tullius Cicero, *M. T. Cicero de Oratore: His Three Dialogues upon the Character and Qualifications of the Orator,* ed. William Guthrie, 1708–1770 (Boston: R. P. and C. Williams, 1822); translated into English with notes, historical and explanatory, and an introductory preface, 1.64. Book may be found online at http://onlinebooks.library.upenn.edu (accessed 8 January 2009).

[6] Fred B. Craddock, "Is There Still Room for Rhetoric?" in *Preaching on the Brink: The Future of Homiletics,* ed. Martha Simmons (Nashville: Abingdon Press, 1996) 66–67.

generations. Then, in *The New Rhetoric: a Treatise on Argumentation*, Chaïm Perelman and Lucie Olbrechts-Tyteca said, "Since argumentation aims at securing the adherence of those to whom it is addressed, it is, in its entirety, relative to the audience to be influenced."[7] Perelman and Olbrechts-Tyteca also discuss the constant fluctuation in an audience, as well as other rhetorical variables such as the orator, the content, the goals of the argument, and the necessity of making rhetorically present for an audience what might be absent when an orator begins speaking. Taken together, Aristotle, Cicero, Augustine, Broadus, Perelman, and Olbrechts-Tyteca define rhetoric as the methodology by which one persuades through various linguistic devices, approaches, or arrangement; awareness of one's audience, subject matter, and proper occasion; making the absent present; and careful attention to the desired result from the listener.

All this applies to rhetoric as used by the preacher. Yet in the case of Gardner Taylor—and much of the best preaching of the black church—two additional aspects of rhetoric should be included. The first is the prominence of the inductive approach, where the preacher takes the listeners on a verbal quest for discovery. The listeners are led to a certain conclusion that they can own for themselves. The second is an emphasis on the enhancement of the self-esteem of the hearers. Preaching that intentionally enhances self-esteem is a consistent hallmark of Dr. Taylor's pulpit work and thus needs to be highlighted. Gardner Taylor is a son of Africa, and his people are those of the Diaspora. Accordingly, much of his proclamation at the sacred desk has encouraged, urged, and beckoned his people to fight on, pray on, live on, and love on. Gardner Taylor has been acutely aware of the necessity of preaching that will provide hope and inspiration for downtrodden people.

---

[7] Chaïm Perelman and Lucie Olbrechts-Tyteca, *The New Rhetoric: A Treatise on Argumentation*, trans. John Wilkinson and Purcell Weaver (Notre Dame: University of Notre Dame Press, 1969) 19.

Gardner Taylor's homiletic was fashioned during a period of American history when an appreciation for rhetoric dominated pulpit oratory. His rhetorical genius was formed at his father's knee. His father, Washington Monroe Taylor (1870–1931), was a product of a culture that still highly valued rhetoric. Washington Taylor was one of the ablest orators of his day by all accounts. Unfortunately, only one or two of his written sermons have survived, and none were recorded.

Washington Taylor was the president of the Louisiana Baptist State Convention and the vice president at-large of the National Baptist Convention, USA. He also was the preacher of his generation called upon to do the funerals of national black preachers and leaders (a mantle his son inherited) such as E. C. Morris, who served for twenty-seven years as the president of the National Baptist Convention, USA. We cite below the opening and closing words of Washington Taylor's eulogy of E. C. Morris:

> Dr. E. C. Morris has gone to heaven. He left this world for glory at the rising of the sun on September 5, 1922. And from the known tendency of his soul heavenward and his joyous haste to be gone here, there can be little doubt that his chariot of fire reached its destination speedily, and the triumphant saint has taken his seat with the heavenly company....
>
> The sacred ties that bind us together, the whole family in heaven—these constitute the happiness of the redeemed. These immortal minds will contemplate with never-failing delight the wonders of creative power, the mysteries of redeeming love. Every faculty will be developed, every capacity increased in the Beautiful City, where all the treasures of the sky will be opened to the blood-bought army unfettered by immortality. We shall wing our tireless flight to worlds afar, and the years of eternity shall roll by with richer and still more glorious revelation of God in Christ. And Jesus will open before us the riches of redemption and the amazing achievements in the great controversy with Satan. And the hearts of the redeemed shall thrill with more fervent devotion as the sweep of

the harps of gold and ten thousand times ten thousand and millions
of billions and quadrillions of voices unite in the chorus of praise to
him who has redeemed us with blood. And then we shall see our own
Morris robed in heavenly regalia, accompanying Jehovah's only Son
back to commemorate Calvary's stained mountain.[8]

Gardner Taylor heard such rhetorical splendor from birth until
his father died when he was thirteen. Few young black boys (and, for
that matter, few boys of any ethnicity) had daily exposure to such
oratory and poetry in their homes in the 1920s and 1930s (or even
today). The significance of being reared in an atmosphere that is
extremely conducive to one's future success is incalculable. No one
would have been surprised if a child of Hank Aaron was at least a
good baseball player. No one would think it unusual if a daughter of
Barbara Jordan had political acumen. No one would find it atypical if
a child of Wynton Marsalis showed aptitude for a musical
instrument.

So it is with this preacher, Gardner Taylor. Those who knew
Gardner Taylor's father or who have read his father's preaching are
not surprised by the depth of thought, flair for language, timing, and
passion that have come forth in the father's son. With this beginning,
Gardner Taylor then attended Leland College for undergraduate
studies, where he was a debate master. His rhetorical skills were
further refined by the president of Leland, Alvin Bacoats, who also
followed Gardner Taylor's father as pastor of Mt. Zion Baptist
Church.

Dr. Taylor then completed seminary at Oberlin, a school that
was founded by two ministers and where the evangelist Charles
Finney left a large rhetorical footprint as president. At Oberlin, Dr.
Taylor not only studied rhetoric, but also he met his now deceased
wife, Laura Scott, who was a Phi Beta Kappa with a great love for

---

[8] "The Eulogy of Reverend E. C. Morris," delivered by Washington Monroe
Taylor, reprinted in *The African American Pulpit* 5/4 (Fall 2002): 35–36.

language, literature, and theater. To anyone who asks, he would certainly reveal that Laura added much to his desire to offer sermons with depth, height, and powerful language.

While at Oberlin, Dr. Taylor began studying the preachers who were then most admired, such as Samuel Ringgold Ward (1817– c.1866), who was called the black Daniel Webster and who Frederick Douglass thought was the best orator of their day.[9] Of course, Dr. Taylor was aware of that great preacher, Frederick Douglass (1818– 1895), whose pulpit was the world. Douglass's speeches were a mainstay among black preachers before and during the modern civil rights movement, as they peppered their sermons with his eloquent and profound quotations concerning justice and freedom.

Dr. Taylor also was aware of the legend of another august black Baptist preacher possessed of great rhetorical skill, Joseph Charles (J. C.) Price (1854–1893). In 1881, Price gained national and international fame for his speech during the World Methodist Conference in London. The *London Times* called him "the World's Orator." Price was the first black preacher to stand in the pulpit of Henry Ward Beecher.[10] Price also was co-founder and the first president of Livingston College. Then there were the contemporaries of Dr. Taylor's father: E. C. Morris; C. T. Walker (1858–1884); E. Arlington Wilson (1876–c.1943); L. K. Williams (1871–1940); and J. C. Austin (1887–1968).[11] Gardner Taylor then studied great white preachers: Charles Spurgeon, Alexander Maclaren, Frederick Norwood, Leslie Weatherhead, and others. He read without ceasing

---

[9] Frederick Douglass, *Life and Times of Frederick Douglass: His Early Life as a Slave, His Escape from Bondage, and His Complete History to the Present Time* (Hartford CT: Park Publishing Co., 1881) 32.

[10] Edward Austin Johnson, *A School History of the Negro Race in America from 1619 to 1890* (Raleigh: Edward & Broughton, Printers and Binders, 1891) 178.

[11] This list is taken from the "Eulogy of Sandy F. Ray: A President of Preaching," delivered by Gardner C. Taylor, *The African American Pulpit* 4/1 (Winter 2000–2001): 58.

everything he could about preaching and preachers, oratory, poetry, and prose.

While the study of rhetoric is rarely a staple of modern seminary training, the current generation will need to re-imagine rhetoric to make it relevant for the present moment, as Broadus did for Taylor's generation and as Perelman and Olbrechts-Tyteca have done for later generations. As an introduction to current studies on rhetoric and preaching, this generation of preachers should familiarize themselves with such works as David Buttrick's *Homiletic: Moves and Structure*, Paul Scott Wilson's homiletics textbook, *The Practice of Preaching* (revised edition); Lucy Hind Hogan and Robert Reid's book, *Connecting with the Congregation: Rhetoric and the Art of Preaching*, and Tex Sample's book *Powerful Persuasion: Multimedia Witness in Christian Worship* (especially Part Two: "Rhetoric in Image, Sound, Beat, Light, Move and Dance").

What Is Sacred Eloquence?

We now turn specifically to the matter of sacred eloquence— what it is and how it functions. By sacred eloquence we mean at least three things: (1) a speaker who is filled with and guided by the Holy Spirit; (2) a speaker who is authentic and original; and (3) a speaker who is a persuasive and highly skilled wordsmith.

The Holy Spirit—undoubtedly, some readers will be surprised that we begin a discussion of sacred eloquence with the role of the Holy Spirit. Many preachers trained in some of the most prestigious seminaries will readily attest that the Holy Spirit's connection to preaching is rarely explored in preaching courses. Preachers are taught narrative preaching, emotive preaching, character studies, how to build suspense, how to gain the attention of listeners, and how to introduce and conclude sermons. But there is rarely a word about the Holy Spirit and preaching.

We learn names such as Augustine, John Broadus, David Buttrick, Fred Craddock, Henry Mitchell, Edwina Hunter, and

Eugene Lowry, to name a few. But rarely is a word said in class about the Holy Spirit's essential role in the holy task of preaching. The black church, perhaps more than many other faith communities, frequently attempts to invoke the presence of the Holy Spirit in church services. Yet we wonder how many black preachers prioritize a discussion of the Holy Spirit as it relates to the preparation and delivery of sermons.[12]

Preachers will drift in a dangerous direction if we remove the Holy Spirit from our preaching and our teaching of preaching. The goals of sacred eloquence are to: (1) deliver people from sin; (2) remind persons that they are created in the image of God for the good of themselves and all creation; and (3) equip persons to enrich their families and communities as a testimony to God's abundance. Accordingly, preachers must recognize that sacred eloquence has its life force in the Holy Spirit. Furthermore, preachers must be mindful that eternity often hangs in the balance for someone when we speak, including the preacher if she or he fails to take seriously the weightiness of the moment.

Preachers cannot bring forth sacred eloquence on their own merit or talent. The Holy Spirit bestows sacred eloquence upon preachers who earnestly care about the holistic salvation of people. The primary purpose is the winning of souls, the redeeming of lives, and the transforming of communities—all for the glory of God.

Sacred eloquence works on hearts as well as minds. A well-reasoned sermon with superbly poetic language and a magnificent delivery will be ineffective unless the Holy Spirit breathes upon the preacher in his or her daily life and sermon preparation. Furthermore, the Spirit must use the words of the preacher to move the hearts and minds of hearers in the preaching moment. Thomas Potter insisted,

---

[12] For recent works by black homileticians who prioritize the ministry of the Holy Spirit in preaching, consult James A. Forbes, *The Holy Spirit and Preaching* (Nashville: Abingdon Press, 1989) and Brad R. Braxton, *Preaching Paul* (Nashville: Abingdon Press, 2004) 69–96.

"True eloquence does not consist in the mere graces of style, in skillfully rounded periods, or in elegant figures of speech; but in the power of acting upon the minds and hearts of men; enlightening the one by means of solid instruction and reasonable conviction, and moving the other by those strong emotions which influence the will and reduce it to subjection."[13] The eloquent preacher must be constantly cognizant that the success or failure of preaching is dependent upon how much the preacher has yielded to the will of the Holy Spirit.

Many congregants bring the following questions with them to the preaching moment: Has the preacher spent time with God? Is the preacher possessed by the Holy Spirit in a way that draws people to him or her? Do the preacher's bearing and words urge me to ask ultimate questions such as, "Can I know the Savior the preacher knows? Can that Savior lift me from this condition as the preacher has been lifted?" Sacred eloquence is meant to provide serious, convincing answers to these probing questions. Sacred eloquence is not a means to inflate the preacher's ego, but is instead a mechanism that urges people to inquire about life's ultimate meaning.

Sacred eloquence also is as much about the preacher's life outside the pulpit as it is about the preacher's words inside the pulpit. Apparently, this wisdom is not being heeded enough since the number of moral scandals involving clergy appears to be escalating. While all have sinned and fallen short of the glory of God, the preacher who seeks to consistently deliver sacred eloquence must live in a manner that does not place his or her words in direct conflict with his or her behavior. Thus, the Holy Spirit must constantly remind each proclaimer of the gospel, especially those with gifts of rhetorical eloquence, that to preach a *life-changing* word requires a preacher with a *changed life*—a life that is pointed in the direction of Christ and the cross. All other directions are mazes.

---

[13] Potter, *Sacred Eloquence*, 134.

While every Christian is to be an evangelist, the proclaimer of sacred eloquence has been ordained of God, affirmed by a community of believers, and has accepted the responsibility of standing forth and declaring, "This is my calling." Therefore, the expectations of the community are higher, rightly or wrongly. Consequently, one's calling to be an orator of the sacred gospel requires, at a minimum, an abiding commitment to holy living. As Thomas Potter said, "When the preacher ascends the pulpit he [or she] represents the divine Majesty, he [or she] is the ambassador charged with the great and all-important interests of the glory of God, and the salvation of immortals souls."[14]

Furthermore, the Holy Spirit imparts to preachers the passion that is necessary for effective proclamation. By passion we do not mean whether one speaks loudly, sweats profusely, performs acrobatically, or whoops melodically as part of delivering the word. By passion we refer to the Holy Spirit-imbued energy that awakens in the preacher a fiery zeal for the souls of people and for the uplift of the community. This fire touches the hearts and passions of listeners. If listeners are headed for a life of destruction, this fire can compel them to make a u-turn. If they are meandering through life, this fire can awaken in them meaning and clear direction. If they are possessed of a vice that has been their lifelong thorn unremoved, the fire can provide freedom and release from bondage.

Proclaimers of sacred eloquence are cognizant of and moved by the eternal implications of every sermon. They are ablaze with words of grace, words of comfort, words of judgment, words that cut and those that cure. Such preachers are never nonchalant about their task, for nonchalance awakens no passion in others.

Originality—is the second component of sacred eloquence. By originality we mean several things: (1) the preacher's attempt to be authentic and to allow God to mediate truth through him or her; (2)

---

[14] Ibid., 73.

the preacher using models of effective preaching without stealing from other preachers; and (3) the preacher's dedication to the hard work that gives rise to homiletic creativity.

First, the proclaimer of sacred eloquence allows God to mediate truth through him or her. Such a preacher is authentic. Commenting on the need for homiletic authenticity, Claudette Copeland declares,

> The task of preaching "in authentic voice" is to give honor to the life-long developmental process. It is unfolding life, and *unfolding of truth* as we discern it. Preaching is discerned differently as a twenty-two year old, than as a fifty year old. It is discerned and interpreted differently as one is riding the crest of ambition, good health, solid marriage and an unchallenged future ahead. Preaching is heard and sung with a different voice, a changed melody, after having weathered loss, deaths, failure, ill health, broken relationships and faded dreams—-and still being a prisoner of one's call to herald "Good News."
>
> To find one's own voice in preaching, a woman [or man] must be willing to handle not only "Truth" inside the text, but the nuances of "truths" as they emanate from her [or his] real life, in the shadow of the Almighty. The woman [or man] who preaches with her [or his] own voice, dares to slay the idols of certitude about texts and techniques, in favor of openness, and seeking God's face anew, at every season of her [or his] journey. "As *we find* the light, we walk therein…" And we are honest about what the light has shown to us.
>
> Secondly, preaching is a *continual tension and ongoing integration.* It is a journey back and forth, between intellect and inspiration, mind and heart. It is a journey between the polarities of *relational context* (I know, tenderly, intimately, who *you* are) and *prophetic conscience* (I know what *God* demands). Preaching in one's own voice is a stretch *between,* and a grasp *of.* It is faithfulness *to* the texts, and integrity *about* the self. The "self" that is us all. It is hearing the

witness of men [and women] long dead, and being a fully alive woman [or man] whose experience must interpret this witness.[15]

Once preachers understand the significant role that authenticity plays in the Christian life in general and sacred eloquence in particular, preachers will yearn for authenticity all the more. Even amid our personal and professional failings, authenticity enables preachers to present themselves more openly and freely to a God who desires to be in an ever-deepening relationship with every preacher and every creature.

Unfortunately, authenticity is an increasingly rare virtue among preachers. Timidity is one reason for its scarcity. Timidity has crept into the American pulpit. Preachers are afraid to stand in opposition to prevailing notions in the culture or in religious traditions (especially if it means bucking a denominational edict or pronouncement).

If the president of the United States announces that troops are to be sent into yet another war, many preachers have no comment, other than to pray for the president and the troops. If a flood threatens to wipe away a city as a government watches, many preachers are silent, other than to pray for those who are drowning and for the government; or, even worse, some preachers offer ill-conceived theological reasons for the disaster. If thugs show up determined to take over a community through the dual death dealers of drugs and violence, many preachers are silent, other than praying for the community under siege. If another school closes or a school that remains open fails to educate children, many preachers sound no alarm from the pulpit, other than praying for the children and the school.

The backbone of sacred eloquence is authenticity. Authenticity allows us to stand as ambassadors representing God and God's people

---

[15] Claudette Copeland, "Preaching in the Key of F," *The African American Pulpit* 7/1 (Spring 2003): 36.

and declare, "Thus saith the Lord." Producing sacred eloquence requires authentic courage because souls are at stake. The preacher who conveys sacred eloquence does not possess all truth about all things, but has enough truth to speak life to the world, though such speaking may put that preacher on the hit-list of the dream stealers and the death dealers.

Next, while preachers possessed of sacred eloquence have ministry models, they pride themselves on honestly presenting what the Lord has given them. This leads us to a brief discussion concerning plagiarism. Such a discussion is appropriate and timely in a festschrift honoring a preacher from whom so many preachers have stolen. Our short, common-sense instruction is this: If you use the words of others, give them credit, and do not take credit for yourself!

Plagiarism is not new among sacred orators. It has long been one of the dark sides of preaching. Preachers often attempt to justify it with excuses such as fatigue, or the stolen sermon was so good that it had to be preached again, or the springs of sermonic inspiration refused to bring forth fresh water by Sunday morning. In an Internet-dominated world, the inexcusable practice of plagiarism has run amok. One no longer has to visit a library or a bookstore to steal from the greatest preachers of all times. With a few keystrokes and the move of a mouse, preachers can cut and paste whatever they can find and claim it and proclaim it. Preachers who do this are neither authentic, nor honest, nor original. In *The Little Book of Plagiarism*, Richard Posner says that plagiarism "is a species of intellectual fraud."[16]

Are we being too harsh or unrealistic? It is commonly suggested that there are only a few original ideas in the world. So whenever we preach, aren't we simply rehashing and reissuing ideas of others anyway? Yes and no. Certainly, we were not the first to promote the idea of grace abounding. Or to say faithfulness is required of the

---

[16] Richard A. Posner, *The Little Book of Plagiarism* (New York: Pantheon Books, 2007) 106.

Christian unto death. Or to say that love conquers all. Or to say that life has harsh seasons and tender moments. So when we build on such well-known truths, we are rehashing and reissuing the statements and thoughts of others. But that is precisely the point. The world knows that we did not first conceive such truths. Our listeners only ask that we reissue these truths in a fresh way for our time as God reveals them anew to us.

Furthermore, preachers who fail to give attribution to others when using their work defame the craft of sacred oratory and stain the sacred desk. People are not impressed by thieves or ungrateful borrowers. Sacred eloquence and homiletic ethics must go hand in hand. Simply put, preachers should use the words of exemplary preachers with attribution. Congregants will appreciate your honesty and laud your earnestness in study.

This brings us to the difficulty of being original. Originality requires hard, tedious work. The sheer intensity of labor needed to be original is the reason there are so few preachers who are consistent producers of sacred eloquence. There is no substitute for hard work. Each of us occasionally desires a shortcut from strenuous effort. But there is no shortcut by which one can arrive quickly at the destination of sacred eloquence. Thomas Potter once queried, "How often have we listened to preachers bury us under a deluge of empty verbiage?"[17] Equally problematic are those preachers who consistently repeat the same ideas in their sermons because the work of careful sermon preparation was not done.

The marks of an ill-prepared sermon emerge very quickly: Each move of the sermon was not studied and dissected, verified by commentaries, sages, and the wisdom of the ages. If the sermon raises major theological and social issues at all, those issues were not given any more than a passing thought. Grace in the sermon was not balanced by justice. Love in the sermon was not met by personal

---

[17] Potter, *Sacred Eloquence*, 72.

responsibility. The metaphors, if there were any, were puny and unimaginative. No great doctrines of the faith were taught, and no grand themes of the faith were presented anew for another generation. A proverb says, "A sermon which costs the preacher little to compose costs the audience a great deal to listen to, and that which costs little is worth precisely what it costs."

Eloquence requires a loss of sleep, the relinquishment of a measure of leisure time, and a voracious appetite for reading. The Holy Spirit often meets the one from whom sacred eloquence will flow in a study or a library, then in meditative moments and hours of prayer. The Spirit never tires of visiting if the orator never tires of working to present the revelation that God has to give to him or her. We paraphrase Fred Craddock's words to a student who complained to him that he had "a family, a church, other classes, and a long drive" and therefore could not find the time for study that Craddock required: "Why not tell God that you are just too busy to prepare sermons and go and do something else. God will not mind."

If preachers are willing to endure the sacrifice necessary to proclaim sacred eloquence, God will reward their attentiveness to the craft. After many seasons of arduous work, those preachers are able to speak increasingly from the overflow of what has been stored in their minds and hearts. The proclamation comes forth as fresh bread from heaven, even though God and the preacher know that this heavenly bread has been baking in the preacher's mind and heart for decades.

Sacred eloquence is also hard work because even the most trained, experienced preacher has seasons of lack, seasons of coldness, seasons of emptiness, and seasons of futility. It is never always summer homiletically; nor are we always surrounded by a quiet culture conducive to creative preaching. Imagine the weight on Dr. Martin Luther King, Jr., as he prepared to preach at the Dexter Avenue Baptist Church in Montgomery, Alabama, with the hell hounds of racism chasing him, his family, his friends, his church, and his community.

This same weight is borne by every eloquent sacred orator, for he or she also is surrounded by the hell hounds of his or her day. Those hounds neither sleep nor slumber. Thus, in light of this inevitable truth, the eloquent sacred orator must prepare well as often as life permits. Indeed, the salvation of souls is ever at stake. How can one step forward to the sacred desk without due diligence in preparation when so much hangs in the balance? How can one not study hard and pray harder when he or she knows that an ultimate account of one's pulpit work must be given at the judgment bar of the Almighty?

Wordsmith—we begin this section with the words of John Henry Cardinal Newman, whose characterization of a poet and orator summarizes brilliantly the work of a master wordsmith:

> If he is an orator, then too he speaks, not only "distinctè" and "splendidè," but also "*aptè*." His page is the lucid mirror of his mind and life.... He writes passionately, because he feels keenly; forcibly, because he conceives vividly; he sees too clearly to be vague; he is too serious to be otiose; he can analyze his subject and therefore he is rich; he embraces it as a whole and in its parts, and therefore is consistent; he has a firm hold of it, and therefore is luminous. When his imagination wells up, it overflows in ornaments; when his heart is touched, it thrills along his verse. He always has the right word for the right idea and never a word too much. If he is brief, it is because few words suffice; if he is lavish of them, still each word has its mark, and aids not embarrasses, the vigorous march of his elocution.[18]

Two of Newman's observations are especially germane for our purposes—the first is knowing one's subject and embracing it in whole and in part and therefore being consistent; the second is having the right word for the right idea.

A wordsmith dabbles in the laboratory of words. In the case of the producer of sacred eloquence, the main book in his or her laboratory is the Bible. A vocabulary of depth and significance is first

---

[18] John Henry Cardinal Newman, *The Idea of a University Defined and Illustrated* (London: Longmans, Green and Company, 1905) 212.

gained by reading scripture. Amazingly, there are those who preach as if they have never read a Bible, or at least not in a long time. Their sermons show little understanding of text and context of biblical narratives. The Bible is not an easy book to read and decipher. But it is the most significant tool in the toolkit of one who would produce sacred eloquence.

No Christian preacher speaks apart from a tradition that has preceded the preacher. A large part of that tradition is the biblical text, with its stories of love, revenge, rape, forgiveness, family, confusion, jealousy, war, humor, prophecy, hope, justice, selflessness, and renewal. There are also many other sources for sacred revelation in the culture, from Saturday conversations in barbershops and beauty salons to TV sitcoms and Broadway musicals.

The subject matter of the Christian faith is found in its great affirmations, which allow for loftiness, hyperbole, and an august stance toward language. Fred Craddock aptly chronicles some of these affirmations:

> God is one; God creates, sustains, judges, and redeems creation; God loves all persons but at the same time calls for ethical earnestness and responsible relationships among us; creation, history, and prophets reveal God, but in Jesus of Nazareth, crucified, risen and glorified, God is known supremely; God's Spirit dwells with the faithful community to comfort, guide, correct, and purify; God is not only the source but the end and meaning of all life which is purposely moving toward God's good and final purpose.[19]

Sacred eloquence requires thick subject matter rather than puny topics that change as rapidly as the next news cycle on cable television. The speaker of sacred eloquence is familiar with the latest conventional wisdom and the newest religious treatise on *The New York Times* best-sellers list or Oprah's Book Club selection. They are in tune with the new approaches to religion by popular pastors and

---

[19] Fred B. Craddock, *Preaching* (Nashville: Abingdon Press, 1985) 145.

the latest "theologian of the year." Still, the eloquent sacred orator recognizes that preaching must not only be relevant, but it must also be rooted in the deep soil of the biblical story. Preaching that is both relevant and rooted will speak powerfully to the current generation and likely even to generations yet unborn.

We now comment briefly on the right word for the right idea. Many preachers might wonder if sacred eloquence requires a large vocabulary. The short answer is "no." The long answer follows: it requires a vocabulary of depth and significance. Such a vocabulary shuns platitudes and appreciates hyperbole, metaphor, and other tools of creative expression. Sacred eloquence avoids weak, worn verbs, since those verbs do not enable listeners to viscerally experience and be moved by God's good news.

Sacred eloquence strives to be specific. So much contemporary preaching is vague. Many sermons present possibility after possibility but lack the courage or intellectual precision to name the sin or address the issue head-on. Consequently, the sermon is simply a series of band-aids applied to the surface of wounds—wounds that are left unattended to fester. The real issues were actually never addressed.

Vagueness will never create sacred eloquence because it lacks the concreteness that arouses the senses. It is not necessary to call people's names in the pulpit to ensure that listeners know the identity of the perpetrators who trespass against the justice of God and the well-being of humanity. Name-calling is an act of last resort for the speaker of sacred eloquence. However, sacred eloquence is *clear* about the culprits of violence and injustice and God's abiding commitment to peace and justice.

In sacred oratory, the right word for the right idea requires careful and mature decision making. Consider these memorable statements from scripture and history: "David, you are the man" (2 Samuel 12:7). "Power concedes nothing without a demand" (Frederick Douglass). "I found God in myself, and I loved her fiercely" (Ntozake Shange). These are more than statements. They are the outcomes of sober consideration about one's position in the world, what matters most, and one's destiny.

Sacred eloquence requires that we pay more attention to our words. While there are other professions where attention to words is crucial (e.g., lawyers, editors, and playwrights), the preaching profession involves an unabashed claim that the orator is speaking for God. This claim carries a grand responsibility. Failure to consistently honor this responsibility can cause grave harm. Consider the preacher who takes this matter lightly. For him or her the preaching moment becomes a trite task instead of a marvelous opportunity. Thus, their words are carelessly flung about, unaware of the soul who has arrived at the preaching moment in need of salvation, comfort, or deliverance.

Many cultural commentators have discussed the "dumbing down" of America and the decreasing literacy in a technological age saturated with gadgets. The pulpit has not escaped unscathed. One has only to turn on the television on any Sunday in any state in our country to hear sermons that are difficult to decipher at best, and sermons that people have no interest in deciphering at worst. Far from sacred eloquence, we hear a chorus of jumbled, boring, theologically suspect, and poorly worded sermons. What happened to sacred eloquence?

Eloquence in a Post-Gardner Taylor Age

Where does all of this leave us? The paucity of educational opportunities that prepare persons to think for themselves and to express themselves clearly does not bode well for sacred eloquence. To add to the difficulty, preachers are now bombarded with television and Internet images of wealthy pastors who have little or no seminary training and who do not value eloquence. Preachers are subtly and blatantly encouraged to venture into televangelism. The prevailing ecclesial wisdom often goes like this: "Get a broadcast; a website; a ministry separate from the church; a MySpace page; a gimmick if you can think of one; and a blog; but whatever you do, get yourself out there. If your church does not make you famous, you can toot your own horn with help from technology."

There are, indeed, sizeable barriers against the return of sacred eloquence. Let's face it; sacred eloquence will not return in any significant way to the American pulpit. The odds are stacked too high against that. So what can be done in the face of such overwhelming odds?

If the 2008 presidential campaign taught us anything, it taught us that change is possible when buttressed by hope, a great deal of planning, hard work, and a bit of suffering. We conclude this essay with three suggestions that we believe might help sacred eloquence to remain a viable homiletic option.

First, those of us who believe in sacred eloquence must do more to model it, teach it, and pray for it. Second, seminaries must become more accountable to churches as they prepare persons for proclamation, and churches must be more accountable to seminaries by offering more financial and other support to those seminaries. Third, by increasing the presence of sacred eloquence through a small number of preachers who have access to large audiences and professors who have access to large numbers of students, we can ensure that sacred eloquence will survive, if not thrive, well into the twenty-first century.

Modeling Sacred Eloquence

For several decades, many homileticians have suggested that preaching should be more conversational, understandable, and accessible. We wholeheartedly agree with this suggestion. However, in the last several decades, few seminaries have presented cogent classes or programs that make the vocabularies and the proclamation of preachers more robust, lofty, and eloquent. We are not recommending that persons want to hear each Sunday the "Gettysburg Address," the "I Have a Dream" speech, or similar oratorical masterpieces. We are saying that hearers deserve preaching possessed of loftiness occasionally, if not regularly. Pastors need to be more concerned with the power of words and not just the latest sermon illustration.

In light of the local, national, and global challenges we face, we need serious words from the pulpit that cling to the hearts and captivate the minds of listeners. Now is the time for compelling language that demands listeners' attention and response. Now is the time for a grand word from the pulpit that insists that God's salvation is stronger and bigger than the problems we face. These are not the days for "It Is Your Season" prosperity messages, which insist that the season is always summer. These are not the days for "Don't Worry Be Happy" messages poured like fresh sugarcane syrup upon starving souls. These are not the days for pulpit messages that equivocate about this possibility, ruminate about that possibility, and vacillate about the main things. Instead, these are opportune times for sacred eloquence.

Those of us lamenting the loss of clear language, a love of words, and passionate oratory that demands a decision must do more of this type of preaching ourselves; ask it of students and recommend it to peers and colleagues. If sacred eloquence continues to recede in our culture, we who know better are most blameworthy. We must use our opportunities in pulpits, seminaries, divinity schools, lecture halls, and certainly in the public square to provide hearers with sacred eloquence that shows and tells the world, in the words of Tex Sample:

> The story of the world is that of a Triune God who creates and redeems the world and who will finally take it to its completion.... God's story is not a mere entrant into the world; it is the story of the world itself so that the world cannot be understood rightly except in terms of the story of God. When Christ enters the world, the world

is changed, history is changed, the powers are defeated on the cross, and their ultimate fate is clear.[20]

The Mutual Accountability of Seminaries and Churches

Debate has long raged concerning the role of seminaries in preparing persons to preach well. Increasingly, neither homiletics courses nor basic public speaking courses are required in seminaries. Many students come to seminary precisely because they want to preach and serve as pastors. Those students cannot graduate from seminary without taking a battery of courses in Bible and theology; yet they can graduate without taking a course in preaching, even though preaching will be one of the most significant, consistent professional duties they perform. The diminishing significance of preaching in the theological curriculum might indicate that seminaries feel more accountable to their accrediting associations and denominational bodies than to local congregations.

Also, many seminaries offer preaching courses that are lecture-hall size (meaning fifty to seventy-five students). After a few sessions in the lecture-hall-size classes, students are placed for the majority of the semester in smaller groups typically led by Ph.D. students who have never served as pastors and often know little about the joys and complexities of preaching. Seminaries can begin to make sacred eloquence a priority by hiring professors who preach regularly and are connected to a church! While it can be helpful in certain ways if these preaching professors hold Ph.D's in homiletics or other related academic disciplines, seminaries should insist that their preaching professors are expert practitioners.

---

[20] Tex Sample, *Powerful Persuasion: Multimedia Witness in Christian Worship* (Nashville: Abingdon Press, 2005) 21–22.

Preaching courses must also again be treated as "bread and butter" courses in the seminary curriculum. We mean this in more than a metaphorical way. A large number of persons who attend seminary will at some point attempt to literally earn their bread and butter behind the pulpit. Consequently, competence in the pulpit should be considered a professional survival skill.

Undoubtedly, we want clergy to have sound theology, basic knowledge of pastoral care, biblical literacy, and especially knowledge of church administration. However, at the end of the day, they will be paid to be pastors and preachers. So why not build seminary curricula as if this is the case? Why not treat preaching as the bar examination is treated for lawyers? If a person wants to be a lawyer, she or he must pass a bar examination. A person can attend law school only for the information and then move to another field and not sit for the bar examination. But to practice law, certain professional competencies are expected and required.

A similar thing can happen with seminary and preaching. A person can attend seminary for the profound theological information a seminary education affords. If that person has no interest in preaching, preaching knowledge would not be required. But if a student's career is to be one of proclamation or instruction in proclamation, seminaries should treat preaching courses as preparation for the "homiletic bar examination." As many fledgling pastors soon discover, a congregation can be tougher and more scrutinizing than any judge or jury. More importantly, all preachers will ultimately stand before God, the Great Judge, in order to give an account of every word spoken in the pulpit.

No matter how broad a minister's theological education might be, churches will have been cheated and preachers will have been ill prepared to face the real challenges of leading a congregation if we do not insist on excellence in preaching in our seminaries. Furthermore, seminaries will continue to experience declining enrollments if they do not make preaching a priority and give students the attention and training necessary to achieve homiletic competence, and better still, homiletic excellence.

Having presented our expectations of seminaries, we, in fairness, must also lay some responsibility upon congregations. In order for congregations to expect pastoral and homiletic excellence from seminary-trained ministers, these same congregations must be willing to significantly invest in the financial well-being of seminaries. Theological schools, especially those not affiliated with wealthy research universities, are under enormous financial pressures. Often, those pressures result in schools having to downsize their faculty and curtail their curricular offerings. The faculty and curriculum related to the practical arts of ministry, such as preaching, are frequently the first to be sacrificed on the altar of economic exigencies. If congregations, irrespective of size, began including in their yearly budgets a substantial, even sacrificial, financial commitment to a seminary, those contributions would be a tangible investment in the future of sacred eloquence.

A Little Sacred Eloquence Goes a Long Way

We accept that there might never again be the amount of sacred eloquence that we witnessed in the nineteenth and early twentieth centuries. Thankfully, however, sacred eloquence is like the mustard seed in Jesus' parable (Mark 4:30–32). A small amount of it can produce big results, especially when harnessed with a responsible use of media and technology. If we only increase the presence of sacred eloquence through a small number of preachers who have access to large audiences and through professors who have access to large numbers of students, this will go a long way to impacting twenty-first-century preaching.

There are many compelling examples of the long lifespan of sacred eloquence: Augustine is still read more than 1,500 years after his death. Charles Spurgeon is quoted more than 100 years after his death. The sermons and speeches of Martin Luther King, Jr., are as powerful as they were when preached more than forty years ago. And even though he retired eighteen years ago from his pastorate, the preaching of Dr. Gardner Taylor remains the gold standard of sacred eloquence for past, present, and emerging generations of preachers.

Yale Divinity School celebrated the poetry and power in Dr. Taylor's sacred eloquence by inviting him to serve as the one hundredth Lyman Beecher lecturer in 1976. In the last of those lectures, which is titled "Preaching the Whole Counsel of God," Dr. Taylor recounts the experience of a beloved deacon who, upon his deathbed, said that he wished he could hear Dr. Taylor preach one more time. Reflecting pastorally and homiletically on that experience, Dr. Taylor said to those attending the lectures,

> Now, no preacher has of himself or herself anything of real significance to say to anyone who is within the view of the swelling of Jordan. But there is a Gospel, and you are privileged to be summoned to declare it. It can stand people on their feet for the living of their days. And, also—what a privilege almost too precious to be mentioned—it may be that the Gospel which you preach will then steady some poor pilgrims as they come to where the bridgeless river is and some of them, feeling the spray of Jordan misting in the face, might thank God as they cross the river that He made you a preacher.[21]

---

[21] Gardner C. Taylor, *How Shall They Preach: The Lyman Beecher Lectures and Five Lenten Sermons* (Elgin IL: Progressive Baptist Publishing House, 1977) 93–94.

We know not how close either of us is to the Jordan River right now. But this one thing we know: we are glad, mighty glad, that God made Gardner Calvin Taylor a preacher and a preacher's preacher!

THE MEASURE OF PROPHETIC MINISTRY: TRAJECTORIES IN CONTEMPORARY AFRICAN-AMERICAN PREACHING AND THE LEGACY OF GARDNER C. TAYLOR

Cheryl J. Sanders

The African-American prophetic preaching tradition originates in the experience of suffering. The capture and transport of millions of Africans to the Americas was accomplished over a period of four centuries by European slave traders. Eventually, the masses of slaves on plantations in North America were evangelized via revivals and plantation missions. There emerged from among these early black evangelicals preachers who responded to the call to proclaim the good news of Jesus Christ to people in chains. Typically, these slave preachers had to summon their congregations to the hush harbors and forests of the South in the middle of the night to escape detection and avoid punishment. To proclaim freedom to the captives was to emulate Jesus and the prophets of the Old and New Testaments who spoke the word of God to the people of God with a full awareness of their past and present suffering and their hopes and dreams for the future. Most of these slave preachers are unknown and undocumented, but the fruits of their labors have been multiplied through generations of Americans of African descent who are at the same time the offspring of chattel slavery and aspirants to the unfulfilled American promise of life, liberty, and the pursuit of happiness. However, the African-American prophetic preaching tradition was established as a public witness against slavery by men and women whose legacy of courageous confrontation in the name of Christ has been celebrated and preserved, including David Walker, Sojourner Truth, Frederick Douglass, and Maria Steward.

Although slavery in the United States was abolished at the end of the Civil War, successive generations of preachers have responded to the call to minister to persons living under conditions of segregation, discrimination, and poverty. Dr. Martin Luther King, Jr., remains the greatest exemplar of the tradition to date, and the sermon he preached during the 1963 March on Washington, often referred to as the "I Have a Dream" speech, provided a twentieth-century benchmark for prophetic preaching as public witness. The fall 2008 issue of *The African American Pulpit* features sermons and essays on prophetic preaching produced by African-American preachers and scholars who are highly esteemed representatives of Dr. King's generation and legacy. This essay seeks to demarcate some trajectories in modern African-American prophetic preaching.

Generally speaking, the word "trajectory" has three meanings: (1) the path of a projectile or other moving body through space; (2) a chosen or taken course: "What died with [the assassinated leaders] was a moral trajectory, a style of aspiration" (Lance Morrow); (3) mathematics: a curve that cuts all of a given family of curves or surfaces at the same angle.[1] The sermons under consideration here signify a path taken by African Americans in the wake of massive forced migration from the coasts of West Africa to the plantations of North America, beginning more than 400 years ago, along a chosen course of spiritual and moral aspiration for freedom and justice. Moreover, this trajectory bears the mathematical sense of cutting across a given family of Christian traditions at "the same angle," which is to suggest that African-American prophetic preaching cuts against the grain of a peculiar mode of incongruous Christian preaching and practice that has simultaneously denied and reinforced social practices of racism and segregation.

---

[1] "Trajectory," *The American Heritage Dictionary of the English Language*, 4th ed. (Boston: Houghton Mifflin Company, 2004). Found online at http://dictionary.reference.com/browse/trajectory (accessed 11 December 2008).

What is prophetic preaching? How is it different from other types or traditions of preaching? Marvin McMickle's brief essay "Prophetic Preaching in the 21st Century: It Is Not Just about the Words" provides a helpful and necessary definition of prophetic preaching from the vantage point of homiletics. His understanding of what makes a sermon prophetic is based upon one or more of three specific things a prophetic preacher does. The prophetic preacher: (1) takes a text from the biblical prophets; (2) emphasizes themes of justice and righteousness; and (3) delivers the sermon with zeal and fervor.[2] As the subtitle of his essay would indicate, McMickle draws a further distinction between what makes a sermon prophetic and what makes a preacher prophetic, citing the measure of the preacher's commitment to living and doing what is preached as the definitive criterion for prophetic preaching.

What kinds of sermons do African Americans preach? Assuming that the preachers whose sermons are under scrutiny here inhabit the intersection of prophetic discourse and African-American life, we must inquire about the nature of African-American preaching. To assess the preaching of African Americans in particular, we can turn to my essay, "The Woman as Preacher," which is actually a comparative analysis of thirty-six published manuscripts of sermons preached by African-American men and women in terms of several key categories: (1) sermon form, (2) biblical texts, (3) central themes, (4) use of inclusive language with reference to God and persons, and (5) homiletical tasks the sermons were designed to perform, such as affirmation, celebration, critique, interpretation, storytelling, teaching, and invitation to Christian commitment. Although the original intent of that essay was to highlight the distinctive characteristics of sermons preached by African-American women, the approach undertaken in the analysis illumines our understanding of the preaching of African Americans in general. Only seventeen

---

[2] Marvin A. McMickle, "Prophetic Preaching in the 21st Century: It Is Not Just about the Words," *The African American Pulpit* 11/4 (Fall 2008): 16–18.

percent of these thirty-six sermons would meet McMickle's initial criterion for prophetic preaching, that is, taking a text from a biblical prophet. However, it is especially noteworthy that the male and female preachers were identical in this regard, there being no difference in the proportion of men and women in the sample who took their texts from the Bible prophets. With respect to content, the most prevalent themes found among the sermons preached by both male and female African-American preachers were (1) the church and its mission, (2) Christian virtues, and (3) racial identity.[3] Although McMickle and I have adopted different rubrics for our understanding of African-American preaching, each of the themes I have noted enables the emphasis upon justice and righteousness that denotes prophetic preaching in McMickle's scheme. Rather than to designate prophetic preaching as a discrete theme in my analysis, instead I employ the expressions "criticizing the church" and "criticizing the society" as homiletical tasks, signifying essentially the same thing as McMickle's notion of justice and righteousness. Criticizing the church means "pointing out the problems and shortcomings of a particular body of Christians, or of the church at large," while criticizing the society entails "pointing out the problems and shortcomings of the society and especially the unjust social structures and systems."[4]

Both expressions constitute what prophetic preachers do, and it so happens that the particular sermon used in the essay to illustrate criticizing the church cites what is probably the most popular scripture passage preached by African Americans in the prophetic tradition, namely, Luke 4:18–19. In this text Jesus reads from the book of the prophet Isaiah to announce his ministry in the synagogue. I concluded my focused comparison of the preaching of African-American women and men by advocating an ethic of mutual

[3] Cheryl J. Sanders, "The Woman as Preacher," *Journal of Religious Thought* 43/1 (Spring/Summer 1986): 6–23.
[4] Ibid., 11–12.

appreciation and shared learning between the two groups of preachers: "Women's sermons can teach men to temper social criticism with compassion. At the same time women can learn from men how to sharpen their own testimonies and calls for Christian commitment with the cutting edge of prophetic indignation."[5] Because my earlier essay examined sermon manuscripts and not live or recorded performances of sermons, I make no attempt to measure the "zeal and fervor" McMickle ascribes to prophetic preaching. However, it is not difficult for the reader of these manuscripts to imagine the emotion and energy with which these sermons were actually preached. Similarly, I do not have sufficient data to examine these sermons in light of McMickle's claim that prophetic preaching must be tied to prophetic ministry, for "the work of the prophet is in both word and deed.... Our words are meaningless unless they are matched by our actions."[6]

Informed by the findings of my previous analysis of African-American sermons, then, and with some added insights from McMickle's work, I propose a simple framework for highlighting the prophetic character of the 2008 collection of sermon manuscripts: (1) the statement of a social problem, (2) the analysis of its causes, and (3) the offer of a remedy from scripture. These three features provide a convenient way to frame a brief overview of each of these sermons. The prominence of these features in the six sermon manuscripts I have selected from *The African American Pulpit* points us to the conclusion that the African-American prophetic preaching tradition is alive and well in the twenty-first century.

Mack King Carter is pastor of the New Mount Olive Baptist Church in Fort Lauderdale, Florida. The title of his sermon states a social problem: "Why Racism Continues." He offers an explanation for the persistence of racism in American society in response to the 2007 incident where radio announcer Don Imus referred to black

---

[5] Ibid., 22.
[6] McMickle, "Prophetic Preaching in the 21st Century," 17.

female athletes on the Rutgers basketball team as "nappy-headed hos." Carter's extensive analysis of the causes of racism is informed by a broad and sophisticated understanding of the problem, with insights drawn from history, philosophy, and the social sciences. He gives twelve reasons for the persistence of racism in American culture: parental dysfunction; ignorance; pigmentocracy (skin-color prejudice); the need to feel superior (white supremacy); theological and ecclesiastical sanction; philosophical insinuations (especially Immanuel Kant); the political system; self-interested economics; mis-education (failed stewardship of educational opportunity); media (including hip hop music with degrading lyrics); juridicial injustice; and self-hatred. Based upon two passages from the New Testament, 1 John 4:20 and Colossians 4:6, Carter offers two remedies to the problem of racism, love and faith: the love you must have for your brother and sister if you say you love God, and faith that transforms your public attitude.[7]

Cynthia Hale is the senior pastor of the Ray of Hope Disciples of Christ Church in Decatur, Georgia. Her sermon "It's Time for the Silent Giant to Speak Up" begins with a blanket statement: "Our world is in a mess," as indicated by pornography, black male incarceration and unemployment, and the high rates of HIV infection among black women. The remedy is a church assuming its role in the society as "salt and light," following Jesus' teaching in Matthew 5:13–16. Hale outlines a number of initiatives the church should take to rectify a broad canvas of social problems, beginning with the exhortation to be bold in our witness, to reclaim our prophetic voice, and to speak truth to power. She sets forth an ambitious agenda of social advocacy and intervention to be undertaken by the church, including: (1) advocacy of policies and programs to end homelessness and hunger; (2) provision of greater employment opportunities, training, housing, health insurance, and

---

[7] Mack King Carter, "Why Racism Continues," *The African American Pulpit* 11/4 (Fall 2008): 52–58.

day care; (3) restoration of the health of the black family by providing programs to teach parenting skills, mentoring, and motivating of black youth; (4) addressing inequities in the criminal justice system; (5) reconciling persons to God.[8]

Frederick D. Haynes, III, is pastor of Friendship West Baptist Church in Dallas, Texas. He begins his sermon "Are You the One Making Waves?" with a defense of a statement made by Michelle Obama during her husband's 2008 presidential campaign, namely, that she was proud to be an American for the first time in her life. Haynes uses her as an example of one who was labeled, defined, and attacked because of her "anointed audacity to step out of the box." He goes on to identify the social problem in terms that are reminiscent of Cynthia Hale's sermon: the prison system; redlining to preclude economic development in black neighborhoods; AIDS as the number one killer of black women from ages eighteen to twenty-five; and the rise in reports of racism to the EEOC (federal Equal Employment Opportunity Commission), which have doubled since 1991. Haynes's proposed remedy is a threefold exhortation: be conscious of your identity, confront the powers that be, and "make some waves to bring the people of God back to God." From the text 1 Kings 18:17, he retells the story of Elijah's prophetic encounter with Ahab in the vernacular of contemporary black culture. The sermon ends with a roll call of "troublemakers," beginning with Elijah and Jesus, and contrasting the "troublemakers" with "titleholders" from the Bible to the present (e.g., Saul was the titleholder, David was the troublemaker; Lyndon Johnson was the titleholder, Martin Luther King, Jr., was the troublemaker, and so forth).[9]

---

[8] Cynthia L. Hale, "It's Time for the Silent Giant to Speak Up," *The African American Pulpit* 11/4 (Fall 2008): 59–63.

[9] Frederick D. Haynes, III, "Are You the One Making Waves?" *The African American Pulpit* 11/4 (Fall 2008): 64–70.

H. Beecher Hicks is the senior servant of Metropolitan Baptist Church in Washington, DC. The title of his sermon is taken from the song written for the film *Hustle and Flow*, which won an Academy Award: "You Know It's Hard Out Here for a Pimp." Hicks's message is laced with references, quotes, and allusions from popular culture, and his complaint is that the church is silent in the face of an increasingly vulgar, virulent, abusive culture, a condition indicative of "spiritual wickedness in high places." The particular problem is the glorification of the dehumanization of women, and Hicks laments that life has become nothing but sex and sensuality, an endless parade of pushers, pimps, and "hos." His remedy is rooted in Paul's exhortation to holy living in Romans 12:1, to be holy, separate, set apart for a sacred purpose, to "come on up a little higher above raggedy living, fast funny money, vulgar language and examples." The alternative perspective and purpose he offers are drawn from the wellsprings of traditional Christian hymns such as "Guide Me, O Thou Great Jehovah," "My Hope Is Built" and "Higher Ground."[10]

Otis B. Moss, III, is pastor of the Trinity United Church of Christ in Chicago, Illinois. In his sermon "Why the Black Church Won't Shut Up," he brings a comprehensive historical perspective to his analysis of the social problems the black church should be addressing, inclusive of past and present concerns, beginning with the trans-Atlantic slave trade, Reconstruction, Jim Crow segregation, and more recently, redlining, subprime lending, and disrespect. His rationale for the necessity of speaking up is grounded in the example of Jesus (Luke 19:29–30), who addressed the poverty in Bethphage "house of unripe figs" and Bethany "house of affliction" before his triumphal entry into Jerusalem, a city of wealth. In addition, Jesus ordered his disciples to untie a "colonized colt" so that it would be free to do the things that God wanted it to do. While exhorting the

---

[10] H. Beecher Hicks, "You Know It's Hard Out Here for a Pimp," *The African American Pulpit* 11/4 (Fall 2008): 72–77.

black church not to "shut up," Moss makes a barely veiled allusion to his controversial pastoral predecessor at Trinity United Church of Christ, Reverend Jeremiah Wright, whose prophetic speaking was severely criticized and silenced during the course of the 2008 campaign for president of the United States. Moss concludes that the church should keep telling the truth and keep speaking about the love of Jesus, because "God has done too much for us as a people to keep our mouths shut."[11]

James Perkins is pastor of Greater Christ Baptist Church in Detroit, Michigan. His sermon "A Resurrection in the Ghetto" is based on one of the favorite prophetic texts of African-American preachers throughout the history of the black church tradition, the story of Ezekiel and the dry bones (Ezekiel 37:1–10). Perkins characterizes the social problem in terms such as hopelessness, apathy, polarization, alienation, fragmentation, and brokenness. By comparison, Ezekiel faced the impossible task of reviving the hopes of a lifeless people who lived in captivity in the Babylonian "ghetto," and the hand of the Lord came upon him in a ghetto of dry bones.

Perkins takes the same critical question Ezekiel raised to direct attention to the current situation in African-American churches and communities: Can these bones live? Can a church broken by cliques and factions come together and be the powerful spiritual force it ought to be in the lives of people? Can a people who believe they have no potential ever become what God knows they can be? His remedy is profoundly spiritual; the ultimate aim of the Spirit is not to make us shout but to make us useful. We have neglected God's life-giving Word and we need God's Spirit. Perkins proclaims that Jesus was resurrected in a ghetto outside the metropolis of Jerusalem. If we get in touch with Jesus, then God will "resurrect the ghetto," and the

---

[11] Otis B. Moss, III, "Why the Black Church Won't Shut Up," *The African American Pulpit* 11/4 (Fall 2008): 78–82.

impact will be felt by drug addicts, stray husbands, negligent mothers, and dead churches.[12]

The six sermons surveyed provide clear and convincing evidence that the prophetic tradition in African-American preaching remains intact in the present age. In these sermons, each of these prominent pastors addresses and analyzes social problems, biblical texts, and proposed remedies. In light of McMickle's essay, however, we observe that content alone is insufficient as an indicator of prophetic ministry. Borrowing from the writings of Cornel West, he presents a three-step action agenda as a means of authenticating the preacher's prophetic ministry. McMickle's criteria can be posited as three questions we may employ to guide our evaluation of the prophetic agenda undergirding the proclamation. Namely, does it (1) develop the courage to care? (2) to change our lives? (3) to impact our historical circumstances? The great preaching legacy of Gardner C. Taylor offers us the opportunity to examine a great exemplar of both the prophetic word and the prophetic agenda. First we will evaluate the content of one of his prophetic sermons, and then scrutinize his prophetic agenda in light of the three queries suggested by McMickle.

Taylor's sermon "Three Women and God" was published in *Women: To Preach or Not to Preach*, a collection of sermons edited by Ella Pearson Mitchell in 1991. The entire volume has a prophetic orientation and agenda, namely, to support the preaching ministry of women. Taylor cites the book of Ruth to address the exclusion of women from preaching and leadership in the church. He also compares Ruth's story to the predicament of the African Americans who were pressured by racism and sexism to leave the South in the massive social relocation known as the Great Migration. Ruth was a Moabite woman who insisted upon returning to her mother-in-law's Jewish homeland after both women's husbands died. Taylor's poignant analysis of the problem of race attributes the failure of the

---

[12] James Perkins, "A Resurrection in the Ghetto," *The African American Pulpit* 11/4 (Fall 2008): 83–88.

democratic vision of America to the "wicked liaison between greed and racism":

> But how tragic that a land like America, so blessed, so great, would now be so imperiled by a wicked liaison between greed and racism, so that the nation has penalized itself and paralyzed its energy. And how sad that the heirs of the people who braved the uncertainties of migration, and who came out of the dark night of slavery with a bright vision of who they were and what they might become, should be succeeded in our day by so many who seem to have lost all sense of direction and purpose. I weep for the black American community when I remember whose descendants we are.[13]

Taylor's devastating critique of America's failed democratic vision includes an indictment of the sexist practices in the churches:

> As the nation has chosen to turn away from its democratic vision by its choice of racism and sexism, so have we in our churches chosen to distort the vision of the kingdom of God by limiting the full exercise of the gifts of women. We have excluded women from the pulpit and other areas of church leadership and dared to claim that this is God's will. We are guilty of an unholy liaison between sexism and the privilege of power. This is not of God. There is in Christ neither Jew or Greek, neither bond or free, neither male nor female.[14]

The scriptural text is Galatians 3:23, cited as a rebuke and a remedy in response to the problem of exclusive practices in the church and society. Taylor commends as a solution to the problem the "covenant of grace," signified by the presence of Ruth in the genealogy of Jesus:

> When I turn to the fifth verse of that first chapter of the book of Matthew, there her name stands. She becomes the mother of Obed,

---

[13] Gardner C. Taylor, "Three Women and God," in *Women: To Preach or Not to Preach*, ed. Ella Pearson Mitchell (Valley Forge: Judson Press, 1991) 85.

[14] Ibid., 86.

Obed becomes the father of Jesse, Jesse becomes the father of David, and there in that lineage comes the Savior of the world. This Moabite girl, this alien child of the hills, this foreigner, this woman in a society that devalued and oppressed women, by loyalty to love and to duty, enters the covenant of grace.... Who could have imagined that God would choose to use a humble foreign woman in such a way? God's ways are not our ways. Yet some of us are trying even now to choose for God who should preach and who should not. How arrogant. How outrageous.[15]

Taylor narrates from the Old and New Testament scriptures the bestowal of covenantal grace and divine favor upon an oppressed alien who ultimately is ascribed a place of honor in the genealogy of Jesus. From this vantage point he defends the ability of women to preach, by acknowledging God's prerogative to choose who preaches and who leads. The story of Ruth's triumph over tragic circumstances fuels Taylor's prophetic indictment of those who would deny the ministry of women.

In her 2003 study *Contemporary African American Preaching*, author L. Susan Bond devotes an entire chapter to the preaching of Gardner Taylor. She takes note of Taylor's critique of America's failure to honor its national vision of "a more perfect union" in another sermon where he laments the lack of hopefulness in a nation that has settled into "predictably ruinous patterns of greed and selfishness." In this tragic scenario the role of the church is to be the prophetic community that "continues to manifest mercy and justice in its own corporate life and to call for mercy and justice in the broader social sphere."[16]

Gerald Thomas's doctoral dissertation, published under the title *African American Preaching: The Contribution of Dr. Gardner C. Taylor*, includes a brief assessment of the prophetic preaching of

---

[15] Ibid., 87.

[16] L. Susan Bond, *Contemporary African American Preaching: Diversity in Theory and Style* (St. Louis: Chalice Press, 2003) 56.

Gardner Taylor. Thomas discerns several ways in which Taylor embodies prophetic ministry in his preaching and spiritual leadership as he has consciously experienced the redemptive love of God for an oppressed people: "Those drained, weary, faithful pilgrims who came to hear his declarations of the gospel were spiritually strengthened and morally motivated to trust in the power of God."[17] Taylor's personal experience of the tragedies of the American way of life have authorized his prophetic stance as one committed to the proclamation of a gospel intended for everyone: "During the early years of Taylor's pastoral ministry, he came to the conclusion that the gospel was intended for every race, creed, and color. The situations in society required a prophetic voice for change and commitment. Taylor had first hand experience of second class citizenship and the tragedies of the American way of life.... It was necessary for Gardner Taylor to become a spokesperson against the social conditions of Black people and their situation in America."[18] Thomas further observes that Taylor's sermons conveyed his sense of urgency to advance the cause of human dignity and personhood.[19]

It is my view that Taylor's own assessment of prophetic preaching as presented in the Lyman Beecher Lectureship on Preaching at Yale Divinity School in 1975–1976 and published in 1977 under the title *How Shall They Preach* secures his legacy as the consummate exemplar of the prophetic preaching tradition:

> The preacher has no warrant to speak to our social ills save in the light of God's judgment and God's grace. For instance, racism is not merely an oppression by one people of another with all of its resultant group guilt, group degradation and social disorder. Racism is set against the "one blood" tie which God ordained in our creation. Racism, whether it be the rapacity of a majority position or

---

[17] Gerald Lamont Thomas, *African American Preaching: The Contribution of Dr. Gardner C. Taylor* (New York: Peter Lang Publishing, 2004) 141.

[18] Ibid., 142.

[19] Ibid.

the reactionary toughness and terrorism of an outraged minority, assaults the mandate of our creation that we human beings are to have dominion over the "fish in the sea, the birds of the air, and every living creature that crawls on the earth," not over each other.[20]

The courageous and life-changing circumstances of his prophetic ministry span World War II, the Cuban missile crisis, and the civil rights movement, and in each era he has ministered to his hearers from the deep recesses of his personal experience, wisdom, and hope: "'As I preached during those difficult days, I wanted people to know that God is still on the throne,' he says. 'I couldn't predict the future; I could only give them the assertion made by my old theology dean, Thomas Graham: 'Faith is reason gone courageous'.'"[21]

The ultimate measure we can offer to validate Gardner Taylor's prophetic ministry over nine decades of fruitful longevity is to view his own testimony as trajectory. Beginning with the call and choice to preach, Taylor's prophetic testimony has marked a critical path through space and time from the old segregated South through the cosmopolitan challenges of the urban North, in all cases and all places binding the words of the preacher to the aspirations of the people at an angle that brings the divine mandate of justice and love to bear firmly upon their social condition. In 1995, the evangelical magazine *Christianity Today* quoted Taylor's apt summary of this divine-human dynamic in preaching: "Taylor insists that, whatever a sermon does, it must bring humanity in touch with its Creator. 'There's no excuse for the preacher if he or she is not speaking to people for God,' he asserts. 'Preaching that does not bring in the vertical aspect of the sermon—the impact of God upon human life—cannot be called a

---

[20] Gardner C. Taylor, *How Shall They Preach* (Elgin IL: Progressive Baptist Publishing House, 1977) 84. See also Evans E. Crawford's review of *How Shall They Preach* in *Journal of Religious Thought* 34/2 (Fall 1977/Winter 1978): 72–73.

[21] Edward Gilbreath, "The Pulpit King," *Christianity Today* 39/14 (11 December 1995): 27.

sermon.'"[22] It is my hope that succeeding generations of preachers will continue to extend the trajectory of African-American prophetic preaching, not only by incorporating social criticism, biblical exegesis, and remedial advocacy into their sermons, but also by emulating the authenticity of soul and voice that, in Taylor's words, "sounds in varying tones of joy and sorrow in every preacher's inmost self, challenging, summoning, examining, accusing, encouraging."[23]

---

[22] Ibid., 27.

[23] Taylor, *How Shall They Preach*, 53.

A SELECT BIBLIOGRAPHY OF THE PUBLISHED WORKS OF GARDNER C. TAYLOR AND ASSESSMENTS BY OTHERS OF HIS MINISTRY

Compiled by James Earl Massey

I. Books

Taylor, Gardner C. *How Shall They Preach: The Lyman Beecher Lectures and Five Lenten Sermons.* Elgin IL: Progressive Baptist Publishing House, 1977.

———— and O. C. Edwards. *Pentecost 3.* Aids for Interpreting the Lessons of the Church Year, edited by Elizabeth Achtemeier, Gerhard Krodel, and Charles P. Price. Philadelphia: Fortress Press, 1980.

————. *The Scarlet Thread: Nineteen Sermons.* Elgin IL: Progressive Baptist Publishing House, 1981.

————. *Chariots Aflame.* Nashville: Broadman Press, 1988.

———— and Samuel D. Proctor and Gary V. Simpson. *We Have This Ministry: The Heart of the Pastor's Vocation.* Valley Forge: Judson Press, 1996.

———— and Avery Lee. *Perfecting the Pastor's Art: Wisdom from Avery Lee and Gardner Taylor.* Valley Forge: Judson Press, 2005.

II. Contributions to Books by Others

1950. "They Shall Ask the Way." In *Eighth Baptist World Congress,* edited by Arnold T. Ohrn. Philadelphia: Judson Press, 1950, 50–55.

1959. "Hearts Waiting for What?" In *Best Sermons,* edited by G. Paul Butler. New York: Thomas Y. Crowell Co., 1959, 276–81.

1965. "Why I Believe There Is a God." In *Why I Believe There Is a God: Sixteen Essays by Negro Clergymen,* edited by Howard Thurman. Chicago: Johnson Publishing Co., Inc., 1965.

1965. "Some Comments on Race Hate." In *The Pulpit Speaks on Race,* edited by Alfred T. Davis. New York: Harper & Row, 1965, 184–91.

1966. "Freedom and Responsibility." In *The Truth That Makes Men Free: Official Report of the Eleventh Baptist World Congress,* edited by Josel Nordenhaug. Nashville: Broadman Press, 1966, 66–70.

1969. "Some Spiritual Reflections on the John Kennedy Era." In *The Cry for Freedom: An Anthology of the Best That Has Been Said and Written on Civil Rights Since 1954*, edited by Frank W. Hale, Jr. New York: A.S. Barnes and Co., 1969, 303–308.

1972. "Introduction." *Best Black Sermons*, edited by William M. Philpot. Valley Forge: Judson Press, 1972, vi.

1979. "Foreword" in Wyatt Tee Walker. *"Somebody's Calling My Name": Black Sacred Music and Social Change*. Valley Forge: Judson Press, 1979, xi–xii.

1979. "The President's Message to the Progressive National Baptist Convention, Inc., September 1968." In *Black Theology: A Documentary History, 1966–1979*, edited by Gayraud S. Wilmore and James H. Cone. Maryknoll NY: Orbis Books, 1979, 262–67.

1982. "His Own Clothes." In *Outstanding Black Sermons*, edited by Milton E. Owens, Jr. Valley Forge: Judson Press, 1982, 63–68.

1983. "Shaping Sermons by the Shape of Text and Preacher." In *Preaching Biblically: Creating Sermons in the Shape of Scripture*, edited by Don M. Wardlaw. Philadelphia: Westminster Press, 1983, 137–52.

1983. "Foreword." *Dynamic Preaching*, edited by Chevis F. Horne. Nashville: Broadman Press, 1983, vii–viii.

1991. "Three Women and God." In *Women: To Preach or Not to Preach: 21 Outstanding Black Preachers Say YES!*, edited by Ella Pearson Mitchell, Valley Forge: Judson Press, 1991 83–88.

1994. "Foreword" in Samuel D. Proctor. *The Certain Sound of the Trumpet: Crafting a Sermon of Authority*. Valley Forge: Judson Press, 1994, ix–xi.

1994. "His Own Clothes." In *A Chorus of Witnesses: Model Sermons for Today's Preachers*, edited by Thomas G. Long and Cornelius Plantinga, Jr. Grand Rapids: Eerdmans, 1994, 286–92.

1995. "Titles." In *Concise Encyclopedia of Preaching*, edited by William H. Willimon and Richard Lischer. Louisville: Westminster John Knox Press, 1995, 491–92.

1996. "Foreword." *Preaching on the Brink: The Future of Homiletics*, edited by Martha Simmons. Nashville: Abingdon Press, 1996, 11–12.

2000. "Make Goals, Not Excuses." In *Ten Great Preachers: Messages and Interviews*, edited by Bill Turpie. Grand Rapids: Baker Book House, 2000, 141–50.

2000. "Foreword." *A Mighty Long Journey: Reflections on Racial Reconciliation*, edited by Timothy George and Robert Smith, Jr. Nashville: Broadman & Holman Publishers, 2000, ix.

2001. "A Question Out of the Darkness" and "Living with Change." In *Keeping the Faith: African American Sermons of Liberation*, edited by James Haskins. New York: Welcome Rain Publications, 2001, 19–25, 87–93, respectively.

2001. "Reconciliation: Beyond Retaliation." In *9.11.01: African American Leaders Respond to an American Tragedy*, edited by Martha Simmons and Frank Thomas. Valley Forge: Judson Press, 2001, 33–36.

2001. "Foreword" in Mervyn A. Warren. *King Came Preaching: The Pulpit Power of Dr. Martin Luther King, Jr.* Downers Grove IL: InterVarsity Press, 2001, ix.

2002. "A Holy Pursuit" and "Look Up." In *Power in the Pulpit: How America's Most Effective Black Preachers Prepare Their Sermons*, edited by Cleophus J. LaRue. Louisville: Westminster John Knox Press, 2002, 145–55, 156–60, respectively.

III. Commemorative Collections

Sermons, Lectures, Speeches, Interviews

Taylor, Gardner C. *NBC Radio Sermons, 1959–1970*. Volume 1 of *The Words of Gardner Taylor*, compiled by Edward L. Taylor. Valley Forge: Judson Press, 1999.

———. *Sermons from the Middle Years, 1970–1980*. Volume 2 of *The Words of Gardner Taylor*, compiled by Edward L. Taylor. Valley Forge: Judson Press, 2000.

———. *Quintessential Classics, 1980–Present*. Volume 3 of *The Words of Gardner Taylor*, compiled by Edward L. Taylor. Valley Forge: Judson Press, 2000.

———. *Special Occasion and Expository Sermons*. Volume 4 of *The Words of Gardner Taylor*, compiled by Edward L. Taylor. Valley Forge: Judson Press, 2001.

———. *Lectures, Essays, and Interviews*. Volume 5 of *The Words of Gardner Taylor*, compiled by Edward L. Taylor. Valley Forge: Judson Press, 2001.

———. *50 Years of Timeless Treasures*. Volume 6 of *The Words of Gardner Taylor*, compiled by Edward L. Taylor. Valley Forge: Judson Press, 2002.

IV. Published Interviews

1981. Muck, Terry, and Paul Robbins. "The Sweet Torture of Sunday Morning: An Interview with Gardner C. Taylor." *Leadership* 2/3 (Summer 1981): 16–29.

1995. Strobel, Lee. "Timeless Tension: How Can Preachers Bring the Unchanging Scripture to a Changing World?" *Leadership* 16 (Fall 1995): 18–27.

1996. Duduit, Michael. "Preaching and the Power of Words." In *Communicating with Power: Insights from America's Top Communicators*, edited by Michael Duduit. Grand Rapids: Baker Books, 1996, 206–15. (The interview was reprinted from *Preaching*, January/February 1994 issue.)

1999. Jones, Byron Kirk. "An Interview with Gardner C. Taylor: Part I." *The African American Pulpit* 2/3 (Summer 1999): 87–92.

1999. Jones, Byron Kirk. "An Interview with Gardner C. Taylor: Part II." *The African American Pulpit* 2/4 (Fall 1999): 86–91.

2001. Evans, Joseph. "An Interview with Gardner C. Taylor on the Measure of Nelson Mandela." *The African American Pulpit* 4/4 (Fall 2001): 22–24.

V. Selected Writings about Gardner C. Taylor

"The Dean of Black Preachers: He Didn't Want to Be a Preacher." In *The Irresistible Urge to Preach: A Collection of African American "Call" Stories*, edited by William H. Myers. Atlanta: Aaron Press, 1991, 328–30.

"Gardner C. Taylor." In *Encyclopedia of African American Religions*, edited by Larry Murphy, J. Gordon Melton and Gary L. Ward. New York: Garland, 1993.

Lischer, Richard. "Gardner C. Taylor." In *Concise Encyclopedia of Preaching*, edited by William H. Willimon and Richard Lischer. Louisville: Westminster John Knox Press, 1995, 465–67.

Bond, Susan. "To Hear the Angel's Wings: Apocalyptic Language and the Formation of Moral Community with Reference to the Sermons of Gardner C. Taylor." Ph.D dissertation, Vanderbilt Divinity School, 1996.

"Gardner Taylor: The Poet Laureate of the American Pulpit." In Michael Eric Dyson, *Between God and Gangsta Rap: Bearing Witness to Black Culture*. New York: Oxford University Press, 1996, 40–55. (Reprinted in *The Michael Dyson Reader* [New York: Basic Civitas Books, 2004] 192–201.)

Aguian, Marian. "Gardner Calvin Taylor." In *Africana: The Encyclopedia of the African and African American Experience*, edited by Kwame Anthony Appiah and Henry Louis Gates, Jr. New York: Basic Civitas Books, 1999, 1828.

"Gardner C. Taylor." In Marvin McMickle, *An Encyclopedia of African American Christian Heritage*. Valley Forge: Judson Press, 2002, 84–86.

"Gardner Calvin Taylor." In L. Susan Bond, *Contemporary African American Preaching: Diversity in Theory and Style*. St. Louis: Chalice Press, 2003, 49–63.

"Gardner Taylor." In O. C. Edwards, Jr., *A History of Preaching*. Nashville: Abingdon Press, 2004, 714–16.

Thomas, Gerald Lamont. *African American Preaching: The Contribution of Dr. Gardner C. Taylor*. New York: Peter Lang, 2004.

CONTRIBUTORS

Timothy George (A.B., University of Tennessee at Chattanooga; M.Div., Harvard Divinity School; Th.D., Harvard University) is the founding dean of Beeson Divinity School. He is currently serving as senior editor for *Christianity Today* and is on the editorial advisory boards of the *Harvard Theological Review, Christian History,* and *Books & Culture.* A prolific author, he has written more than twenty books and regularly contributes to scholarly journals. His book *Theology of the Reformers* is the standard textbook in many schools and seminaries on Reformation theology and has been translated into several languages. He has been active in the evangelical dialogue with the Roman Catholic Church and is a highly sought after preacher and conference speaker. He is also the general editor of the *Reformation Commentary on Scripture,* a multivolume work of sixteenth-century exegetical comment. As founding dean, George has been instrumental in shaping the character and mission of Beeson Divinity School. An ordained minister in the Southern Baptist Convention, he has served as pastor for churches in Alabama, Georgia, and Massachusetts. Recent books edited by George include *God the Holy Trinity* (Baker, 2006), the second book in the Beeson Divinity Studies series; and, with Eric Mason, *Theology in the Service of the Church: Essays Presented to Fisher H. Humphreys* (Mercer University Press, 2008).

James Earl Massey (B.R.E., Detroit Bible College; M.A., Oberlin Graduate School of Theology; D.Div., Asbury Theological Seminary; Hum.D., Tuskegee University; Litt.D., Anderson University) is dean emeritus and Distinguished Professor-at-Large of the Anderson University School of Theology, honors bestowed on him after more than twenty-five years of service in theological education on that campus. From 1984 to 1990, and then again from 1997 to 1998, he was dean of the chapel and university professor of religion and society at Tuskegee University. A native of Detroit, he is pastor emeritus of

Metropolitan Church of God, a congregation of which he was the founding pastor and served from 1954 to 1976. Massey has preached and lectured in America, the Caribbean, England, Europe, Egypt, Australia, and Japan, and on the campuses of more than 100 colleges, universities, and seminaries worldwide. A productive scholar, Massey has contributed many chapters for publication and authored twenty-four books, including: *Designing the Sermon: Order and Movement in Preaching* (Abingdon); *Sundays in the Tuskegee Chapel: Selected Sermons* (Abingdon); *The Burdensome Joy of Preaching* (Abingdon), which was named by *Preaching* magazine as its 1998 Book of the Year. Most recently he published his autobiography, *Aspects of My Pilgrimage* (Anderson University Press), and *Stewards of the Story: The Task of Preaching* (Westminster John Knox). He has served on the editorial boards of *Preaching, Leadership,* and as a senior editor of *Christianity Today.*

Neville Callam has served as general secretary of the Baptist World Alliance (BWA) since 2007. He was BWA's vice president from 2000–2005, serving on numerous committees, commissions, and workgroups, including the general council and executive committee. Callam served as president of the Jamaica Baptist Union (JBU) from 1985–1987 and from 2000–2002 and held all senior positions in the Jamaican Baptist Convention, including that of general treasurer and acting general secretary. He is also former vice president of the Caribbean Baptist Fellowship. An educator and ordained minister, Callam graduated from the United Theological College of the West Indies, the University of the West Indies, and Harvard Divinity School. He is a specialist in Christian ethics and theology and taught at the United Theological College of the West Indies, the Caribbean Graduate School of Theology, and Jamaica Theological Seminary. He has sat on the university council of Jamaica, the country's accreditation body for colleges and universities. He founded, managed, and chaired the board of the religious radio station, The Breath of Change (TBC FM). He served as founding director of the National Religious Media of Jamaica and was chairman of the board of the Public Broadcasting Corporation of Jamaica. Callam has written five books, including *Moral Responsibility: Issues in Church and Society* (Kingston, Jamaica: Tarrant Baptist Church, 1993); *Deciding Responsibility: Moral Dimensions of Human Action* (May Pen, Clarendon, Jamaica: Grace Social Ethics Books, 1985); *Voicing Concern: the Social Witness of the Jamaica Council of Churches* (Kingston, Jamaica: Pelican Publishers, 2004), and has published articles in academic journals as well as written chapters for books published by others.

Joel C. Gregory (B.A., Baylor University; M.Div., Southwestern Baptist Theological Seminary; Ph.D., Baylor University, Baylor Law School) is professor of preaching at George. W. Truett Theological Seminary. Gregory, a former president of the Baptist General Convention of Texas, was pastor of Travis Avenue Baptist Church before serving as pastor of First Baptist Church of Dallas. He was the keynote speaker for the Panhandler Plains Pastors' and Laymans' Conference at Wayland Baptist University for thirteen years. His books include *Too Great a Temptation: The Seductive Power of America's Super Church* (Summit Group); *Growing Pains of the Soul* (Thomas Nelson, Inc.); and *Gregory's Sermon Synopses: 200 Expanded Summaries* (Broadman & Holman).

Donald E. Demaray (B.A., Los Angeles Pacific College; B.D., Asbury Theological Seminary; Ph.D., Edinburgh University; D.Litt., Los Angeles Pacific College; Sr. Scholar, Cambridge, UK) is Senior Beeson Professor of Biblical Preaching (retired) at Asbury Theological Seminary. A prolific preacher and writer with years of experience in both areas, his preaching experience includes sermons/lectures at Seattle Pacific University Church; B. T. Roberts Church, NY; Spring Arbor University Church; Wilmore Free Methodist; Centenary

United Methodist; Tuskegee University; and many leading retreats/conferences. Worldwide circulation of books and articles, Demaray has contributed to journals, including *Chrsitianity Today*, *The Seminarian*, *The Christian Digest*, *The Evangelical Christ*, *Arnold's Commentary*, and *The Sermon Builder*. A few of his books are *Mile Markers: 40 Intimate Journeys with Jesus* (Evangel Publishing, 2007); *Spiritual Formation for Christian Leaders: Lessons from the Life & Teaching of E. Stanley Jones*, with Reginald Johnson (Abingdon Press, 2007); *A Robust Ministry* (Evangel Publishing, 2004); *The Wesley's Hymns and Poetry: A Daily Devotional* (Bristol House, 2003).

Michael Duduit is executive editor of *Preaching* magazine and founding dean of the Graduate School of Ministry at Anderson University in Anderson, SC, where he also serves as professor of Christian ministry. Prior to this role, Duduit served as an administrator and teacher at three Christian colleges and a seminary, most recently as executive vice president at Union University. A graduate of Stetson University and Southern Baptist Seminary, he received a Ph.D. in humanities from Florida State University. He is the author or editor of several books, including the *Handbook of Contemporary Preaching*, *Preaching with Power*, and *Communicate with Power*. He directs the National Conference on Preaching, the International Congress on Preaching, and produces *Preaching Now*, a weekly e-mail newsletter read by more than 20,000 pastors and church leaders. He and his wife, Laura, have two sons, James and Stephen.

Thomas G. Long (B.A. and M. Div., Erskine Seminary; Ph.D., Princeton Theological Seminary) is the Bandy Professor of Preaching at Candler School of Theology at Emory University. A Presbyterian minister, Long has served churches in Georgia and New Jersey. He has taught preaching for over thirty years—at Erskine Theological Seminary, Columbia Theological Seminary, Princeton Theological

Seminary, and, since 2000, at Candler. Long is the chair of the Day1 advisory board (Day1 is the voice of the mainline Protestant churches on the radio and online, offering outstanding sermons, community interaction, and life-enriching resources to help one grow in one's faith). He is the author or editor of fourteen books on preaching and worship, collections of sermons, and biblical commentaries on Matthew and Hebrews. His most recent books include *Beyond the Worship Wars: Building Vital and Faithful Worship* (Alban Institute 2001); *Testimony: Talking Ourselves into Being Christian* (Jossey-Bass, 2004); *The Witness of Preaching*, 2d ed. (Westminster John Knox, 2005).

Marvin A. McMickle (B.A., Aurora University; M.Div., Union Theological Seminary, NY; graduate work at Columbia University, NY; D.Min., Princeton Theological Seminary; Ph.D., Case Western Reserve University; honorary D.Div., Aurora University) is senior pastor of Antioch Baptist Church, Cleveland, and professor of homiletics at Ashland Theological Seminary, Ashland, OH. During his time in ministry, he led the church in establishing the first ministry for people infected with or affected by HIV/AIDS. Other pastoral experience includes St. Paul Baptist Church while an adjunct faculty member of Princeton Theological Seminary. He served two terms as president of the Montclair branch of the NAACP and the Urban League in Cleveland as well as serving as president of the Shaker Heights board of education and president of Karamu House Performing Arts Center. McMickle has authored eleven books and many articles for professional journals and magazines. He serves as contributing editor of *The Living Pulpit* as well as a featured writer for the *National Baptist Voice, Preaching* magazine, and *The African American Pulpit*. For the winter semester of 2009, he will be a visiting professor at Yale University Divinity School. Some of his books are *Preaching to the Black Middle Class: Words of Challenge, Words of Hope* (Judson Press, 2000); *Living Water for Thirsty Souls: Unleashing the*

Power of Exegetical Preaching (Judson Press, 2001); *Before We Say I Do* (Judson Press, 2003); and *The Star Book on Preaching* (Judson Press, 2006).

William E. Pannell (B.A., Fort Wayne Bible College; M.A., University of Southern California; D.D., Malone College; D.D., Geneva College) serves as special assistant to the president and senior professor of preaching at the Fuller Theological Seminary School of Theology. Prior to joining the Fuller faculty as assistant professor of evangelism, he was the first African American to serve on Fuller's board of trustees. In 1992 he was appointed as the Arthur DeKruyter/Christ Church Oak Brook Professor of Preaching, served as dean of the chapel from 1992 to 1998, and also served as director of the African-American studies program. A gifted preacher and professor of homiletics, Pannell has nurtured several generations of Fuller students from the classroom to the pulpit. Areas of expertise, research, writing, and teaching include preaching in contemporary America, race relations, black church, and evangelism. He currently serves on the board of Taylor University in Indiana and is the author of numerous articles and books, including *The Coming Race Wars? A Cry for Reconciliation* (Zondervan, 1993); *Evangelism from the Bottom Up* (Zondervan, 1992); and *My Friend, the Enemy* (Word Books, 1968).

Henry H. Mitchell (B.A and L.H.D, hon., Lincoln University, Pennsylvania; B.D. and M.Div., Union Theological Seminary, NY; M.A. in linguistics, California State University at Fresno; Th.D., Claremont School of Theology, California; and D.D., hon., The American Baptist Seminary of the West, Berkeley, CA). Prior to semiretirement, Mitchell served as academic dean and professor of history and homiletics at Proctor School of Theology, Virginia Union University (1982–1987); founding director of the Ecumenical Center for Black Church Studies, in Los Angeles; and briefly as professor of religion and pan-African studies at California State University, Northridge. Prior to this he was the first Martin Luther King, Jr., Professor of Black Church Studies at Colgate Rochester Divinity School, Bexley Hall (Episcopalian) and Crozer Theological Seminary, 1969–1974. He was appointed professor emeritus by this consortium in 1992. He previously served from 1945–1959 as an American Baptist regional staff person in northern California, and as pastor of Second Baptist Church, Fresno, CA (1959–1966) and Calvary Baptist Church, Santa Monica, CA (1966–1969). Mitchell is the author of *Black Preaching: The Recovery of Preaching and Celebration and Experience in Preaching.* He co-authored *Soul Theology and Preaching for Black Self-Esteem* with Dr. Emil M. Thomas.

Robert Smith, Jr. (A.S., God's Bible College; B.S., Cincinnati Bible College; M.Div. and Ph.D., The Southern Baptist Theological Seminary; STD hon., Temple Community Bible College), serves as professor of Christian preaching at Beeson Divinity School. Previously, he served as the Carl E. Bates Associate Professor of Christian Preaching at The Southern Baptist Theological Seminary. A popular teacher and preacher, he received Southern's 1996 Findley B. Edge Award for Teaching Excellence. An ordained Baptist minister, he served as pastor of the New Mission Missionary Baptist Church for twenty years before returning to complete his Ph.D. He is a contributing editor for *Preparing for Christian Ministry.* Dr. Smith received Beeson's "Teacher of the Year Award" in 2005. He is a member of the Academy of Homiletics and the board of consulting editors for *Preaching* magazine. He co-edited with Timothy George *A Mighty Long Journey: Reflections on Racial Reconciliation,* published in 2000. His newest book, *Doctrine That Dances: Bringing Doctrinal Preaching and Teaching to Life* (Nashville: B & H Publishing, 2008) was selected as *Preaching* magazine's 2008 Preaching Book of the Year and the 2009 Preaching Book of the Year by *Christianity Today's* PreachingToday.com.

Wallace Charles Smith (graduate of Villanova University; M.Div. and D.Min., Eastern Baptist Theological Seminary) is the president of Palmer Theological Seminary of Eastern University and senior minister of Shiloh Baptist Church of Washington, DC. Smith's ministerial career spans service at both First Baptist Church of Capitol Hill in Nashville, TN, and Calvary Baptist Church in Chester, PA. He has served as professor of the practice of ministry at Vanderbilt University Divinity School and assistant professor for practical theology at Eastern Baptist Theological Seminary, as well as an adjunct faculty member at Howard Divinity School and Wesley Theological Seminary. Smith has traveled extensively and preached on four continents, giving much of his time and efforts to fostering racial reconciliation. He received the 1994 Distinguished Service Award from the Anti-Defamation League of B'nai B'rith. Smith was a contributing editor for *The Pulpit Digest* from 1986 to 1997. Smith's latest contributed chapters include "Revisiting the Church in the life of the Black Family," in *Multidimensional Ministry for Today's Black Family* by Johnny B. Hill (Judson Press, 2007). He is the author of *The Church in the Life of the Black Family* (Judson Press, 1985).

Cleophus J. LaRue, Jr. (B.A and M.A., Baylor University; M.Div. and Ph.D., Princeton Seminary), serves as Princeton Theological Seminary's Francis Landey Patton Associate Professor of Homiletics. An ordained minister in the National Baptist Convention of America and a member of the Academy of Homiletics, LaRue is the former pastor of churches in Texas, Harlem, and Jamaica Queens, NY. LaRue has participated in many lecture series, such as Black Alums Princeton Theological Seminary; St. Andrews, Scotland; Eastern Baptist Theological Seminary School of Theology; Virginia Union University; Dubuque Theological Seminary; United Theological Seminary; St. Nersess Armenian Seminary; George Truett Seminary; Lipscomb University; Pleasant Hill Harvest Festival; and the Pastors'

Conference, Phoenix, AZ. Publishing in various scholarly journals, his newest books include *The Heart of Black Preaching* (Westminster John Knox Press, 1999); editor of *Power in the Pulpit: How America's Most Effective Black Preachers Prepare Their Sermons* (Westminster John Knox Press, 2002); editor of *This Is My Story: Testimonies and Sermons of Black Women in Ministry* (Westminster John Knox Press, 2005); and *More Power in the Pulpit: How America's Most Effective Preachers Prepare Their Sermons* (Westminster John Knox Press, 2009).

William H. Willimon (B.A., Wofford College; M.Div., Yale University; S.T.D., Emory University; with many D.D. and other honorary degrees from various colleges and universities from 1968–2006) served as pastor in churches in Georgia and South Carolina and was elected bishop of the United Methodist Church in 2004. Prior to becoming bishop, he served as dean of Duke University chapel and assistant professor of liturgy and worship at Duke University; director of the ministerial course of study school at Duke and presiding minister in the divinity school chapel. He has served as vice chairman of the board of trustees, Wofford College; chairperson of the University Council Committee for the Institute of Sacred Music at Yale; and on the board of overseers for Memorial Church, Harvard University, and boards of Emory, Birmingham-Southern, and Huntingdon Colleges. Bishop Willimon has served on the editorial boards of *Christian Century, Christian Ministry, Preaching, The Wittenburg Door,* and *Leadership.* Author of some 600 articles and nearly sixty books (selling more than one million copies), his *Worship as Pastoral Care* was selected as one of the ten most useful books for pastors in 1979 by the Academy of Parish Clergy. Baylor University named him one of the twelve most effective preachers in the English-speaking world in 1996. In 2005, Pulpit and Pew Research Center found Bishop Willimon is the second most widely read author by mainline Protestant pastors. His latest books include

Thank God It's Friday: The Seven Last Words of Jesus from the Cross (Abingdon, 2007); *United Methodist Beliefs: A Brief Introduction* (Westminster John Knox Press, 2007); and *Who Will Be Saved?* (Abingdon Press, 2008).

David G. Buttrick (graduate of Haverford College; Union Theological Seminary, NY; further studies at Garrett Biblical Institute and Northwestern University) served since 1982 as the Drucilla Moore Buffington Professor of Homiletics and Liturgics, Emeritus, Vanderbilt University. He is a former chair of the Pittsburg Theological Seminary's Church and Ministry Division and an adjunct graduate professor of rhetoric at the University of Pittsburg. Buttrick has served as visiting professor at St. Meinrad School of Theology; St. Francis Seminary; SS. Cyril & Methodius Seminary; Southern Baptist Seminary; Lexington Theological Seminary; and Iliff School of Theology. Buttrick has lectured at more than eighty colleges and universities and has given the Lyman Beecher Lectures at Yale University. He has authored or edited eighteen books, twenty-five chapters in books, and published more than 150 articles and reviews. Other positions of interest include chief writer/editor for the *Presbyterian Worship Book* (1970), consultant on worship to the Commission on Church Union (COCU), and member of the Catholic Bishops' Ad Hoc Committee on the Homily. Memberships include the Academy of Religion, the Academy of Homiletics, the Religious Speech Communication Association, the North American Academy of Liturgy, and the International Societas Homiletica. Buttrick was honored with a festschrift titled *Preaching as a Theological Task*, edited by Thomas Long and Edward Farley (Westminster John Knox Press, 1996). His many writings include *The Mystery and the Passion: A Homiletic Reading of the Gospel Traditions* (Fortress Press, 1992); *Proclamation 5: Easter* (Fortress Press, 1993); and *A Captive Voice: The Liberation of Preaching* (Westminster John Knox Press, 1994).

Richard A. Lischer (B.A., Concordia Senior College; M.A., Washington University; B.D., Concordia Seminary; Ph.D., University of London) is an ordained minister in the Evangelical Lutheran Church and serves as the James T. and Alice Mead Cleland Professor of Preaching at Duke University Divinity School. Lischer has taught and lectured widely in the areas of practical theology, ministry, religious autobiography, and preaching and has held distinguished lectureships, including the Lyman Beecher Lectures at Yale Divinity School. He served as president of the Academy of Homiletics (1997–1998) and received the Academy's Lifetime Achievement Award in 2007. Lischer's writings include numerous articles, sermons, book reviews, and book chapters. Recently authored and edited books include *The Company of Preachers: Wisdom on Preaching from Augustine to the Present* (Eerdmans, 2002); *Open Secrets: A Spiritual Journey through a Country Church* (Doubleday, 2001); and *The End of Words: The Language of Reconciliation in a Culture of Violence* (Eerdmans, 2005). Publishing awards include Book of the Year award for 1995 by *Preaching* journal for *Concise Encyclopedia of Preaching;* Outstanding Book Award for 1995–1996 by the Religious Speech Communication Association for *The Preacher King: Martin Luther King, Jr., and the Word That Moved America;* and the Best Book on Ministry/Leadership award in 2003 by *Christianity Today* for *The Company of Preachers.*

O. C. Edwards, Jr. (A.B., Centenary College; STB, The General Theological Seminary; STM, Southern Methodist University; M.A., Ph.D. University of Chicago; D.D., Nashotah House; D.D., University of the South), is a retired and ordained Episcopal priest and seminary educator and served as curate, vicar, or rector in churches in Louisiana, Texas and Illinois. He served as president and dean of Seabury-Western Theological Seminary from 1974–1983 and was professor emeritus of preaching from 1983–1993. Edwards preached, lectured, and conducted workshops and retreats for many dioceses, churches, seminaries, and agencies. Board service includes Episcopal Council of Seminary Deans, the Board of Theological Education, General Board of Examining Chaplains, Council for the Development of Ministry, the Joint Lutheran-Episcopal Coordinating Committee, the Native American Theological Association, and Friends of St. Benedict. His writings include numerous chapters, articles, and book reviews in edited books, reference works, journals, and magazines. As author, co-author, or editor of more than a dozen books, some of the authored books include *How It All Began, The Bible for Today's Church* [Church Teaching Series] (Seabury Press, 1973, 1977); *Luke's Story of Jesus* (Fortress Press, 1981); *Elements of Homiletic: A Method for Preparing to Preach* (Pueblo Press, 1982); *How Holy Writ Was Written* (Abingdon Press, 1989); and *A History of Preaching* (Abingdon Press, 2004). Edwards has received many awards, including 2005 Book of the Year Award, Academy of Parish Clergy; Academy of Homiletics Lifetime Achievement Award, 2007; General Assembly of the National Council of Churches and Church World Service, Joseph Cardinal Bernardin Award, 2008

Teresa L. Fry Brown (B.S. and M.S., University of Central Missouri [formerly Central Missouri State University]; M.Div., Iliff School of Theology; Ph.D., Iliff School of Theology and the University of Denver) is an associate professor of homiletics at the Candler School of Theology and director of black church studies at Emory University. Dr. Fry Brown has served as a teacher and speaker in ecumenical settings across the United States and internationally, holding workshops and seminars in the areas of homiletics, church administration, African-American health and family issues, ministerial relationship, voice and diction, and worship. Fry Brown is a prolific writer with numerous journal articles, lectures, and books. Her recent books include *Delivering the Sermon: Voice, Body and Animation in Proclamation* (Fortress Press, 2008); *Can A Sister Get a Little Help?:*

Advice and Encouragement for Black Women in Ministry (Pilgrim Press, 2008); *God Don't Like Ugly: African American Women Handing on Spiritual Values* (Abingdon Press, 2000); *Weary Throats and New Song: Black Women Proclaiming God's Word* (Abingdon Press, 2003); and *The 2006 African American History Devotional* (Abingdon Press,2006).

Martha Simmons (B.S., Bradley University; M.Div., Emory University; Jurist Doctor, New College of California School of Law; D.Th., Boston University) is an associate minister at Rush Memorial United Church of Christ, Atlanta. She is publisher and co-owner of *The African American Pulpit Journal* (TAAP). She also serves as a general editor of *Preaching with Sacred Fire: African American Sermons 1750 to the Present* (W. W. Norton Publishers, anticipated publish date winter 2009). Simmons is creator and director of the *African American Online Lectionary Project* (2006), funded by the Lilly Endowment in partnership with Vanderbilt Divinity School. She has served as a lecturer in the area of homiletics at United Theological Seminary, The Interdenominational Theological Center of Atlanta; the Pacific School of Religion in Berkeley, CA. She also served as a visiting professor at the American Baptist Seminary of the West, Berkeley, CA, and at St. Paul School of Theology, Kansas City. A prolific writer, she has published numerous articles and chapters and has served as co-editor of *9.11.01: African American Leaders Respond to an American Tragedy* (Judson Press, 2001); editor of *Preaching on the Brink* (Abingdon Press, 1998); and co-author of *Making a Sermon Come Alive* (Abingdon Press, 1994). In 1997, she was named on *Ebony* magazine's Honor Roll of Outstanding African-American Women Preachers in America.

Brad R. Braxton (B.S., University of Virginia; M.Phil. [New Testament], University of Oxford; Ph.D., Emory University), a former Phi Beta Kappa and Rhodes Scholar, is the former senior minister at the Riverside Church in New York City. Prior to his call to Riverside, he served as associate professor of homiletics and New Testament at Vanderbilt University Divinity School and was the Jessie Ball DuPont Assistant Professor of Homiletics and Biblical Studies at Wake Forest University Divinity School. Braxton, a frequent guest preacher and lecturer at churches and conferences, recently lectured in Ghana and preached at Westminster Abbey, London, as part of the bicentennial commemoration of the abolition of the slave trade in the British Empire. He serves on the advisory board of *The African American Pulpit*, a quarterly journal. His books include *The Tyranny of Resolution: 1 Cor. 7:17–24* (Society of Biblical Literature, 2000); *No Longer Slaves: Galatians and African American Experience* (The Liturgical Press, 2002); and *Preaching Paul* (Abingdon Press, 2004).

Cheryl J. Sanders (B.S., Swarthmore College; M.Div. and Th.D., Harvard Divinity School; Honorary D.Div., Asbury College, honorary D. D., Anderson University) is professor of Christian ethics at the Howard University School of Divinity, teaching courses in Christian ethics, pastoral ethics, and African-American spirituality, camp meetings, conventions, conferences, and revivals. Sanders has ministered nationally and internationally for more than thirty years, including the 2005 C. Eric Lincoln Lectureship at Clark Atlanta University and the Staley Distinguished Christian Scholar Lectureship. She has served as senior pastor of Third Street Church of God in Washington, DC, since 1997. In 2005, she was honored as one of the elders in the fall issue of *The African American Pulpit: Those Preaching Women*. A prolific writer with more than 100 published articles, Sanders has authored several books, including: *Minister in the Margins: The Prophetic Mission of Women, Youth and the Poor* (InterVarsity, 1997)*; Saints in Exile: The Holiness-Pentecostal Experience in African American Religion and Culture* (Oxford University Press, 1996); and *Empowerment Ethics for a Liberated People* (Fortress Press, 1995).

INDEX

NAMES

INDEX
SCRIPTURES

OUR SUFFICIENCY IS OF GOD

ADDENDUM

BEESON DIVINITY SCHOOL

The Inaugural William E. Conger, Jr. Lectures on Biblical Preaching (1993) presented by Gardner C. Taylor

1.   *Show Us the Father* (24.04)

2.   *The Privileges and Perils of Preaching* (34:50)

CD originally produced by Robert Willis, Manager, Media & Technology Services, Beeson Divinity School, Samford University, 800 Lakeshore Drive, Birmingham, AL 35229. Reproduced with permission of Timothy George, Dean, Beeson Divinity School as an addendum to *Our Sufficiency is of God* (Mercer University Press, 2010).